Spectacular
Blackness

Spectacular Blackness

THE CULTURAL POLITICS OF THE BLACK POWER MOVEMENT AND THE SEARCH FOR A BLACK AESTHETIC

Amy Abugo Ongiri

University of Virginia Press   *Charlottesville and London*

University of Virginia Press
© 2010 by the Rector and Visitors of the University of Virginia
All rights reserved
Printed in the United States of America on acid-free paper

First published 2010

9 8 7 6 5 4 3 2 1

LIBRARY OF CONGRESS CATALOGING-IN-PUBLICATION DATA

Ongiri, Amy Abugo, 1968–
    Spectacular blackness : the cultural politics of the Black power movement and the search for a Black aesthetic / Amy Abugo Ongiri.
        p.   cm.
    Includes bibliographical references and index.
    ISBN 978-0-8139-2859-3 (cloth : alk. paper) — ISBN 978-0-8139-2860-9 (pbk. : alk. paper) — ISBN 978-0-8139-2960-6 (e-book)
    1. Black power—United States—History—20th century. 2. Black Arts movement. 3. Black Panther Party—History. 4. Black nationalism—United States—History—20th century. 5. African American arts—20th century. 6. African Americans—Intellectual life—20th century. 7. African Americans—Race identity. 8. Arts—Political aspects—United States—History—20th century. I. Title.
    E185.615.O63 2010
    322.4´20973—dc22   2009023618

To the loving memory of my late aunt Pamela Atieno Oteng

And to my parents, David Onyango Ongiri and Nancy Hunt Ongiri, and my sister Bessie Ongiri

Contents

Acknowledgments

Like the Notorious B.I.G. said in "Juicy," the last really great hip-hop song: "It was all a dream." In that song, Biggie Smalls told the story of the impossibility of all he had achieved given the conditions he had had to overcome. I haven't had quite the experiences or the achievements of Biggie Smalls, but I am the first to acknowledge that I would never have achieved anything at all without the support of the many people along the way. My committee greatly assisted in the early development and completion of this project in its incarnation as a dissertation. Sunn Shelley Wong provided a model for scholarly and pedagogical integrity. The project could not have been completed without her tireless support and understanding at every stage. Hortense Spillers repeatedly provided critical challenges to my ideas that forced me to reconceptualize, refine, and hone my arguments. Timothy Murray offered an invaluable critical perspective on race and visual culture. Karlton Hester not only helped me to have a fuller understanding of the cultural and aesthetic production of music but he also introduced me to jazz, which became a lifelong love and probably the single most important thing that I have gained from my education. I have had the benefit of great teachers and mentors throughout my education. Salah Hassan, Ann Cvetkovich, Rajeswari Mohan, Joyce Miller, Dawit Woldu, and Helena Woodard have been models of excellence in teaching and mentoring.

This project also benefited enormously from the support of my colleagues in the "Historicizing Identities" seminar at Duke University's John Hope Franklin Center of International and Interdisciplinary Studies. Priscilla Wald, Trina Jones, and Lee D. Baker were particularly generous and giving of their time. Several people read drafts of this project while it was in progress, and my colleagues at the University of Florida have been exceptionally helpful throughout its final stages. Marsha Bryant, Kim Emery, Pamela Gilbert, Mark Reid, Lamonda Hortons Stallings, Debra Walker

King, Wayne Losano, Jodi Schorb, Stephanie Evans, and Andrew Gordon all offered advice, support, and valuable input. Carol Anne Tyler, Michelle Raheja, Charles Nero, Jurgen Donnerstag, Tiffany Ana Lopez, Diedrich Diedrichson, Nancy Kok, Ingeborg Majer O'Sickey, Hank Okazaki, David Hilliard, and Rickey Vincent offered invaluable insights and encouragement. A. B. Spellman and Evelyn Neal generously allowed me permission to reprint material. The support and encouragement of my University of Virginia Press editor, Cathie Brettschneider, was invaluable, as was the input of the two anonymous readers. Their concern and attention was matched by the efficient help and consideration of my copy editor, Beth Ina. Claude Marks at the Freedom Archives continues to offer insight and inspiration. Mary Fahnestock-Thomas helped not only with editing the manuscript but also with really great advice and support. Bessie Ongiri read and edited a late version of the manuscript in a pinch and saved the day as usual.

It is always my hope that any work that I do honors my ancestors and my biological and chosen family here and abroad. This project would not have been completed without the love, care, and commitment of Barbara Mennel, who not only read multiple drafts but also introduced me to the work of Chester Himes. Without her, this project would not have been possible. I will always be forever grateful to my parents for instilling in me a love of family and a commitment to education. Their openness to the world taught me new ways of seeing. My brothers and sisters John, Elizabeth, Mary, Allen, Laura, Jennifer, Catherine, Sarah, and David inspire, provoke, and praise in a way that I simply can't live without. My nieces and nephews Ashley, Alicyah, Olivia, Little Ray, Jabari, Jack, Zachary, Lauren Mariana, Anjett, Janiyah, and David belong to me and the world in a way that is just lovely. My brothers-in-law Ravi Howard and Raymond Sullivan are always there when I need them most. Todd Reynolds, Rosi Reyes, Nora Gutierrez, Lisa Dusenberry, Martha Ehrenfeld, Carla McKay, Katherine Baker, Jennifer Ongiri, Anne Wolf, Elisa and Sion Rodriguez y Gibson, Kimerly Cornish, Kimberly Brown, Marisol Arriola, and Jackie Byars provided the very necessary moral and material support to see the project through to completion.

Spectacular
Blackness

Cotton Comes to Harlem

AN INTRODUCTION

March against Fear   The Civil Rights Movement and the Birth of Black Power

In 1966 James Meredith, a nonviolence advocate, a veteran of the Civil Rights Movement, and the first African American to graduate from the University of Mississippi, began a symbolic walk across the state of Mississippi that he called "The March against Fear."[1] Meredith hoped that his act would "tear down the fear that grips the Negroes in Mississippi," but the march ended abruptly when on the second day, he was shot by a sniper and so severely injured that he was unable to continue. Like the King assassination that was to come later, the attack on James Meredith seemed to many African Americans to point to the ultimate futility of nonviolent resistance as a direct-action tactic against racism and fear. The Civil Rights Movement responded to the attack on James Meredith by sending representatives from the mainstream civil rights organizations to finish the March against Fear, including Martin Luther King Jr. from the Southern Christian Leadership Conference (SCLC) and Stokely Carmichael and Willie Ricks from the Student Nonviolence Coordinating Committee (SNCC). In film footage of the march, King can be seen to be physically holding Carmichael back from responding to police and anti–civil rights protesters.[2] When the march arrived in Greenwood, Mississippi, Carmichael was arrested for trespassing on public property, and when he was released later that evening, he galvanized the audience that gathered with calls for "Black Power"—a call that Ricks had first uttered that evening—rather than the chant of "Freedom Now" that was customary for the Civil Rights Movement.

The notion of Black Power galvanized those within the Civil Rights Movement who perceived it to be stagnating behind the radical legislative change the movement had provoked. The passage of the Civil Rights Act of 1964 barred discrimination in public accommodations, education, and employment, and the Voting Rights Act of 1965 ended discriminatory practices in relation to voting. On 10 December 1964, Martin Luther King was awarded the Nobel Peace Prize, but neither legislative acts nor public accolades seemed to assure the freedom that the Civil Rights Movement— originally called the Freedom Movement—had promised. King began to plan the "Poor People's March" at least partly in response to those in the Civil Rights Movement, epitomized by Ricks and Carmichael, who wanted to create a vision of the civil rights struggle beyond legislative and court gains. King's assassination on 4 April 1968, the day after he delivered his iconic "I Have Been to the Mountaintop" speech in support of a garbage workers strike, caused widespread urban rioting and was widely grieved.

Black Power, an idea conceptually diffuse enough to be claimed by Black capitalists as well as Black communists, revolved around the notion of economic independence and cultural self-determination.[3] Carmichael and Ricks declared the need for "Black Power" on 16 June 1966, and by October of the same year, Bobby Seale and Huey Newton responded by founding the Black Panther Party in Oakland, California. That same month, in the context of widespread campus unrest, James Garrett founded the first Black Student Union, at San Francisco State University, paving the way for the establishment of a black studies program the next year. According to the historian Jeffrey O. G. Ogbar in *Black Power: Radical Politics and African American Identity*, "by 1967, most major universities and colleges formed Black Student Unions and Black Student Associations" (136). While the Civil Rights Movement had argued for inclusion in educational institutions, the Black Student Union movement insisted on defining the parameters for that inclusion.

In the political arena, the Nation of Islam, which had been founded in the 1930s, experienced a meteoric rise in membership throughout the late 1950s and into the 1960s, so much so that at the death of its founder, Elijah Muhammad, in 1975, it was the wealthiest African American organization in U.S. history.[4] Increasing attention to the Black Power movement in popular culture and the news media bolstered existing groups and created new ones. For example, membership in the Nation of Islam doubled after Minister Malcolm X appeared on a Mike Wallace CBS special on the "Black Muslim movement" entitled *The Hate that Hate Produced* in 1959. Though Black nationalism could claim a history in the United States dating back to the 1700s, membership in new radical Black nationalist groups such as the US Organization, the Revolutionary Action Movement (RAM), and the Republic of New Afrika skyrocketed.

In *The Black Power Movement*, Peniel E. Joseph warns against seeing the rise of Black Power as the death of the Civil Rights Movement and views it instead "as an alternative to the ineffectiveness of civil rights demands in critical areas of American life" (3). A perspective that regards Black Power as having "simultaneously triggered the demise of civil rights and the New Left's descent into destructive 'revolutionary' violence" not only severely limits the historiography of the Civil Rights Movement and African American radicalism, as Joseph claims, it also disables possibilities for seeing African American culture of the 1960s and 1970s in relation to an understanding of culture as "a noun of process," as Raymond Williams has declared in *Keywords* (3, 87).

Chester Himes and the Question of Culture

In *Black Power* Stokely Carmichael asserts: "It is absolutely essential that black people develop an awareness of their cultural heritage. . . . And they will soon learn that the Hollywood image of man-eating cannibals waiting for, and waiting on, the Great White Hunter is a lie" (38–37). Three years later, in 1970, Metro-Goldwyn-Mayer Studios released *Cotton Comes to Harlem*, a film adaptation of Chester Himes's popular Coffin Ed and Grave Digger Jones series of detective novels from the 1950s and 1960s. Set in Harlem, the film's intricate plot revolves around the exploits of a colorful messianic religious leader, two equally colorful African American Harlem detectives, Harlem's criminal underworld, and a lost bale of cotton. Generally regarded by film historians as either the first film in the Black film explosion of the late 1960s and 1970s that spawned the genre of Blaxploitation or an important precursor of it, *Cotton Comes to Harlem* is high on "local color" and documents the intricacies of lower-class African American urban life.[5] Drawing on Himes's vividly absurdist portraits of ghetto life, the film both created and recycled a canon of visual images that would come to define the contours of African American life in U.S. popular culture for decades to come.

In an essay in *The Wretched of the Earth* entitled "On National Culture," Frantz Fanon speaks of the "impossible contradictions" inherent in the assertion of a culture of liberation in the midst of political struggle for liberation (237). Himes's work for major Hollywood studios and as a fiction writer epitomizes the "impossible contradictions" that came to characterize the uneven embrace of Black Power culture in the 1960s and 1970s. He never achieved the financial success or artistic legitimacy he sought in his lifetime, though he would be courted by both major publishers and Hollywood studios. Like Black Power culture in general, Himes's work formed the unacknowledged contours for contemporary understandings of racial exchange and conflict and perceptions of African American culture and cultural production. Chester Himes not only provided an important catalyst for the Black Power–era cultural revolution when he created the African American urban underclass in *Cotton Comes to Harlem* as the prototype for African American authenticity, but, in shifting from the literary metaphors of protest fiction to an emphasis on the visual, he prefigured cultural trends in African American culture that continue to the present moment.

Chester Himes had come of age as a writer just after the time "when the Negro was in vogue," as Langston Hughes famously wrote in *The Big Sea*, his landmark autobiographical examination of the African American literary, social, and artistic renaissance that flowered in Harlem in the 1920s and 1930s, only to come to a radical standstill as taste and market conditions changed in the late 1930s and 1940s (41). Himes experienced firsthand the vagaries of the U.S. cultural market's relationship to African American cultural production throughout his career. Born in 1909, he had begun writing as the Harlem Renaissance waned, but not long after it had created the conditions for the widespread popular reception of African American protest fiction in the 1940s and 1950s that would come to be defined almost solely by the unprecedented success of Richard Wright. Himes described Wright as "afraid of his imagination" (*My Life of Absurdity*, 201), but Wright would consistently outsell and outshine Himes as a writer.

Wright, who helped create the influential journal *New Challenge* with the Harlem Renaissance luminary Dorothy West and was friends with Langston Hughes, had also begun writing just as the Harlem Renaissance drew to a close (Kinnamon, 68–69). His first published short story collection, *Uncle Tom's Children*, was excitedly received by such important Harlem literary figures as Countee Cullen and Sterling Brown as a necessary challenge to existing literary norms that failed to explore the political, so- cial, and cultural realities of the African American lower classes. Perhaps sensing and hoping to ward off the shifts in taste that would characterize the post–Harlem Renaissance era, Zora Neale Hurston was alone in writ- ing a searing critique of the book that stated: "One wonders what he would have done had he dealt with plots that touched the broader and more fun- damental phases of Negro life instead of confining himself to the spectacu- lar" (qtd. in Reilly, 9). Even if praise was not completely universal within Harlem's literary establishment, in a sense Wright's forcing of the African American literary establishment into the realm of what Hurston termed "the spectacular" prefigured new directions in African American literary and cultural aesthetics that would culminate in the 1967 filmic recreation of *Cotton Comes to Harlem* and the attendant craze for the images of spec- tacularized African American urban violence embodied by the Blaxploita- tion film boom of the 1960s and 1970s.

Spectacular Blackness

Saidiya V. Hartman writes about the ways in which the spectacular na- ture of African American sufferance informed the establishment of Afri- can American subjectivity in the context of slavery, historically connecting African Americans to visuality, public display, and a discourse of suffering in relationship to the limits of the body and the boundaries of the self and other. Forced to "step it up lively," sing, and smile as they processed in shackles up to the auction block, enslaved African Americans were forced to perform "merriment" and "the entertaining" in situations of complete abjection (33). W. E. B. Du Bois labeled this performative duality "double consciousness" in his landmark 1903 treatise on African American subjec- tivity, *The Souls of Black Folks*, in which he argued, "the Negro is a sort of seventh son, born with a veil, and gifted with second sight in this Ameri- can world—a world which yields him no true self-consciousness, but only lets him see himself through the revelation of the other world" (16). By the time Hurston criticized Wright's choice to portray African Americans in a manner that was "spectacular," the cultural and political shifts that had created the Harlem Renaissance were already renegotiating the pa- rameters of performativity that Hartman describes in relationship to slave subjectivity or that Du Bois chronicled in 1903.

Collectively, the popular reception of writers such as West, Hurston, Cullen, and especially Hughes had enabled the conditions for Wright's unprecedented success with mainstream American readers. But when Wright's second book, *Native Son,* became a Book of the Month Selection in 1940, the first book by an African American author to be so distinguished, it was granted a popular success unimaginable to any of the Harlem Renaissance writers. The novel was "a literary phenomenon" according to Sterling Brown, who noted: "Its first edition sold out within three hours, a quarter million copies called for within six weeks" (qtd. in Reilly, 22). The success of Wright's work proved that it was not only possible for African American writers to have a broadly based mainstream success, but that they could also do so while writing social critique involving lower-class African American life.

Native Son had been significantly altered by the Book of the Month Selection Committee to suit the tastes of its readership, as would happen with Wright's second novel, *Black Boy,* which would also become a runaway bestseller with the Book of the Month Selection Committee's help (see Rowley). Richard Wright's success, mediated as it had been by the mainstream literary and publishing establishment, assured that the social protest formula for African American literary production that he outlined in a *New Challenge* editorial entitled "Blueprint for Negro Writing" came to displace for the majority of American readers and writers all other artistic and aesthetic concerns of the Harlem Renaissance, a movement Wright characterized as resulting from "a liaison between inferiority-complexed Negro 'geniuses' and burnt-out white Bohemians with money" ("Blueprint," 315). What Hurston had termed the "spectacular" nature of Wright's fiction—his interest in what he described in "Blueprint" as "the long complex (and for the most part, unconscious) struggle to regain in some form and under alien conditions of life a whole culture again"—lay at the heart of the social protest formula (316).

In this same editorial Wright commanded African American writers to use African American culture to overturn the existing social order rather than to simply mine African American folklore for its aesthetic or artistic merits as Hurston had done. Though Chester Himes started out writing social protest fiction, this sense of social mission would be displaced by an interest in what he termed "the absurdity of the Negro condition" (*My Life of Absurdity,* 203). Himes did not write to "do no less than create values by which his race is to struggle, live, and die," as Wright had dictated the African American author must in "Blueprint for Negro Writing" (316). Rather than seeking models in the "consciousness and mobility for economic and political action" of the African American working class, as Wright had "in the Negro workers' struggles to free [Angelo] Herndon and the Scottsboro boys," Himes wrote about a palpable, colorless, and futile racialized fear that was, finally, "absurd." Himes eventually achieved the economic and critical success that had eluded him in the United States through the publication of his popular detective fiction in Europe.

This success in a popular, commercially driven genre stood for Himes in marked contrast to the critical literary acclaim achieved by Richard Wright in the U.S. cultural arena. Despite his eventual success overseas, in the end Himes felt a profound rejection by the U.S. publishing industry and reading public that had lionized Wright. He wrote in the second volume of his autobiography, *My Life of Absurdity:* "Nothing in all my life hurt me as much as the American rejection of my thoughts" (110). However, when he reacted to the perceived rejection of his work by a U.S. reading public with a decision to leave the country permanently for Europe, he was aided and encouraged by Richard Wright.[6] Himes's work—with its emphasis on lower-class urban vernacular culture—and Wright's ability to make the African American struggle popular in a broad mainstream context would end up defining the parameters of postwar African American cultural expression. Zora Neale Hurston's fears that Wright "confin[ed] himself to the spectacular" would prefigure the creation of a postwar African American culture that was profoundly visual, aggressively vernacular, and grounded in urban lower-class cultural and political expression.

Cotton Comes to Harlem, Black Authenticity, and the New "Black Aesthetic"

As *Cotton Comes to Harlem* went into production in 1967, the United States stood on the brink of a cultural transformation initiated by the Civil Rights Movement and marked by the postsegregation call for Black Power and the search to define the contours of a discrete Black aesthetic. Himes would unwittingly leave the United States in 1953 at the culmination of a revolution in the production of African American literary culture and return in 1965 as part of a developing revolution in the relationship between African American literary culture, visual culture, and American popular culture. Frustrated over the reception of his own early racially themed social protest novels and by the realist contours that were coming to define African American literary production, Himes left the United States in the early part of his career to live in permanent exile in Europe, where he would continue his writing career almost exclusively for European presses. Chief among Himes's complaints about the American literary scene was what he viewed as its inability to integrate his work into the rigidly developing contours of realism being set for African American fiction, which he considered overly restrictive, formulaic, and proscriptive. He wrote in his autobiography: "To Americans I was a nigger lost from home—as *Time* wrote, 'Amidst Alien Corn'—and I wasn't supposed to write anything of value. . . . But I took myself seriously as a writer of absurd stories and the Americans could go to hell. Maybe that's why they resented me so much" (201).

The passage of the Civil Rights Act of 1964 marked the beginning of institutionalized desegregation in its sweeping gestures of reform, but it also marked the beginning of a significant shift in the consumption, distribution, and production of African American popular culture. Just as it signified the symbolic beginning of African American inclusion in wider U.S. culture, Himes's brief return to the United States to fulfill a landmark contractual agreement with the Hollywood mogul Samuel Goldwyn Jr. to complete three films based on his novels also marked the quiet beginning of a wider U.S. interest in production and consumption of popular visual images of African American culture. These cultural currents would give birth to the genre of Blaxploitation film, the creation and crossover of soul music from an amalgamation of older genres and traditions, and vibrant literary and poetic movements that sprang from the desire to articulate a new Black aesthetic. As did Himes's work, African American culture after 1964 would blur the lines between popular culture and high art and complicate even as it attempted to delineate notions such as realism, authenticity, experience, and commercially driven expression.

Despite Himes's claims that he was writing absurdist fiction, the popularity of his detective series—which would spawn two Blaxploitation-era films in the United States, film adaptations in Europe, and translations into several European languages—relied heavily on the conventions of authenticity and realism that determined the consumption of African American literature in a period dominated by the dictates of protest fiction as defined by the work of Richard Wright. In many ways Himes saw himself as working much more in the tradition of William Faulkner, whose characters he also labeled "absurd," than in the realist tradition of African

American writing epitomized by Wright (*My Life*, 217). Despite this, the reception of Himes's literature as a realist documentation of ghetto life persisted throughout his career, even though the very conditions leading to the creation of his Harlem detective series were antithetical to that reality. Living in exile and in dire need of money, Himes undertook the now celebrated detective series at the behest of the French publisher Marcel Duhamel, primarily because Duhamel was willing to pay large sums of money upfront for the unwritten novels. Himes described the process of accepting Duhamel's offer to publish his work in *La Serie noire* as "consenting to being seduced" (*My Life*, 103).

According to Himes, Duhamel "asked me to write my first thriller, and advised me on the structure of a detective novel, the importance of dialogue, and suggested how I should develop the plot, characters, general atmosphere, and suspense. As a result, I wrote exclusively for *Serie noire* . . . the catalyst was Marcel Duhamel . . . It's Duhamel who created Himes, the writer of detective fiction" (see Cullaz). Himes's writing during this period was very much driven by the constrictions of the detective fiction genre as defined by Duhamel, including the choice of Harlem as a locale and the gangster underworld as the thematic nexus. Himes would later claim about his detective series that "without Duhamel's instruction and financial help I would never have written it" (*My Life*, 111).

While Himes was unequivocal about Marcel Duhamel's role in the creation of his detective series, he was less clear about his own relationship to the symbolic landscape of Harlem and the question of authenticity, and he made the almost contradictory claims that "what makes me happy is that the people of Harlem can recognize each spot in the city, and see themselves mirrored in one character or another in my books" (qtd. in Cullaz, 144), and also, "I didn't really know what it was like to be a citizen of Harlem; I never worked there, raised children there, been hungry, sick or poor there. I had been *as much of a tourist as a white man from downtown changing his luck. The Harlem of my books was never meant to be real; I never called it real; I just wanted to take it away from the white man if only in my books*" (*My Life*, 126, emphasis added). In labeling himself "as much of a tourist as the white man from downtown changing his luck," Himes was not only challenging the notion of himself as a documentarian of Harlem life, he was also significantly rescripting his encounters in Harlem through the language of vice, commerce, and exploitation.[7]

Chester Himes had been born in Jefferson City, Missouri, while his father was a professor in an African American industrial college, and he grew up mostly in Ohio, where he also served a lengthy stint in prison for petty larceny as a young man. He had, however, spent relatively little time in Harlem.[8] While his early writings in prison on criminality were hard-bitten social realist texts, the Harlem detective series he produced for Marcel Duhamel was by contrast a heavily stylized and ironic product. It is marked by what Himes himself would call "absurd" situations, such the one indicated in the title *Blind Man with a Pistol,* or by motivation and action, as in *Run, Man, Run,* in which the chief protagonist spends the entire novel being chased by variously malevolent characters throughout the streets of Harlem. Himes's detective novels are less "whodunnits" in the classical detective novel sense than representations of the stylized portrait of African American life that he wished to create. His first novel, *For the Love of Imabelle,* which became *A Rage in Harlem* in its U.S. translation, contains many of the key tropes and stock cast of characters that would characterize and consequently signify African American ghetto life for generations of consumers of African American popular culture to come: hustlers, con men, greed, vice, and the struggle of ordinary people to stay alive and "make it."

Undoubtedly influenced by the rising world visibility of African American political activism in the United States, Himes added politically radical "Black militants" to his stock cast of tropes for the stylized social chaos of 1965's *Cotton Comes to Harlem,* the seventh novel in the series, which imagines Harlem's Black militants as the proponents of a corrupt, self-serving, Marcus Garvey–styled "Back to Africa" movement. *Cotton Comes to Harlem* moves the Harlem Precinct's "ace" Black detectives Coffin Ed Johnson and Grave Digger Jones rapidly through a series of confrontations with a newly articulated Black consciousness, urban African American despair, the cruelty and indifference of white city officials, and a viciously articulated Harlem criminal underworld. In characteristic fashion, Himes represents Harlem as a place of absurd lawlessness, the logic of which is decodable only to those who possess an African American vernacular sense of American culture, an intimate understanding of African Americans themselves, and a knowledge of the urban terrain on which African Americans were forced to compete, not only with corruption and white injustice, but with each other as well.

However, even given its critical seriousness and its depiction of the social injustice and racism of the United States, the novel is hardly a documentation of social reality. Instead, *Cotton Comes to Harlem* offers a cartoonishly ironic romp through the symbols, signs, and language of African American cultural history. At one point Grave Digger Jones and Coffin Ed see "democracy at work" in the image of two elderly white men shining "colored" men's shoes under an awning that reads "American Legion Shoe Shine," while nearby, white men get their shoes shined by elderly "colored" men under an awning announcing "Father Divine Shoe Shine," and in the next moment, a ribald dancer at Harlem's notorious Cotton Club writhes obscenely against a bale of cotton while crying out, "ohhh, daddy cotton!" (129, 147). *Cotton Comes to Harlem* doesn't so much parody African American representation in mainstream culture as call attention to the absurdity of a history of representation based on what Himes claims are essentially faulty racial presumptions. For this reason, the corruption of the "Back to Africa" movement is juxtaposed in the novel with the cartoonish retrogressiveness of the "Back to the Southland" movement, which seeks to send homesick, newly urban African Americans back to the cotton fields of the South. Cotton coming to Harlem is not a metaphor for a pastoral bounty arriving in an urban wasteland of poverty and despair. Instead, Himes's cast of characters maim and execute one another in a vain search for a bale of cotton stuffed with money that has already been claimed by an elderly African American junk dealer named Cotton Bud, who uses his ill-gotten gains to finance his own return to Africa.

In its novelistic form, *Cotton Comes to Harlem* both anticipated and helped to create several important trends in the articulation of African American popular culture during the Black Power era, especially as it was translated through the idioms of visual culture. Chief among these concerns was negotiating a rhetoric of Black empowerment through a discourse of Black masculinity, especially in relation to the law. Coffin Ed Johnson and Grave Digger Jones's status as "outlaw" lawmen who stand in an always fraught relationship to the law became a standard, oft-repeated trope during the Black action-film boom of the 1970s that *Cotton Comes to Harlem* helped initiate. But Himes's concern with the relationship of Black masculinity to U.S. culture through a discourse of law and order also became a major organizing principle for Black radical discourse, as epitomized by the Black Panther Party's call to "the brother on the block" to "pick up the gun" (Foner, 212).

By 1967, scriptwriters for the film version of the novel at MGM Studios, which included at various times Himes himself, the actor and social activist Ossie Davis, and the playwright LeRoi Jones, would imagine Harlem's activists not as followers of Marcus Garvey but rather as proponents of a Black Power ideology obviously modeled after the stylized visual rhetoric of the Black Panther Party. As had Himes's Harlem detective series, Black Power culture as epitomized by the Black Panther Party would valorize urban identity and street culture as primary expressions of Black authenticity and also resistance. The Black Panthers Party's particular fascination with the visual rhetoric of urban culture and its ongoing involvement with African American vernacular style were very much in keeping with the version of African American culture being commodified by projects such as the film adaptation of *Cotton Comes to Harlem*. The party's engagement with issues of urban poverty, policing, and social justice were negotiated through a rewriting of African American vernacular cultural symbols such as the gun, the criminal as the "bad nigger," and the righteous outlaw, which turned them into potent visual metaphors of urban injustice.

The vision of African American culture as urban, outlaw, and vernacular so powerfully affected developing notions of race, urbanity, and culture that it would greatly contribute to the distillation of that vision throughout American popular culture at large. The Blaxploitation genre would seemingly cement in the lexicon of U.S. popular culture the vision of African American cultural authenticity as primarily constituted by the vernacular archetypes of the glamorous gangster, the pretty pimp, the Black radical, the hustler, the beautiful "bad" woman, and the con man mixing it up in the unrelentingly mean streets of the urban ghetto. However, this vision of African American urban culture stems as much from Himes's ironic, market-driven, expatriate vision of African American urbanity as it did from the social protest movement in which Black Power ideology was disseminated across popular culture.

Himes, in his role as a consultant for the filming of *Cotton Comes to Harlem*, relished the opportunity to return to New York City, especially for extended visits to Harlem. Although Himes had figured large in the formulation of Harlem's reputation internationally, he was, admittedly, not intimately acquainted with it. Himes had not intended the "Harlem Series," as the detective novels became known, to provide a strict documentation of Harlem life. Though the novels were lauded internationally for their gritty, poetic street realism, the "Harlem" of Himes's detective novels is most accurately seen as an amalgamation of his earlier social protest agenda, a reflection of a now past experience of U.S. racial injustice, and a poet's complex sensibility for the cadences and rhythms of African American vernacular culture fused to a strong, editorially driven sensibility about what version of African American social reality would sell abroad.

Unlike Himes's earlier novels, these books did not represent an attempt to document the social realities of racial injustice, though they were largely received that way in Europe. "I would sit in my room and become hysterical thinking about the wild, incredible story I was writing. But it was only for the French, I thought, and they would believe anything about Americans, black or white, if it was bad enough," Himes wrote in *My Life of Absurdity* (109). Ultimately, it could be argued that Himes's detective series was not really about Harlem at all, but it could also be argued that it was all about Harlem if we accept, as Himes appeared to, that the postwar African American urban social and aesthetic reality was concentrated in the seamy nexus of commerce, vice, and disposable culture. Himes observed in his autobiography that though the *La Serie noire* "was considered the junkyard of writers, Richard Wright had never earned as much money from a book published by a trade publisher in France as I was earning from [it]" (124). But regarding Wright's work, Himes also grudgingly acknowledged that "at least his books were accepted as literature."

Himes's first novel, *If He Hollers Let Him Go* (1945), was a portrait of the downward spiral of the life of a young African American dockworker at a Los Angeles shipyard recently integrated by African American and female workers because of the conscription of white male workers during World War II. It stands as a strong indictment of Black patriotism, wartime ambivalence about legally sanctioned policies of segregation, and African American prospects for inclusion in the "American Dream." *Lonely Crusade* (1947), a novel about an alienated African American intellectual hired to help unionize African American workers at a shipping factory, is a hard-bitten indictment of the racial politics of the labor movement in the United States and the Communist Party.

Himes's work continuously challenged the boundaries for inclusion and exclusion of African American cultural production within mainstream U.S. culture. He experienced the reception of *Lonely Crusade* as so vicious that he characterized it in an interview as "a terrible humiliation"; this would be the catalyst for him to join the ranks of permanent expatriates living first in France and then in Spain, where he died in 1984 (see Fabre, 129). Himes's detective novels, for which he was awarded the prestigious French *Grand prix de la littérature policiere*, were characterized much more by their high stylization, absurdity, and comedic irony—exemplified by the title

Real Cool Killers—than by any obvious social protest message. A "working writer" who often angered other writers and intellectuals with his claims that he wrote simply to make a living, Himes was forced to largely abandon social protest fiction after he began writing his Harlem detective series. Of the ten novels Himes completed between the time he began the series in 1957 and his death in 1984, only *A Case of Rape* lies outside the popular detective genre.[9]

Himes's removal from African American vernacular culture to Europe and his somewhat belated realization that African American writing could be commercially viable did not remove him from the much vaunted realm of "Black authenticity" that became the hallmark of Black Power–era cultural expression. Himes was often grouped with popular African American "street realist" writers such as Donald Goines and Iceberg Slim (Robert Beck). In fact, Donald Goines claimed that he had been inspired to write while serving one of many long prison terms and reading the work of the pimp-turned-novelist Iceberg Slim and Chester Himes.[10] The main character of Goines's first novel is named "Chester Hines," in an obvious tribute to this inspiration. Donald Goines and Iceberg Slim, however, came of age as writers when the parameters of Black authenticity had already been set by Chester Himes and Black Power culture, so much so that their personas were more those of the pimp or street hustler who wrote than that of a former prisoner who wrote, as Chester Himes described himself. But Himes, Goines, and Beck would participate in and help create the postwar African American culture that popularized African American vice by making it commercially viable, and then mystified that process of commodification by designating it as the "authentic" expression of African American culture.

Melvin Van Peebles, the financial success of whose own controversial first film, *Sweet Sweetback's Baadasssss Song!*, is generally credited with sparking Hollywood studios' commercial interest in African American film, had early seen the powerful visual potential of African American vice. He had become a personal friend of Himes while living temporarily in France and had even turned Himes's *Serie noire* novel *For the Love of Imabelle* into a comic strip for a French magazine. In his initial instruction on how to write for the *Serie noire*, Marcel Duhamel had instructed Himes to "start with action . . . always action in detail. Make pictures. Like motion pictures" (*My Life*, 102). In this way, Duhamel had unintentionally helped Himes to anticipate visual culture's burgeoning place of importance in African American postwar culture. Both Van Peebles and Himes were also visionary in their ability to see the iconographic power of images of African American urban criminal culture in postwar America. While African American writers and artists had long been interested in African American urbanity and also in African American criminality, Himes and Van Peebles were prescient in seeing the powerful potential of those cultures and then linking them to emerging possibilities in visual culture, particularly in popular film. Between the release of *Cotton Comes to Harlem* in 1970 and the end of the Black film boom in 1976, an unprecedented number of "Black cast" films would be released, and most of these would be violent action films.

Cultural Change and the Black Arts Movement

By 1968, the cultural, social, and political landscape had changed so much that artists, politicians, and cultural workers alike were not only declaring "a new day in Babylon" with regard to violence and empowerment but also witnessing the birth of a Black Arts Movement and its attendant proclamation of a uniquely Black aesthetic. In the Black Arts Movement's manifesto, "The Black Arts Movement," Larry Neal wrote:

> The political values inherent in the Black Power concept are now finding concrete expression in the aesthetics of Afro-American dramatists, poets, choreographers, musicians, and novelists. A main tenet of Black Power is the necessity for Black people to define the world in their own terms. The Black artist has made the same point in the context of aesthetics. . . . The Black artist takes this to mean that his primary duty is to speak to the needs of Black people. Therefore, the main thrust of this new breed of contemporary writers is to confront the contradictions arising out of the Black man's experience in the racist West. Currently, these writers are re-evaluating Western aesthetics, the traditional role of the writer, and the social function of art. Implicit in this re-evaluation is the need to develop a "black aesthetic." It is the opinion of many Black writers, I among them, that the Western aesthetic has run its course: it is impossible to construct anything meaningful within its decaying structures. We advocate a cultural revolution in art and ideas. (257–58)

Neal's declaration of the need for separate cultural spaces and separate spheres of symbolic articulation was more than the rejection of white culture and the West as which it was often read. It represented an almost utopian longing for a discrete space of cultural expression free from the corruption that he saw as linked explicitly and implicitly to participation in U.S. commodified culture. In defining the Black aesthetic later in the essay, Neal asserts the aesthetic not only as an overturning of an existing cultural order—"the destruction of the white thing, the destruction of white ideas, and white ways of looking at the world"—but as a moral imperative. Describing the Black Arts Movement as "an ethical movement," he states: "The new aesthetic is mostly predicated on Ethics which asks the question: whose vision of the world is finally more meaningful, ours or the white oppressor's?" (259).

In 1970, Gil Scott-Heron famously articulated this longing for a separate, uncorrupted sphere of articulation with an indictment of commodified culture and a declaration that "the revolution would not be televised." Using a series of references to current popular product-endorsement campaigns, Heron asserted that "the revolution" would "not put a tiger in your tank," "go better with Coke," "give your mouth sex appeal," or "kill the germs that cause bad breath." Like Neal, who believed that the Black Arts Movement envisioned "an art that speaks directly to the needs and aspirations of Black America" (257), Scott-Heron sought to articulate an arena of "pure politics" into which commodified U.S. culture would no longer fit.

The Black Arts and Black Power movements' investment in a utopian world outside of the Babylon of commodification occurred, ironically, precisely at the moment when African American vernacular culture experienced a massive crossover commodification through popular film, music, and visual culture. The Black Arts Movement's goal of overturning established aesthetic and cultural norms across a variety of African American representational and expressive traditions and establishing a market-free cultural space occurred just as the Civil Rights Movement was creating unprecedented opportunities for African American social, cultural, and political expression. When the migration from the rural south to urban locations that had been occurring since the turn of the century was heightened by the official desegregation of wartime industries by Franklin Delano Roosevelt in 1944, African Americans were poised on the cutting edge—albeit at the lowest levels of production—of urban industrialization. African American cultural creators were uniquely positioned to capture the imagination of commodified U.S. culture while at the same time making claims to a culture of resistance that was figured as purely and authentically ideologically free from the contamination of the urban industrialized world.

Enter the Black Panther Party

In the postwar period, according to Kobena Mercer, Black identity took on a heightened significance as "an iconic expression of oppositional identities" that would be very much linked to the visual and expressive expression of urban African American street culture documented by *Cotton Comes to Harlem* in its novelistic form and even more so in Ossie Davis's filmic version (300). Mercer links the Black Panther Party's "highly visible oppositional appearance, which clearly differentiated [it] from other strands in black politics," to the development of myriad liberation groups and strategies:

> The political positions of the Black Panthers had an empowering effect in extending the chain of radical democratic equivalences to more and more social groups precisely through their dramatic and provocative visibility in the public sphere. At the level of political discourse, it was this system of equivalences that helped generate the form of women's liberation and gay liberation out of strategic analogies with the goals, and methods, of black liberation, which were themselves based on an analogy with Third World struggles for national liberation. The ten-point platform of the Black Panther Party, articulated by Huey P. Newton and Bobby Seale in 1966, formed a discursive framework through which the women's movement and the gay movement displaced the demand for reform and "equality" in favor of the wider goal of revolution and "liberation." The ten-point charter of demands of the Women's Liberation Movement, 1968, and the Gay Liberation Front, 1969, were based on a metaphorical transfer of the terms of liberation of one group into the terms of liberation of others. (303)

The Black Panther Party's political and cultural program, one of the most visible articulations of Black Power ideology, was not without antecedents. In fact, its Ten-Point Program closely resembled the Nation of Islam statement "What We Want, What We Believe," which was printed in *Muhammad Speaks* and *The Final Call*, the official papers of the Nation of Islam since its inception in the 1950s. What made the Black Panther Party's articulation of its ideology different from the Nation of Islam's, however, was the fact that cultural spaces had been opened for the party's explosive expression as a multimedia phenomenon by both televisual representations of the civil rights struggle and by postwar cultural shifts in the production of identity. The coalescence of radical ideology as espoused by groups like the Black Panthers and the radically altered postwar social, cultural, and political terrain permitted the emergence of the challenge posed by the Black Arts Movement. This framework linked the articulation of the radical political ethos of Black Power to a radically transformative culture of oppositional creativity. In challenging the ways in which politics can and should engage with culture and art in the U.S. context, the Black Power and Black Arts movements undeniably shaped wider cultural perceptions of what it means to be African American, what it means to engage in social protest, and the interface between identity and political action. This book, *Spectacular Blackness*, is an attempt to assess the long-term implications of these movements for the American cultural and social fabric.

Trying to come to terms with the complicated cultural legacy of the Black Panther Party raises questions about the construction and subsequent commodification of African American radical political culture, which the party created and by which it was also consumed. In "'Don't Believe the Hype': Debunking the Panther Mythology," Charles E. Jones and Judson L. Jeffries cite the belief that "the BPP was a media created organization" as number three in their list of the most prevalent misconceptions about the party and conclude that this myth leads to an assessment of the party in which "BPP visibility and prominence are attributed to a sensationalist-driven media captivated by the revolutionary theatrics of the Panthers" (41). They correctly note that this perception "not only underestimates community support, it also depreciates the dedication of the organizational membership." What Jones and Jeffries fail to appreciate, however, are the ways in which this perception also greatly underestimates the Black Panther Party's own participation in and manipulation of the media cult that sprang up around it.

As Manthia Diawara has said in the edited collection *Soul: Black Power, Politics, and Pleasure*, "Popular culture has always been where Black people theorize Blackness in America" (qtd. in Simon, 236), and popular culture played a central role in the Black Panther Party's propagation of a Black Power political culture. In fact, the Black Panther Party evinced a better understanding of popular culture than many similar organizations, cultural workers, and critics. Since it was not only invested in influencing American popular culture of the period but was also in the business of creating it, the party's engagement with African American popular culture has had a widespread effect. A major reason that the Panther legacy continues to live on long after the ideas and contributions of similar organizations such as the Revolutionary Action Committee or the Student Nonviolent Coordinating Committee have long been forgotten is the party's consciousness of the importance of media culture and its brilliance in using it to challenge American culture in general. Without a serious reassessment of the Panthers' utilization of media culture, the myth that they were created by the mainstream media will continue. More important, it will be impossible to gain a serious understanding of the ways in which the Black Panther Party influenced and shaped the popular visual culture that followed it. For this reason, *Spectacular Blackness* explores the Black Panther Party's legacy specifically in terms of its interaction with popular visual and media culture and its affiliation with white radicals in order to begin to understand the conscious dissemination of radical Black political culture throughout other cultural forms of the era.

One of the major unacknowledged and unexplored ways in which the Black Panther Party influenced African American culture was through valorizing "the brothers on the block" as the authentic repositories of "the Black experience." Recent essays by Chris Booker, Charles E. Jones, Floyd W. Hayes, and Francis A. Kiene, collected in Jones's *The Black Panther Party Reconsidered*, address the party's influential attempts to organize the African American lumpen-proletariat class as the vanguard of a revolutionary Black freedom struggle. Influenced by Frantz Fanon's attempt in *The Wretched of the Earth* to rescue the lumpen proletariat from its condemnation as an unstable political force in traditional Marxist thought, Hayes and Kiene contend that Newton and the party provided "one of the most controversial aspects of their political ideology and practice" in their attempts to champion "the brother on the block" as possessing the ultimate revolutionary potential (161).

This challenge to traditional Marxist-Leninist practice and thought proved influential in many spheres of African American cultural production, affecting everything from music, art, and film in particular to political and cultural thought in general. The notion that African American culture resides exclusively in the urban ghetto among the poorest and most disenfranchised of the African American population continues to be pervasive in post–Black Power African American culture. The jury is still out as to whether the Black Panther Party's focus on the lumpen proletariat was effective as an organizing methodology or was, as Booker contends, a major contributing factor to the party's rapid demise. However, the valorization of "the brothers on the block" as the guarantors of an authentic "Black experience" and the demonization of the "middle-class Negro" has continued to haunt African American notions of "authenticity" and has not been widely assessed. This remains true despite the fact that class tension continues to be a major shaping force in African American culture today.

The Panthers' presence is still felt in everything from the popularization of the term "Black" to describe African Americans to the multiple insertions of the party's critique of policing into American popular consciousness. Recent books by and about former members of the Black Panther Party, including Mumia Abu-Jamal's *We Want Freedom: A Life in the Black Panther Party* (2004), Johnny Spain's *Black Power, White Blood: The Life and Times of Johnny Spain* (2000), Elaine Brown's *A Taste of Power: A Black Woman's Story* (1992), David Hilliard's *This Side of Glory: The Autobiography of David Hilliard and the Story of the Black Panther Party* (1993), and Hugh Pearson's biography *The Shadow of the Panther: Huey Newton and the Price of Black Power in America* (1994), have sparked a reassessment and analysis of the party's status in African American culture. The 1995 reissue by Writers and Readers Press of Huey Newton's long-out-of-print autobiography, *Revolutionary Suicide,* and a popular but previously hard-to-obtain essay collection *To Die for the People,* along with the inclusion of *Black Panthers* by Herb Boyd in the press's popular "For Beginners" series of documentary comic books has helped revive a wide popular interest in the legacy of the Black Panther Party. Avant-garde artists have explored the imagery of the Black Panther Party since Jean Luc Goddard's 1968 experimental documentary *Sympathy for the Devil* paired actors portraying the Panthers with documentary footage of the Rolling Stones. In 2003, the jazz composer Fred Ho created "The Black Panther Suite" for his Afro Asian Music Ensemble, and Roger Guenveur Smith explored the legacy of Huey P. Newton with a 2001 Obie Award–winning stage play, *The Huey P. Newton Story.* More than ever since the party's official demise, there is an ongoing attempt to assess the challenges present in the party's critique of policing and its Ten-Point Platform.

The most salient critique that the party offered of American society was directed at the justice system and the role played by police and mass incarceration in institutionalizing state repression. The facts that the U.S.

prison population has grown steadily since 1973 and that the state of California currently incarcerates more people than Great Britain, Germany,
Japan, France, Singapore, and the Netherlands combined, the vast majority of these prisoners being nonwhite, make the Panthers' critique of the
prison industrial complex seem almost visionary.[11] Because the jail and
prison population in the United States is composed primarily of members
of racial minority groups, particularly African Americans, the prison crisis
remains a problem of particular importance to African Americans. These
two issues help account for the Black Panther Party's ghostly presence in
African American popular culture and make a reassessment of the Black
Panther Party legacy especially necessary at this time.

The Black Panther Party's critique of policing and its famous demand
that African Americans "pick up the gun" in defense of the African American community were too often scripted into a discourse of "recovering
Black manhood." The image of the Black Panther Party retained by many is
rightfully characterized as highly stylized, hypermasculine, military Black
macho. This image stems directly from cultural memories of the party's
military-style parade drills and the ever-present image of the African American man with a gun, combined with Eldridge Cleaver's command that African American women invoke "Pussy Power" in defense of the Party and his
pro-rape polemic in Soul on Ice. The Black macho mythos of the party often
obscures, now as it did then, the complexity of the party's official stance on
gender politics and the serious nature of its dialogue with and engagement
in issues of gender parity. The facts that the Black Panther Party was the
first, and for many years the only, national African American organization
to speak out in favor of gay rights or to make open alliances with a homo-
sexual rights group, and that the organization had many women in positions of power are hidden by the macho mythos that surrounds the party.
Recent work by Angela Y. Davis, Joy James, Regina Jennings, Elaine Brown,
Angela Brown, and Tracye Matthews highlights the role of women within
the party, bringing necessary complexity and insight to our understanding
of its gender dynamic both as a lived reality and as articulated in its official
position papers. Such work suggests an urgent need to redefine the group's
relevance to popular culture.

A cultural analysis of the Black Panther Party provides the crucial van-
tage point from which to begin a reassessment of the cultural movements
of the 1960s and 1970s. The discourse of Black liberation fueled a great deal
of post–civil rights African American culture, including popular music in

its varied forms of rhythm and blues, soul, and funk. The party's engagement with popular culture and the subsequent critique of that engagement are reenacted in the Black Arts Movement's attempts to delineate a Black aesthetic as well as in the debates surrounding the commercialization of African American popular music and Hollywood's rescripting of Black Power into Blaxploitation films.

Black to the Future

The Black Arts Movement, which was labeled the "sister to the Black Power concept" by Larry Neal (*Visions of a Liberated Future*, 257), significantly shaped the way in which an entire generation of cultural and artistic critics and practitioners defined their roles within society and culture, but its legacy has been more misunderstood and obscure than that of the Black Panther Party, despite its equally pervasive influence. By presenting the culture of the everyday African American struggle as one worthy of serious scholarly recognition and analysis, the movement contributed to the current formation of African American studies and to a general understanding of what is valuable about African American culture. Problematic as it would become, the decision to make "the Black experience" of "the average Negro" the central determinant in the figuration of a "Black aesthetic" was a truly critical break with past conceptualizations of the ways in which African American art was constructed. The movement consciously dispensed with the idea that African American artists and intellectuals should be busy formulating a plan for the creation of a "New Negro" or that they should operate as a "Talented Tenth" to lead the race to conclusions that they did not already possess. Though the movement was relatively short-lived, its challenges to the status quo helped institutionalize African American literature and culture as legitimate objects of intellectual scrutiny. It continues to exert a powerful influence on artists' ideas about themselves and their art. In his introduction to *The Leroi Jones Reader*, William J. Harris rightfully claims, "No post–Black Arts artist thinks of himself or herself as simply a human being who happens to be black; blackness is central to his or her experience and art" (xxvi).

African American popular culture's tributes to icons of the 1960s and 1970s represent the ascendancy of the aesthetic that was championed by the Black Arts Movement. Members of the Black Panther Party were often openly suspicious of those (including Black Arts spokesman LeRoi Jones) whom they deemed to be overly invested in cultural politics; the Panthers derisively labeled them "cultural nationalists." The Black Arts Movement's valorization of everyday African American urban culture, however, was very much in keeping with the Black Panther Party's elevation of "the brothers on the block" to vanguard status in radical African American politics. In contemporary culture, that which is urban, black, and poor continues to be marked as the most authentic manifestation of African American culture. Everyone from conservative pundits such as John McWhorter and Shelby Steele to politically progressive cultural workers such as *The Boondocks* cartoonist Aaron McGruder constructs urban authenticity as the dominant mood of African American cultural articulation.

The notion that the urban poor experience is definitional in the construction of African American identity is largely a result of the Black Arts/Black Power moment. The central questions first cogently posed by the Black Arts Movement continue to remain unanswered and mostly unexplored. How would African American artists and intellectuals be accountable to the masses of African American people? How would the masses of African American people be integrated into the dominant culture? What stood to be lost and what stood to be gained for African American culture if the project of integration was a success?

The Black Arts Movement was very much concerned with actualizing its demands for self-determined African American cultural production through the creation of independent venues for cultural exchange. Though many of these journals, artistic spaces, theater companies, writing groups, and collectives did not survive the 1970s, the imperative to create independent avenues for African American culture has yet to die down. One of the most significant failures of the Black Arts Movement was the failure of the Black Arts Repertory Theater School of Harlem. Created by an artists' collective spearheaded by LeRoi Jones to be a self-sustaining showcase for the artists, writers, musicians, and intellectuals of the movement, the Black Arts Theater had a brief but mercurial history. Sonia Sanchez, Sun Ra, John Coltrane, Ed Bullins, and LeRoi Jones himself showcased their work there until the theater's demise less than six months after opening its doors. Rather than signaling the radical impossibility of the Black Arts proposition, Larry Neal argues that the Black Arts Theater's history "proved that there was a definite need for a cultural revolution in the Black community" ("Some Reflections," 262).

Though much of the work is currently out of print, the anthologies of the Black Arts Movement remain as tributes to the notion of radical collectivity embodied by the spirit of the Black Arts Theater and other efforts like it. Like so many others of the era, Larry Neal and LeRoi Jones responded to the failure of ventures like the Black Arts Theater of Harlem with the creation of anthologies such as *Black Fire! An Anthology of Afro-American Writing.* These anthologies recreated, in a condensed, retainable, and sustainable form, the highest ideals of the Black Arts Movement—a revolutionary, communal, and collective effort. In the five-year period between 1967 and 1973, more than thirty new anthologies were published, many by small or independent presses. Ranging in subject matter from prisoners' literature to collections of African American women's literature and poetry, they represent the flowering of the Black Arts principle of self-determined, independent Black creation.

Black Fire! An Anthology of Afro-American Writing, published by Neal and Jones in 1968, presented the work of some of the most important artists and intellectuals of the Black Arts Movement, among them John Henrik Clarke, Calvin C. Hernton, Stokely Carmichael, Sun Ra, K. William Kgositsile, David Henderson, Sonia Sanchez, Harold Cruse, A. B. Spellman, Stanley Crouch, Lorenzo Thomas, and Victor Hernandez Cruz. The anthology represented an attempt to counter the attack against African American collectivity occurring in both political and artistic circles. While efforts to destroy African American political organizations such as the Black Panther Party are now well known, the difficulties encountered by artistic and cultural ventures is less so. In "The Black Arts Movement," Larry Neal documents the problems the Black Arts Theater faced in dealing with governmental agencies, which were at least partially responsible for its funding. Efforts such as *Black Fire!* allowed Neal and Jones to propagate the ideas of the Black Arts Movement without interference.

One of the key tenets of the Black Arts Movement was the belief that African American music was the preeminent example of Black aesthetic production. Black Arts poets wrote odes to John Coltrane, Sun Ra, Coleman Hawkins, Sonny Rollins, Billie Holiday, and Pharaoh Saunders. Critics wrote essays in which they professed music to be "the vanguard reflection of black feeling and the continuous repository of black consciousness," as Ron Welburn claimed in "The Black Aesthetic Imperative" (126). Clayton Riley stated that Black music worked to "show Black people . . . how much it is possible to love themselves for being what they are" (297). And LeRoi

Jones simply concluded that the blues "remained the exact replication of The Black Man In The West" (*Black Music*, 297). Although the Black Arts Movement claimed all forms of African American music as nearly sacred manifestations of the Black aesthetic, it was mostly the folk-based African American forms of jazz, gospel, and the blues that were meant when they referred to the "MUSIC of twenty-two million Black souls" (Cobb, 524).

The Black Arts Movement's interest in jazz and the blues and its attendant lack of interest in the African American popular music that was developing in tandem with them is problematic for a number of significant reasons. By the 1960s and 1970s, African American musical forms such as the blues, gospel, and jazz had largely been displaced for "the average Negro" by the popular forms of rhythm and blues, soul, and eventually funk. While Black Arts critics are often quick to acknowledge that "the man standing in line for the Otis Redding show at the Apollo almost certainly never heard of tenor saxophonist Albert Ayler," this fact does not often color their analysis of Black music production or nuance their understanding of a Black aesthetic (L. Neal and L. Jones, 167). Also, at this time, Black Power discourse and the discourse of the Black Arts Movement were seeping into popular music and art. Popular music was replete with celebrations of the new Black Power politics in terms of lyrics as well as stylistic choices in presentation on stage and on album covers. This fact goes mostly unnoted by the Black Arts Movement critics who dismiss popular music either as trivial and corrupted or as more of "the changing same," as LeRoi Jones labeled rhythm and blues in putting it together with contemporary jazz in *Black Music* (180).

This points to an essential problematic of the Black Arts Movement, namely, the critics' inability to theorize the effects of commodification on African American cultural production, which is tied to a fear of the effects of integration on the African American community. The anxiety focuses in particular on the African American middle class and a fear of losing the essential "struggle" quality, which the Black Arts Movement attributes to the Black experience. In "Blackness Can: A Quest for Aesthetics," James A. Emanuel quotes the Black Arts poet A. B. Spellman's image of white colleges in the future "turning out hundreds of black-talking *bourgies* with Ph.D.s in Malcolm X and John Coltrane" (208) and draws on Edward Vaughn's fears that Black studies programs will become no more than "agencies for spying on Black people" (209). While the Black Arts Movement never ultimately settled the issues that arose in the wake of postintegration cultural politics, the negotiations it attempted around cultural production, community, and integration deserve renewed scrutiny.

The final portion of *Spectacular Blackness* deals directly with the much-maligned Black film boom of the 1960s and 1970s that created the genre of Blaxploitation film. Blaxploitation film raises several important questions with regard to consumption, commodification, and African American cultural production, including the possibilities for resistance within commodified culture. By 1965 the images traditionally created in Hollywood to account for African American existence were inconsistent with the images created by the widely televised rebellion in Watts. Images from films such as *Shaft* (1971), *Three The Hard Way* (1974), *Cleopatra Jones* (1972), and *Sweet Sweetback's Baadasssss Song!* (1971) consciously and openly contested images from films such as *Judge Priest* (1934), *Hallelujah* (1929), and *Lilies of the Field* (1963). Yet the question remains, how significantly did Blaxploitation films deviate from the standard script that Hollywood had created of African Americans in relation to visual culture?

In Los Angeles, the lives of African American people had long been ordered by a repressive policing regime structured by an equally oppressive visual regime. This went beyond the standard American practice of criminalizing populations based on racially demarcated visual cues. The Los Angeles Police Department instituted and subjected its African American population to an entire oppressive policing regime based on visuality: recognition, surveillance, and visual identification. Independently produced films made during the Black film boom of this era, such as *Sweet Sweetback's Baadasssss Song!* and *Dolemite II: The Human Tornado* (1976), attempt to provide a counterdiscourse to the visual history of Los Angeles. In "The Revolution Will Not Be Televised," Gil Scott-Heron cautioned: "There will be no pictures of you and Willie Mae pushing that shopping cart down the block at a dead run or trying to slide that t.v. into a stolen ambulance" (61).

Much of Black Power–era politics was negotiated through popular media venues such as the evening news, popular music, and film. Blaxploitation film provides an opportunity to examine the revolutionary possibilities of popular visual culture and also to begin to account for the pleasure possibilities of popular culture for African American that goes beyond "false consciousness" as an explanation. In the last chapter, I view the Black Arts Movement's engagement with jazz and the blues as "Black classical music" and its nonengagement with other African American popular music, such as funk, soul, and rhythm and blues, and African American popular visual culture as symptomatic of its larger failures to address questions about urbanization and the creation and consumption of both folk and mass culture.

Though Chester Himes had been prescient enough in his understanding of developing postwar American culture to see the potential for particular tropes of urbanity that he developed in his Harlem detective series, he ultimately rejected Black Power ideology and aesthetics. In a final, unfinished novel, *Plan B,* Himes resolved longstanding tensions between his two detectives around their relationship to their position as mediators between the white establishment and the African American urban underclass by having one of the detectives kill the other in a dispute over a planned Black Power revolt in Harlem. Rather than suggesting that such an act is heroic, the conclusion of *Plan B* constructs Black Power as an ultimately divisive and destructive force for urban African Americans and faults Black Power culture for failing to form a cohesive strategy for implementing its goal of cultural and political revolution. Rather than portraying Black Power culture as having failed to effect its promised revolution, *Spectacular Blackness* posits that the very contradictions inherent in Black radical notions such as vanguardism and the acceptance of the vanguard model into cultural politics by the Black Arts Movement and Black popular culture critically formed the ways in which we continue to understand Black identity, Black community, and Black cultural production.

1

"Black Is Beautiful!"

BLACK POWER CULTURE, VISUAL CULTURE,
AND THE BLACK PANTHER PARTY

> One does not necessarily have to wait for a
> revolutionary situation to arise; it can be created.
>
> —Ernesto "Che" Guevara, *Guerilla Warfare*

> LITTLE JOHNNY IN SCHOOL
> Little Johnny says, "My brother was in Vietnam and
> got shot in the ass."
> The teacher says, "Hey freeze, freeze. Don't say 'ass,'
> say 'rectum.'"
> Little Johnny says, "'Rect 'um?' Shit, it killed 'um!"
>
> —Richard Pryor, *Bicentennial Nigger*

Guerilla Warfare   Che Guevara's Armed Struggle and the Black Panther Party

Ernesto "Che" Guevara's simple formulation of the factors that enabled the 1965 revolution in Cuba and that could potentially enable revolution throughout the world were widely read and highly influential among all who considered themselves dispossessed and revolutionary during the social and cultural upheaval of the mid-1960s to late 1970s. In a 1968 film, *Black Panther,* created by the Third World Newsreel Collective and the Black Panther Party to highlight their cause and the situation of their imprisoned leader, Huey P. Newton, the camera pauses didactically on a copy of *Venceremos,* a 1969 collection of Guevara's speeches and essays, as Newton describes from his jail cell the goals of the party and its possible sphere of influence by using the Cuban revolution as a metaphor for the possibilities for Black revolution in the West.

Guevara greatly favored military action over political action, and most influential with the Black Panther Party was his claim that, rather than wait for revolutionary situations to arise as traditional Leninist Marxism demanded, the guerilla had a duty to create revolution through his own actions. This also transformed the configuration of revolutionary struggles for "land and freedom" not only throughout the agrarian economies of Latin America and Africa but also throughout the urban, industrialized United States and Europe.[1] Groups influenced by Guevara's concept of armed struggle included not only the Black Panther Party in Oakland, California, but organizations as diverse as the Red Army Faction in West Germany, the Red Brigade in Italy, and the Weather Underground, the Black Liberation Army, and George Jackson's incipient People's Army in the United States.

Throughout *Guerilla Warfare*, Che Guevara maintained a singular focus on revolution as a military possibility alone. However, his "*indispensable* condition" that "the guerilla fighter needs full help from the people of the area" had the unintended consequence of privileging symbolic as much as actual military action (4). This, combined with the Black Panthers' media-savvy approach and the explosion of interest in popular African American culture in the late 1960s and 1970s, expanded Guevara's model of revolution so that it could allow for victories the significance of which Guevara could neither have anticipated nor accounted for. The Black Panther Party would largely fail in its nearly fifteen years of existence at its final goal to "serve and liberate the colony, by the only means necessary—the GUN," as the first issue of the Black Panther Community News Service proclaimed (Foner, 8). In a seeming contradiction to Guevara's fundamental belief that the symbolic actions of revolutionaries, if effective, would necessarily create the conditions for revolution, the more the Black Panther Party seemed to fail in the actual armed struggle, the greater were its successes in convincing U.S. culture of the necessity not only for the party's own existence but for revolution itself. In the end, the Panthers' successes would lie more in the influence they wielded in the arena of popular culture than in military culture. This chapter explores the apparent contradiction between the party's cultural successes and its political failures, as well as its overall role in defining the parameters of postwar African American culture.

Guevara's *Guerilla Warfare* begins with a chapter titled "Essence" that lists "three fundamental conclusions" that "the Cuban revolution revealed": "1) Popular forces can win a war against an army. 2) One does not necessarily have to wait for a revolutionary situation to arise; it can be created. 3) In the under-developed countries of the Americas, rural areas are the best battlefields for revolution" (1). For urban self-styled guerillas like the Black Panther Party, the exact relationship between the "three fundamental conclusions" about the Cuban revolution and the possible contradictions between Guevara's call for a rural revolution and the actual urban industrialized conditions in which they existed were less important than Guevara's claim that revolutionary conditions could be created by small, committed groups bound together by certain strategic revolutionary aims. Guevara's theory, dubbed "focoism," was popularized in the West by the French philosopher Regis Debray, who, along with Fidel Castro, was largely responsible for propagating the work of Guevara after his death while attempting to foment guerilla warfare in the jungles of Bolivia in 1967.

According to focoism, small groups of highly trained guerillas, "focos," could act as agents for socialist revolution by creating through their actions alone the conditions that would enable a large-scale mass revolution. Tactical wins and losses, though important, were less so than the mass identification with revolutionary possibility that such actions could create by proving to the dispossessed, according to Debray, "that a soldier and a policeman are no more bulletproof than anyone else" (51). The inevitable losses incurred when a small fighting force encountered a trained army did not necessarily have to be a deterrent to fomenting revolution: "For a revolutionary, failure is a springboard. As a source of theory it is richer than victory: it accumulates experience and knowledge" (23). The implication of Guevara's theory of revolution as read through Regis Debray was that, win or lose, focos could become through exemplary action alone a revolutionary vanguard for a soon-to-follow revolution.

"Armed Propaganda" and the Vanguard of the Revolution

Groups like the Black Panther Party were not only excited by the possibility that a small-scale organization could provoke a broader engagement with governmental forces and elicit a mass response, they were empowered by the seemingly audacious claim that if small, armed groups created the conditions of revolutionary struggle, ultimately *they could win*. In the short film *Black Panther*, Huey Newton explained from prison:

We're not a self-defense group in the limited fashion that you usually think of self-defense groups. I like to use the example of when Fidel Castro started the revolution along with Che Guevara. There were only twelve of them altogether. They realized they wouldn't be able to topple the oppressive regime in Cuba. What they were was essentially an educational body. They engaged with the Army. They fought with the Army in order to show the people that the army was not bullet proof. The police were not bullet proof and that Batista's regime was not a regime that was impossible to topple. So the people started to feel their own strength. The Black Panther Party feels very much the same way. We think that this educational process is necessary and it's the people that will cause the revolution. . . . And we plan to teach the people the strategies and necessary tools to liberate themselves.

Newton's belief that military action could have a value beyond basic wins and losses by serving as revolutionary propaganda was drawn primarily from the example of the Cuban revolution. Fidel Castro had affirmed in 1962 at the Second Declaration of Havana: "What Cuba can give to the peoples, and has already given, is its example. And what does the Cuban revolution teach? That revolution is possible, that the people can make it." *The Black Panther* would quote Jose Marti's advice that "the best way of showing is doing," while Huey P. Newton would argue in "The Correct Handling of the Revolution," "When the Vanguard group destroys the machinery of the oppressor by dealing with him in small groups of three and four, and then escapes the might of the oppressor, the masses will be overjoyed and adhere to this correct strategy. When the masses hear that a Gestapo policeman has been executed while sipping coffee, and the revolutionary executioners fled without being traced, the masses will see the validity of this approach to resistance" (*Black Panthers Speak*, 41, 20).

Regis Debray labeled this "armed propaganda" in his highly influential *Revolution in the Revolution? Armed Struggle and Political Struggle in Latin America*, which attempted to continue and elaborate on the work begun in Guevara's *Guerilla Warfare* (47). Debray, who had been arrested in Bolivia during Guevara's Bolivia campaign and served three years in prison as a result, greatly favored, as did Fidel Castro and Che Guevara himself, revolutionary praxis over revolutionary theory. Guevara vigorously denigrated "coffee-shop theories" and "the do-nothing attitude of those pseudo-revolutionaries who procrastinate under the pretext that nothing can be done against a professional army" (*Selected Works*, 204, 375). He urged instead, "Where one really learns is in a revolutionary war; every minute teaches you more than a million volumes of books. You mature in the extraordinary university of experience" (386).

The notion of "armed propaganda" suggested that not only could revolutionary war be a learning experience for revolutionaries, it could also be a teaching experience for the masses of people not yet directly involved in the revolution. In his theoretical reworkings of Guevara's writings, Debray would consistently reinforce Castro's theme from *The Second Declaration of Havana* that "the duty of every revolutionary is to make the revolution," first in an essay-length account of the Cuban revolution entitled "Castroism: The Long March in Latin America," which initially appeared in 1964 in *Les Temps Modernes* and was later reprinted in the *New Left Review*, and then in *Revolution within the Revolution*. Both texts would offer the revolutions in Cuba and throughout Latin America as blueprints for revolutionary action worldwide. Castro's maxim was made so central by proponents of Guevara-style revolution that even Carlos Marighella would paraphrase it as the reason for revolution in his highly influential 1969 *Minimanual of the Urban Guerilla*: "No matter what your philosophy or personal circumstances, you become a revolutionary only by making revolution" (39).

Though Debray, Castro, and Guevara consistently denigrated action that was social, political, or strategic rather than strictly military in nature, Guevara had also continuously cautioned that all military action had to have symbolic value that could be easily read and understood by the masses of people not yet involved in the revolution: "The people must be shown that social wrongs are not going to be redressed by civil means alone" (*Guerilla Warfare*, 111). For his part, Debray cautioned: "The guerilla struggle . . . must have the support of the masses or disappear; before enlisting them directly, it must convince them that there are valid reasons for its existence so that the 'rebellion' will truly be—by the manner of its recruitment and the origin of its fighters—a 'war of the people'" (*Revolution within the Revolution?* 47). For groups like the Black Panther Party, whose numbers were initially quite small—the initial Oakland chapter numbered not more than five at its inception—the philosophy of Guevara and its investment in symbolic acts of military violence that could be accomplished in small groups to great results held an obvious appeal. Ultimately, however, it would be the Black Panther Party's interventions into the realm of symbolic, rather than military, culture that would have the most lasting effect in helping to define and position post-1965 African American culture

as hypervisible, radically defiant, and the site of a contradictory empowerment and disempowerment.

Richard Pryor and the Creation of a Revolutionary Cultural Politics

As the Panthers attempted to recreate symbolic culture, they began to
have widespread influence on the transformation taking place in African
American culture and aesthetics. Richard Pryor, whose work came of age
through and with the Black Panther Party, declared in his autobiography,
"I knew that I could stir up more shit on stage than in a revolution" (*Pryor
Convictions*, 121). Pryor embodied the ways in which the cultural politics of
groups like the Black Panther Party were influencing a developing African
American popular culture. Before the 1970s, Pryor's routines were largely
devoid of the explicit political references and references to African American vernacular culture that he would later make famous. After undergoing
a series of personal problems, he relocated to the San Francisco Bay Area,
where he came into contact with a number of radically politicized African
American artists and intellectuals, including Huey P. Newton.[2] In an atmosphere that he would characterize in his autobiography as "a city of spectacles" and "a circus of exciting, extreme, colorful, militant ideas. Drugs.
Hippies. Black Panthers. Antiwar protests. Experimentation. Music, theater, poetry" (115), Pryor had a personal and artistic epiphany: "One night
I served as the disc jockey on a radio station, playing Miles and rambling
on about Nixon, the Vietnam War, the Black Panthers, and shit. I didn't
know anything about that shit. But who better to talk about it?" (118). This
sort of saturation in radical culture resulted in a moment of personal transformation in which, according to Pryor, "I had a sense of Richard Pryor
the person. I understood myself. I knew what I stood for. I knew what I
thought. I knew what I wanted to do" (121).

The Panthers' belief that performative action could serve not only as
a heuristic tool but also as a provocation to revolution enabled them to
understand a variety of activities beyond military action as revolutionary:
"The main purpose of a vanguard group should be to raise the consciousness of the masses through educational programs and certain physical
activities that the party will participate in. The sleeping masses must be
bombarded with the correct approach to struggle through the activities of
the vanguard party. Therefore, the masses must know that the party exists.

The party must use all means available to get this information across to the masses" (Foner, 43). Pryor's belief that he "could stir up more shit on stage than in a revolution" echoed the ambiguities that were developing in the relationship between revolutionary action and revolutionary representation as espoused by the Black Panther Party, whose emphasis on the heuristic and the performative would end up creating revolution as a highly visible and visual affair rather than a series of covert actions that involved anything from public demonstrations to concerts by their in-house group of musicians ("The Lumpen") and the politicizing of popular performers such as Pryor. In "The Correct Handling of a Revolution," Newton explains the process by which revolutionary action will mirror back to the masses images of themselves in the idealized form of revolutionaries:

> The masses are constantly looking for a guide, a Messiah to liberate them from the hands of the oppressor. The vanguard party must exemplify the characteristics of worthy leadership. Millions and millions of oppressed people might not know members of the vanguard party personally or directly, but they will gain through an indirect acquaintance the proper strategy for liberation via the mass media and the physical activities of the party. It is of prime importance that the vanguard party develop a political organ, such as a newspaper created by the party, as well as employ strategically revolutionary art and the destruction of the oppressor's machinery. For example, Watts. The economy and property of the oppressor was destroyed to such an extent that no matter how the oppressor tried to whitewash the activities of the black brothers, the real nature and real cause of the activity was communicated to every black community. (44)

The Panthers' belief that armed propaganda could provoke people to identify with them as the vanguard party caused them to seek to translate every visual encounter with the Panther ideology into a lived experience of the revolutionary utopian possibilities that ideology presented. In *Do It! Scenarios of the Revolution*, the Yippie leader Jerry Rubin would simply declare: "Revolution is theater in the streets. . . . The Panther uniform—beret, black leather jacket, gun—helps create the Panther legend. Three Panthers on the street are an army of thousands" (142). The Panthers thus self-consciously presented individuals and images whose revolutionary representation would provoke the possibility of radical social change by creating an identification between the visual representation and the viewer. The

Panthers used their iconic uniform and images of Newton as a nexus to trigger identification among people who would never wear such clothing and who would identify experiences such as Newton's incarceration as radically outside the realm of their own lives.

The Black Panther Party's emphasis on lower-class urban vernacular culture as the expression of "authentic" Blackness also validated Richard Pryor's own celebration of the aesthetics of a lower-class, urban African American vernacular. Pryor, who lampooned the very possibility of positive African American images in U.S. popular culture with the creation of the character of Clark Washington, "a mild-mannered custodian for the *Daily Planet*" who is able to transform into "Super Nigger," epitomizes the ambivalent possibilities for critical African American images in the post-segregation United States. On the cover of his self-titled 1968 album *Richard Pryor,* the comedian posed naked, mocking the portrayal of African people in magazines like *National Geographic.* The album, from its cover art to routines like "Super Nigger" and "T.V. Panel Show," provides a thorough critique of the overdetermination of African American representation in U.S. popular culture up to that point.

Pryor brilliantly mimicked the Panthers' popular rhetorical style and the unlikely fame they had found by 1968 through frequent appearances in mainstream American television in "T.V. Panel Show," which takes to absurd extremes the Panthers' ability to interject their ideology into even the most banal of settings:

> Black nationalist: I got something to say, man. You dig? You cats been up here rapping and ain't got nothing to say about the real thing. . . . You cats up here rapping about the Jews but what about me? What about my people?
> T.V. Host: I don't believe anybody's said anything about the Jews.
> Black nationalist: You will! You will!

The incongruity of the Panthers' message and the daytime talk-show format, and the obvious limitations of that setting are unmasked, and Pryor continues throughout the routine to foreground the Panthers' attention-getting rhetorical style, such as when the Black nationalist on the panel interrupts the other participant's discussion of religion to interject "God was a junkie, baby! He had to be a junkie to put up with all of this. You don't just walk around feeling nothing behind all of this."

The title of Pryor's popular 1976 album *Bicentennial Nigger* aimed squarely at African Americans' ambivalent position within U.S. symbolic culture and reflects on the status of the African American image in the socially and historically vexed year of the bicentennial celebration of the nation's founding, twelve years after the passage of the Civil Rights Act and ten years after the Black Panther Party's first major public action. By the release of the album, African American images were so soundly incorporated into U.S. popular culture that Pryor's album cover could chain together the litany of representational possibilities open to African Americans at this time, including a naked slave, an emphatic minister, a victorious boxer, a Civil War–era soldier, a Tuskegee airman, a Black revolutionary, a frightened sharecropper, a policeman, a funky hipster, and a Black businessman. The immediate readability that the album presupposes for these images testifies to the extent to which Black images had become a commonplace presence in the shifting terrain of dominant representation between the early 1960s and the late 1970s. While Jerry Rubin would declare that "revolution is theater in the streets" (132), the Panthers would attempt to make a revolution of the limitations of African American representation marked by Pryor's work.

After his sojourn in the San Francisco Bay Area, Pryor reappeared on the comedy scene with a radically reworked comedic persona that included references to the cost of the war in Vietnam, civil discontent, and police violence at home for African Americans, and provided, according to Mel Watkins, "a crucial breakthrough in African American stage humor" (544). Unlike many biographers of Pryor, who tend to attribute the pivotal change in his humor either to the realization of an individual genius or to a personal transformation that finally allowed him to locate himself within an authentic African American subjectivity that he had previously masked, Watkins sees the shift in Pryor's emphasis as reflective of a "shift in the African American mood" that allowed Pryor to build a fan base among "those under thirty-five, who were increasingly rejecting the traditional black middle-class tactic of de-emphasizing cultural differences between the races and embracing Black Power" (545). Attributing these changes to "militant new voices—the Black Panthers and Stokely Carmichael among others," Watkins concludes: "Pryor's switch to an outspoken Black voice occurred at precisely the right time" (545).

Within a shifting cultural climate made ripe for change by both the Civil Rights Movement and the popular urban unrest it had failed to contain, the Black Panther Party would work, like Richard Pryor, with both popular culture and a popular politics of discontent to challenge the dominant motifs of U.S. culture that spectacularized Black suffering and discontent. But while Pryor was largely content to "stir up more shit on stage than in a revolution" with his challenges to the limited parameters of African American representation, the Black Panther Party would seek to reshape those motifs into a radically aestheticized demand for social change. While Pryor would work through the comic absurdity of Black suffering in routines like "Wino and Junkie" and "Niggers vs. the Police,"[3] the Black Panther Party would push a program of "armed propaganda" aimed at demonstrating the necessity for armed struggle and also to argue for a violent visual and discursive moral persuasion that would move African Americans from a position of victimhood to a position of righteous indignation characterized by Carlos Marighella as the "moral superiority" that "sustains the urban guerilla" (47).

Marighella argued in *The Manual of the Urban Guerilla:* "Where the urban guerilla's weapons are inferior, he gains through moral superiority. In moral superiority the urban guerilla has undeniable superiority. . . . Moral superiority allows the guerilla to attack and survive, and to succeed in his main objective" (47). The Panthers would turn Pryor's tragic/comic cry for the positive recognition of racial difference into an unapologetic cry for self-defense through a moral suasion that relied on intense identification provoked by its performance of vanguardism. Their model of identification was dependent on recreating African American identity around revolutionary action. In her autobiography, Assata Shakur explores her transformation from someone who shared the African American middle-class aspirations of the 1950s to a Black revolutionary throughout the 1960s and 1970s with the declaration: "I love Black people, I don't care what they are doing, but when Black people are struggling, that's when they are most beautiful to me" (189).

Seize the Time!   Watts, Armed Self-Defense, and the Death of the Civil Rights Movement in California

For groups like the Black Panther Party, Ernesto "Che" Guevara's dictums, when taken together with the limited success of the Civil Rights Movement and the conditions of widespread social discontent following its failures, social revolution seemed not only possible but inevitable. Amiri

Baraka notes the way in which the fertile political climate of the 1960s and 1970s had been created by earlier movements. In his account of the birth of the Black Arts Theater, Baraka writes about the way in which the vibrant postwar political culture was reflected in the street culture of Harlem:

> The older black nationalists always talked on their ladders across the street from the Hotel Theresa. Larger forums were held in front of Mr. Michaux's bookstore, called, affectionately, the House of Proper Propaganda. Malcolm had spoken in front of the store often and there was a sign in front of the store ringed by pan-African leaders from everywhere in the black world. (208)[4]

Nowhere did possible social revolution seem more plausible than in the symbolically, culturally, and politically loaded terrain of California. Though unrest would break out in cities across the United States throughout the 1960s, "the Watts Riots" in the Watts section of Los Angeles in August of 1965 would become the emblematic moment of racial unrest to which all other subsequent acts of urban discord would be compared. The uprising in Watts held unprecedented symbolic importance because "Watts clashed with the entire organized white world as a collective organism," as Harold Cruse claimed in 1967 in *The Crisis of the Negro Intellectual* (384). For Black radicals like the Panthers, the violence of Watts seemed to be a powerful counterpoint to the symbolic successes of nonviolence as a political and cultural imperative. According to Cruse, "the sobering lessons of the Watts rebellion" enabled a change from a discourse of "self-defense" to a discourse of "guerilla warfare" among Black nationalist groups. This is symbolized in Cruse's argument by the evolving philosophy of revolution espoused by Robert Williams, whose political philosophies as articulated in *Negroes with Guns* (1962) were a major influence on the genesis and evolution of the Black Panther Party (Cruse, 386). Panther cofounder Bobby Seale even went so far as to characterize the party's first major action as "Niggers with Guns in the State Capitol" in *Seize the Time,* his 1968 history of the Black Panther Party (153).[5]

Williams, a local leader in a small chapter of the NAACP in Monroe, North Carolina, came to national prominence in the late 1950s when he began advocating that the organization reevaluate its stance on nonviolence and suggesting that it consider "meet[ing] violence with violence" (*Negroes with Guns,* 26). Like the Deacons for Defense, a group that had armed and organized for "Black self-defense" but ended up primarily providing armed protection for civil rights organizers, Williams constantly ne-gotiated between a civil rights–style engagement with American culture and society and a desire to separate completely from American society and culture. This eventually resulted in his censure by the national leaders of the NAACP and exile, first in Cuba, where he befriended Castro and Gue-vara, and then in China as a guest of Mao Tse Tung.[6]

By 1967, according to Cruse's account, as a direct consequence of the Watts rebellion, Robert Williams began to essentially call for a foco-style revolution by advocating "a new concept of revolution [that] defies mili-tary science and tactics. The new concept is lightning campaigns con-ducted in highly sensitive urban communities with the paralysis reaching the small communities and spreading to the farm areas" (386). For African American radical organizers like Williams, Watts had begun to suggest the limitations of "the good society" of mainstream U.S. social reform and the "beloved community" of civil rights rhetoric. According to Cruse, the con-tradictions inherent in the embrace of guerilla warfare by the leader of an organization that had been created to defend the pro-integrationist aims of the Civil Rights Movement was typical of the ideological confusion ex-perienced by African American intellectuals in the late 1960s. For poets, playwrights, critics, and cultural workers alike, Watts was a watershed mo-ment that brought the civil rights tradition and its attendant mythology to crisis. For Cruse, Williams's embrace of Watts as providing the impetus for "guerilla warfare" foretold a dangerous trend in a African American radi-cal culture, namely, the tendency to adopt the notion of guerilla warfare without fully exploring or creating the necessary conditions for its even-tual success.

In California, the site of several defining moments of the student move-ment, including the Berkeley Free Speech Movement and the long-running student strikes at San Francisco State University, talk of revolution was so much part of the cultural and political discourse by 1968 that further prep-aration or exploration may have seemed completely unnecessary. Even the student struggles at San Francisco State, which began in late 1967 and required the intercession of then California governor Ronald Reagan and the appointment of two chancellors in as many years, had the symbolic violence of Watts at their core.

Students for a Democratic Society (SDS) organizer Todd Gitlin would claim of the student strikes at San Francisco State that "they began, as insurrection does in America, with the blacks" (298). Protests by the Black

Student Union to contest the racist representation in the school's newspaper as well as the suspension of a popular instructor provided the literal but also symbolic impetus for a campuswide shutdown as the Black Student Union formed coalitions with other campus groups, including SDS, the Peace and Freedom Party, and members of the Experimental College. The student strikes grew so large and were so well sustained that Gitlin posited that the "flood might recede, but the countryside will be permanently changed" (298).

Law and Order and Black Power in Conflict

By 1968, California also stood on the brink of transforming its prison system into one of the leading structures of what has come to be characterized as "the prison industrial complex."[7] The assassination of Martin Luther King Jr. and the social unrest that ensued in urban centers throughout the United States brought the confrontation between the dream of a postsegregation culture and its early realities to the forefront of American culture. Nowhere was the conflict between the promises, the actually realizable potential of the Civil Rights Movement, and the intractability of American social and political culture better epitomized than in the clash between radical African American activist culture, which highlighted the police as an "occupying army" and prisons as "modern day slavery," and the culture of "law and order" as pioneered in California by U.S. president Richard Nixon, a former senator from California, and Ronald Reagan, who became governor of California in 1967, just as the Panthers were becoming a powerful force in U.S. public culture.[8] The rhetoric of law and order positioned African Americans firmly within a discourse of lawlessness and disorder that they had traditionally been assigned by the dominant culture. The Black Panther Party would radically reconfigure this discourse, restructuring the relationship between the African American outlaw figure and a romanticized notion of revolution to provoke identificatory possibilities across a broad spectrum of potential supporters. The Black Panther notion of vanguardism successfully created allies out of the formerly uninitiated and apolitical through the wide-ranging appeal of an ideology scripted through an easily decipherable iconic language of images: the raised fist, the black jacket and beret, and the gun.

The industrialization and modernization of California prison technology in conjunction with Nixon's national calls for law and order spawned a cultural climate and economic order that not only endorsed but actually required the incarceration of a large number of its citizenry in order to continue to function.[9] As the postwar booms in industrial production that had attracted large numbers of low-wage southern migrants to California began to fade, African Americans, who had made up the bulk of the southern migrants in what has come to be known as the Great Migration, became fodder for a growing prison system.

In 1978, the U.S. senator Edward Kennedy addressed the NAACP in a speech in which he called "the underclass" both "the great unmentioned problem of America today" and "a group in our midst, perhaps more dangerous, more bereft of hope, more difficult to confront, than any for which our history has known" (Lehman, 282). Kennedy's speech typifies the way in which urban African Americans were beginning to be demonized as an impending threat even by those who considered themselves proponents of the Civil Rights Movement. The growth of radical Black political movements in the 1960s and 1970s in California existed in an immediately confrontational relationship to the growth of a prison industry and a law-and-order culture, which was also radical in its ability to transform the culture of California and eventually the United States. The Black Panther Party's valorization of "the brother on the block" as a potential fighting force played into mainstream ideas about the threat that the urban African American underclass presented. However, the Panthers' desire to present themselves as the vanguard of the revolution, whose job it was to heuristically perform revolutionary behavior for a mass audience also incited an intense identification that ultimately cut across class and racial barriers, redefining the spectacle of urban poverty.

The Black Panther Party, the Media, and Military Action

Though the Black Panther Party would become most strongly associated in its early years with its highly publicized actions to patrol the streets of Oakland in order to monitor police brutality, the party mobilized on multiple fronts. Two such examples include its involvement in local electoral politics, and the party's highly touted "survival programs," which featured screening programs for sickle cell anemia, free breakfast programs, and voter registration drives. The cultural war waged through the Black Panther Party's sophisticated understanding of and engagement with mass media and popular culture created a complex interplay between the radical culture and mainstream American popular culture that it both courted and was courted by. This relationship was simplified and parodied by Tom Wolfe as "radical chic" in his best-selling *Radical Chic and Mau-Mauing the Flak Catchers* (1970) and was also harshly critiqued by Maulana Karenga and his US Organization, the Kuumba Collective, and other cultural nationalists.[10] Much of the contemporary misunderstanding of the Black Panther Party's place in American popular culture and its continuing legacy revolves around the thorny questions of representation, appropriation, and commodification raised by its engagement with American popular and political culture and its embrace of vanguardist philosophy as espoused by Che Guevara, Regis Debray, and Fidel Castro.

Though the specific media training of the early members was limited to cofounder Bobby Seale's professional experience as a stand-up comedian, from the very beginning, the Oakland chapter of the Black Panther Party organized around actions meant to have a specific symbolic cachet that could be easily read when transmitted through dominant media. Seale was working in one of the Johnson administration's Poverty Program job-training offices when he and Huey P. Newton conceived of the Black Panther Party and proceeded to draft the Ten-Point Program after hours in the office on 16 October 1966 (Seale, 59).[11] Newton and Seale met while students at Merritt Junior College in Oakland. Both were active in campus organizing initially in the Afro-American Association, a group organized primarily around the study of African American culture, and later in a breakaway group called the Soul Students Advisory Council. The historian Jeffrey O. G. Ogbar notes the influence of the Revolutionary Action Movement (RAM), which was initially organized on college campuses by African American students involved in SDS, on students like Newton and Seale. Ogbar labels the Soul Students Advisory Council "a RAM front organization" (84). "RAM never attracted the media attention of SNCC or the Panthers," Ogbar notes, and Seale writes that he and Newton became disenchanted with what they perceived as the group's inability to translate their radical political vision off campus to the "brothers on the block" (78). From the beginning, the actions of the Oakland Black Panther Party showed a flair for the audacious and dramatic and a connection to everyday culture. On 21 February 1967, the first real year of action for the fledgling Black Panther Party, the group organized a security detail for the highly publicized visit of Betty Shabazz, the widow of Malcolm X, to the San Francisco Bay Area. The group caught the eye of the Bay Area radical community, including the future high-profile Panther party member Eldridge Cleaver, who would remember as formative to his political education the moment when the Panthers' security detail clashed with police over their refusal to disarm, citing their constitutional right to bear arms (*Post-Prison Writings and Speeches*, 23). A couple of months later, on 27 April 1967, the Panthers released the first crude issue of *Black Panther Community News*, which focused on community outrage over the police murder of an unarmed Black teenager named Denzil Dowell during an alleged arrest attempt in nearby Richmond, California.[12]

Less than a month later, on 2 May 1967, party members garnered national attention when they arrived fully armed on the steps of the state capitol in Sacramento, temporarily diverting media attention from a planned meeting on the capitol grounds between Governor Ronald Reagan and youth groups to Bobby Seale, who read "In Defense of Self-Defense: Executive Mandate Number One," a piece written by Newton in support of the right to bear arms (Seale, 153–55). Because of the strategic and sensational staging and the presence of the media for the youth event, this moment began to form the party's national media profile as not only "armed and extremely dangerous" but also a political force to be reckoned with even though the group was still relatively small at this point. By 29 June 1967, it had consolidated its image as an organization deserving of a national platform—so much so that it was able to name Stokely Carmichael as the "Field Marshall of the Black Panther Party" (Charles E. Jones, 53). Carmichael had been chair of the Student Nonviolent Coordinating Committee (SNCC), one of the most high-profile and radical groups of the coalition of groups that constituted the Civil Rights Movement, when in 1966 it decided to expel its white members in a move to redefine itself as a Black Power group. Highly charismatic, Carmichael was so renowned for his propensity to manipulate media attention that he was nicknamed "Stokely Starmichael" in radical circles.

The Black Panther Party's major action of 1967, which was not strictly tied to the creation of images of militancy and potential power for the group but also had a military component, was the creation of the party's Community Police Patrols, in which armed groups of Panthers patrolled the streets of Oakland in order to provide protection for ordinary citizens against the threat of police violence during traffic stops and arrests.[13] But even these patrols were intended more as guerilla theater than guerilla action, because the confrontation between the Panthers and the police was meant to instruct those who witnessed the confrontations that the police were not above reproach. In the film *Black Panther*, Eldridge Cleaver offers an explanation of why confrontations with the police became the Black Panther Party's primary performative moment for the symbolic staging of their ideology:

> You don't find a guy just remaining the same after really seeing the Panthers. The guys on the block out there, they have never been too impressed by America, by what's been happening. They're not too impressed by that. But they're going to stand there in fear of the cops. This is one of the reasons the Black Panther Party focused on the cops, because the cops are out there and visible. This is the direct contact that Black people have with the white power structure, when the Man, the Pig comes down and bothers them. Here comes two niggers with some guns who step out and talk to the cops just the way they've been talked to. People notice that.

The film, which was created to showcase the Panther platform, established the party's other key visual signifiers by cutting directly from Cleaver's explanation of why the group chose confrontation with the police as their primary performative moment to images of uniformed Panther men and women marching in formation, fists upraised, groups of Panther women chanting the party's slogans, and party members lining the steps of the Alameda courthouse. This visual imagery would become as widely associated with the party as the police patrols because it so successfully translated the Black Panther critique of the justice system in the United States into an easily accessible, visual, symbolic language that still circulates with relevance today, even to those who no longer have access to the party's original Ten-Point Platform.

Free Huey! Mobilizing the Image for Social Change

The arrest of Huey P. Newton on 28 October 1967 inadvertently provided the pivotal symbolic moment around which Panther critique and organizing would focus for the next three years, for Newton's image would be deployed to consolidate support for the notion that unjust police repression justified the necessity for revolution.[14] Newton and Glenn McKinney were driving home from a party late at night in Oakland when their car was stopped by a police cruiser. A firefight broke out: it left Newton critically injured, one police officer dead, and a second injured. Newton was later arrested and charged with a number of felonies, including attempted murder. For the Panthers, Newton's trial would provide the perfect performative moment to stage their dissent. Elaine Brown would write of 1967: "It was the year 'Free Huey' erupted as a kind of universal battle cry that J. Edgar Hoover openly pronounced: 'The Black Panther Party is the single greatest threat to the internal security of the United States'. . . . Huey Newton had become more than just another leader of a black organization. He was the symbol of change for Americans questioning everything sacred to the American way of life" (237). The "Free Huey" campaign would provide not only the organizing opportunity for the coalescence of an international movement, making the Panthers objects of admiration for radicals around the world, but it would also allow the relationship between theatrical militancy and radical dissent that had been inherent in the Panthers from the beginning to emerge. Through the movement to free him from incarceration, Newton's image would become synonymous with radical dissent and vanguardist leadership.

In December 1967, the Panthers, in a coalition with the Peace and Freedom Party, an antiwar group based in Berkeley, coined the slogan "Free Huey," which would become an international rallying cry for the campaign of the same name. The group chose 17 February, Newton's birthday, to stage a large rally as a precursor to demonstrations at the trial (Seale, 208–10). Several thousand people gathered to listen to prominent members of the Student Nonviolent Coordinating Committee and the Panthers, including Stokely Carmichael, H. Rap Brown, James Foreman, and Eldridge and Kathleen Cleaver. In keeping with the vanguardist philosophy of the Panthers, they both spoke about the particulars of Newton's case and used Newton as a vector for understanding the situation of African Americans in general. Stokely Carmichael reminded the crowd: "We're here to celebrate brother Huey P. Newton's birthday. We're not here to celebrate it as Huey Newton the individual, but as Huey Newton parcel of black people wherever we are on the world today. . . . And so, in talking about brother Huey Newton tonight, we have to talk about the struggle of black people, not only in the United States, but in the *world* today" ("Free Huey Rally Speech"). Standing under large photographs of Newton, Carmichael continued to insist on the heuristic value of Newton's experience of incarceration, which he collapsed into the experience of Black people in general by claiming: "We must develop an undying love as is personified in brother

Huey P. Newton. Undying love for our people. If we do not do that then we will be wiped out." For Carmichael, Newton personified Guevara's demand that "the guerilla fighter as a social reformer should not only provide an example in his own life but he ought also constantly to give orientation in ideological problems" (34). As Huey P. Newton's image became the nexus for vanguardist identification, the Black Panther Party quickly became the spectacle through which the experience of revolution could be translated into what the party would label the "brother on the block" or "the lumpen proletariat."[15]

The austere setting of the rally, which resembled a political meeting more than a birthday party, provided a stark contrast to the explosive rhetoric and animated theatrics of the speakers, many of whom were renowned for their ability to stir crowds in the best tradition of African American oratory. H. Rap Brown asked the crowd: "How many white folks you kill today?" reminding them: "You are revolutionaries! Che Guevara says they only two ways to leave the battlefield: victorious or dead. Huey's in jail! That's no victory" ("Free Huey Rally Speech"). Carmichael reiterated the relationship between policing and state control: "They make us fight; they make us steal; they judge us; they put us in prison; they parole us; they send us out; they pick us up again. Where, in God's name, do we exercise any sense of dignity in this country?" ("Free Huey Rally Speech").

The speakers' invocation of the struggle of Huey P. Newton against the police and justice system was in keeping with Che Guevara's dictum in *Guerilla Warfare:* "The people must be shown that social wrongs are not going to be redressed by civil means alone" (111). Brown and Carmichael hoped to use the incarceration of Newton to incite revolution against what they saw as a growing police state. Newton's image would become an iconic shorthand that translated his personal struggles with the police, the court system, and his lengthy incarceration into a treatise on Panther ideology. Organizers of the event hoped to transform the "talk about law and order" into talk about "justice in America," as Carmichael urged, and also to transform discourse about revolution into actual revolution by provoking an increase in Black Panther Party membership as an initial means of securing the "progressive radicalization" that Guevara spoke of as a necessary step toward revolution (81). Earl Anthony, who was only the eighth person to join the party, claims that at the time of the Free Huey Rally, "there were still, actually, only about thirty hardcore members; the Free Huey Campaign would be the ticket to flood the membership rolls" (*Spit-*

ting in the Wind, 43). Between Newton's arrest and trial, membership in the Black Panther Party mushroomed so much that when the actual trial began on 15 July, more than 450 Black Panther Party members were present and over 5,000 spectators ringed the Alameda County Courthouse in what was to become a daily, ritualized display of chants, marches, singing, speeches, and slogans throughout the length of the trial.

Culture as Conduit of Revolutionary Change

When images of the courthouse reached the world via the televisual newsmedia, print media, and alternative journalism, the Black Panther Party successfully transformed the courthouse from its representative role as a vehicle for state power into a theater for the display of a spectacular blackness that was potent in its presentation and seemingly potentially revolutionary in its consequences. The moment the Panthers triumphantly transformed the courthouse into a site for contestation of law-and-order ideology in image culture would become emblematic for the successes of the Black Panther Party, whose biggest victories would largely continue in the terrain of the symbolic through a transformation of image culture in relation to notions of race, power, and potential in the United States.

The conflict between the group's stated goal to become a potential vehicle for "self-defense" and military action along the lines of *Guerilla Warfare,* and the more political or social-reform agendas inherent in its decision to organize as a political "party" with political education goals was present from the start. This tension is apparent even in the potentially contradictory name the group almost gave itself: "The Black Panther Party for Self-Defense." The conflict between those who saw the group as a possible vehicle for radical military intervention and those who saw it as a vehicle for political education, and, therefore, a more potentially social reformist platform, would be a constant and growing problem as the years brought ever increasing levels of governmental and police repression.

The Black Panther Party would successfully, spectacularly appropriate U.S. image culture to their own advantage when they managed to literally "Free Huey" from prison when all charges against him were dropped on 5 August 1970. But had they achieved what Che Guevara outlined as "the essence of guerilla warfare," "the miracle by which a small nucleus of men— looking beyond their immediate tactical objective—becomes the vanguard of a mass movement, achieving its ideals, establishing a new society, ending the ways of the old, and winning social justice" (*Guerilla Warfare*, 114)? At the Free Huey Rally, Stokely Carmichael stressed to the audience that revolution would only be possible through "organizing our people and orienting them towards an African ideology which speaks to our blackness," but the exact relationship between armed struggle and the struggle for a liberated African American radical culture was never clearly articulated by Guevara, Debray, Castro, or the Panthers themselves. They would repeatedly decry those whom they labeled "cultural nationalists," mostly notably the US Organization, a Los Angeles–based group led by Maulana Karenga.

The rivalry between the Panthers and US would eventually lead to an armed confrontation over the direction of the Black studies program on the campus of UCLA on 17 January 1967. During this confrontation, John Huggins and Alprentice "Bunchy" Carter, important leaders in the Southern California chapter of the Black Panther Party, were killed.[16] Scholars such as Ward Churchill, Jim Vander Wall, and Kenneth O'Reilly, as well as Panther accounts of the period, have documented how the conflict between the Panthers and the US Organization was targeted and inflamed by the FBI under COINTELPRO, but with or without FBI interference, a lack of clarity over the role that the cultural struggle would play in the armed struggle was all too real for the Panthers.[17] Newton would repeatedly contrast what he labeled "cultural nationalism" or "pork chop nationalism" with "revolutionary nationalists," which included the Black Panther Party. According to him, cultural nationalists "feel the African culture will automatically bring political freedom," which could potentially lead to political leaders who "oppress the people but . . . promote the African culture"; in contrast, he continued, the Panthers "believe that culture itself will not liberate us. We're going to need some stronger stuff" ("Correct Handling," 50). For the Black Panther Party, the "stronger stuff" was the promotion of an armed struggle through the creation of a dynamic image culture. Ironically, the Panther image culture proved to be such a powerful complement to the party's vanguardist politics that its images would eventually eclipse the party's actual political presence.

Feelings of ambiguity with regard to gains made in the cultural realm were exacerbated by the Panthers' relative success in that realm versus their relative failure to convert those gains into genuine gains in a popular armed struggle. This became especially problematic as violence around the Panthers intensified after the inception of the "Free Huey" campaign in 1967. According to Russell Shoats, "The Panthers were a potentially strong

Black fighting formation that was forced to take to the field before they were ready [because they chose a] high-profile operation, characteristic of the Civil Rights Movement, that relied heavily on television, radio, and print media" (5,7). Consequently, Shoats says, the Panthers floundered "as groups tried to combine the activities of the political and military workers in one cadre" (5).

To view the Panthers' high level of engagement with popular media culture simply as a strategic mistake that preceded immense military and political failures, as Shoats does, not only paints a limited portrait of the Panthers' contribution to U.S. society and culture but also puts unnecessary limitations on what constitutes political and cultural change. The Black Panther Party evinced a more sophisticated understanding of the relationship between African Americans and American popular culture and the centrality of visual culture to African American cultural life than they were or are often given credit for. Examinations of the Black Panther Party legacy continue to be guided by misunderstandings of the central role of cultural work in the Panther struggle, and the Panthers are frequently painted as the victims, unwilling dupes, or scheming manipulators of American media culture. From their first appearance on the front page of the *New York Times* in a photograph showing several Panthers brandishing firearms at the California Statehouse and the inception of the party's official newspaper, the Black Panther Party created an especially sophisticated relationship to broadcast and print media that acknowledged the incipient possibilities for disruption existing in a burgeoning mainstream visual media culture. By doing so, they were able to create a canon of images, slogans, and gestures that codified these symbols into an iconic language of revolution.

The Black migration into northern urban centers paralleled the movement of Black images into mainstream visual culture via television culture; Melvin Patrick Ely has characterized African American presence in postwar television culture as "the Great Black Migration into America's living room" (64). The Panthers were successful in seizing television culture, one of the most important arbiters of public opinion during the Civil Rights Movement and early postsegregation era, and were unquestionably more successful than Karenga and the US Organization or any other organization of the era in manipulating the cultural order against Nixon's notion of law and order.

The Civil Rights Movement's ideology of nonviolence held an obvious appeal for most Americans, but from the onset of the "Free Huey" campaign, the Black Panther Party successfully conveyed the notion that armed struggle was not only justifiable for African Americans but, in fact, mandated by the treatment of African Americans in the United States. In a certain sense, they were successful precisely because they utilized both the romance and the threat of violence endemic to constructions of Blackness in the United States to win support for their cultural war against the notion of law-and-order culture, even though they could never really fulfill either the role of romantic revolutionary or violent impending threat. Their tremendous success in seeming to convince popular culture of the necessity of a mandate against law-and-order culture would be mocked by those who insisted on downplaying gains made by the party in the cultural realm: thus, party members were dubbed "media star revolutionaries," and much focus was placed on the party's inability or unwillingness to be seen as simply fulfilling the role of revolutionary hero or being a dangerous threat.

The Panther Look   A Visual Language for Social Change

In "Afro Images: Politics, Fashion, Nostalgia," Angela Davis herself writes of the manner in which the current circulation of images associated with her political work from the 1960s and 1970s often occurs without reference to its origins in Black radical politics. After an encounter with a young man who directly identifies her with the Afro hairstyle that she wore throughout the 1960s, Davis ruminates, "It is both humiliating and humbling to discover that a single generation after the events that constructed me as a public personality, I am remembered as a hairdo. It is humiliating because it reduces a politics of liberation to a politics of fashion; it is humbling because such encounters with a younger generation demonstrate the fragility and mutability of historical images, especially those associated with African American history" (29). Davis is most deeply disturbed when reconstructed images from her time as a fugitive appear along with images of Che Guevara in a fashion spread of a popular music magazine, "emptied of all content so that it can serve as a commodified backdrop for advertising." For Davis, the mutability of such images is a particular problem because it allows for the specific details of African American radical historicity to be unfixed in such a way that lays it open for a troubling nostalgia. This nostalgia offers a romantic vision of the past that is in the end highly commodifiable.

For Davis's account, the commodification of social movements is a contemporary phenomenon associated with a commodified nostalgia that exists in the place of what might be a more genuine historical memory. According to Davis, the recirculation of the images from the 1960s and 1970s radical culture testifies to the strength of those images to continue to speak in myriad ways to audiences removed from the direct political reality that they portray, but she insists on maintaining a strict boundary between commodification and politicization that risks perpetuating a nostalgia of its own for a political era free of the trivialization and commodification of the raw material of historicity by market forces. This nostalgia for an era "back in the day when everyone was Black and conscious / Freedom was at hand and you could just taste it," as a contemporary song puts it,[18] ignores the ways in which contemporary nostalgia was in fact created and enabled by the visual politics of vanguardism that dominated the radical culture of the time.

Black radical culture of the 1960s and 1970s would continually seek out and define the symbolic language and visual tools that could convey the potential for social and political revolution to African Americans who had grown used enough to oppression to incorporate it into even the everyday language of humor as Richard Pryor had done. The transformation of the symbolic artifacts of everyday culture into potent political symbols was perhaps achieved most consistently by the Black Panther Party, but Angela Davis's Afro spoke as powerfully as their leather jackets and raised fists of the climate of repression and disappointment during the early postsegregation period. Taken together, these symbols created an iconography whose power lay much more in its translatability to commodity culture than in its distance from it.

A vision of the 1960s and 1970s radical culture as one of pure politics free from commodification fails to recognize the complicated role the Black Panther Party played in perpetuating their own mystique throughout commodity culture. Angela Davis's Afro, with which she is now so deeply identified and to which she so greatly regrets being reduced, was cultivated as much for its dramatic performative ability to speak a reductive symbolic political language in a vanguardist manner as "the Panther look." Far from being simple media opportunists, many of the Panthers saw the wide dissemination of their example across U.S. culture as the radical mandate of a vanguard party to model revolutionary behavior. Huey Newton, who seemed to understand the Black Panther Party's primary role as that of educating through symbolic action rather than leading an actual armed insurrection, made it clear in his writings that he believed symbolic action could provide instruction that far outlasted both the action and the teacher.

In "The Correct Handling of the Revolution," Newton emphasized the importance of creating moments of dynamic performative action that would then create the visual symbols that would become shorthand instructions for other revolutionary actions: "The brothers in East Oakland learned from Watts a means of resistance. . . . The first man who threw a Molotov cocktail is not personally known by the masses, but yet the action was respected and followed by the people. If the activities of the Party are respected by the people, the people will follow the example. This is the primary job of the Party" (41). At no time, however, did Newton or the Black Panther Party in general limit their notion of "action" to military action in the streets. While Newton and the party's minister of culture Emory Douglas, a skilled illustrator, placed particular emphasis on the creation and circulation of nontextual visual representations of the Black Panther Party, there were other equally significant nonvisual articulations of it. These ranged from Panther songs and slogans from Elaine Brown's album dedicated to the party, to the chants and slogans created for demonstrations such as "Black is Beautiful / Free Huey!" and "No more brothers in jail / The Pigs are gonna catch hell," which successfully imprinted the party ideology onto American popular culture.

One of the most consistently circulated articulations of the Black Panther Party ideology, however, was the party's official newspaper, the *Black Panther*. In his memoir *This Side of Glory*, David Hilliard records how the paper's prominence quickly grew after Emory Douglas, a skilled graphic artist and illustrator, joined the party: "In a short time, the paper becomes the most visible, most constant symbol of the Party, its front page a familiar sight at every demonstration and in every storefront-window organizing project throughout the country" (149).[19] The paper's circulation eventually grew so large, Hilliard records, that it would at times become the primary source of income for the Oakland chapter of the party (154).

Serving both to provide information and to promote the party, the *Black Panther* combined graphic images of police brutality and urban black misery with uplifting illustrations and textual analysis of events in American popular and political culture. In the 19 June 1971 issue are found an article on the lack of scientific research on sickle cell anemia; a lengthy analysis of the film *Sweet Sweetback's Baadasssss Song!* that includes movie stills alongside illustrations by Douglas; a press statement on the Richmond Five; and an article on and picture of Jo Etha Collier, a young Black woman killed while celebrating her graduation from the white high school in Drew, Mississippi, that she had integrated. The careful mélange of popular and political culture in the *Black Panther* suggests how the party would successfully operate within popular culture to create an enduring critique of U.S. culture in general. At the same time, this mix also suggests how the Black Panther Party's investment in popular culture would leave it open to co-option and appropriation by the same commodity forces driving the popular culture that it critiqued.

Material from the early days of the Oakland chapter of the Black Panther Party, now archived in the Dr. Huey P. Newton Foundation Collection held in Palo Alto by Stanford University, suggests the seemingly limitless extent of the creative nature of its engagement with American popular culture. Whereas Panther efforts to imprint the notion of Black Power and an end to police brutality through the newspaper and rallies is widely known, the extent and sophistication of their engagement with popular culture is not.

In *This Side of Glory,* Hilliard makes brief mention of "large contributions" and "remunerative book deals" as important sources of income for the Black Panther Party (154). The extent of its financial dealings and the sophistication of its interaction with popular culture, however, is not generally acknowledged or explored in the numerous Panther autobiographies and writings about the party. The control of the lucrative book contracts of the prison activist George Jackson, who was seen as a movement martyr; the creation of films to document the Panther struggle and prominent members of the party; and plans for the creation of an Eldridge Cleaver watch dispel myths that members of the Black Panther Party were unaware, unwitting pawns in their interaction with the American culture industry. The name of the entity created to oversee the economic interests of the party demonstrates that the Panthers fully understood the ambiguous nature of such ventures. Elaine Brown notes that Huey P. Newton created "Stronghold Incorporated" as "a one-word idea that captured what the Party intended to erect inside the walls of the citadel of capitalism" (244).

In his final will and testament, George Jackson directed that "anything that I may in capitalist terms seem to possess should be passed on as directed below to further my political ideals." At the time of his death at the hands of California corrections officers in an alleged escape attempt in 1971, he had risen from the ranks of California's ever-growing anonymous prison population to become one of the most widely recognized prison rights activists, and the group best situated to further those ideas was the Black Panther Party. Jackson directed all the proceeds from his latest book, *Blood in My Eye*, to "the Black Panther Survival Programs through the Berkeley Branch of the Black Panther Party." Jackson had already authored one of the most widely circulated antiprison manifestos in contemporary American history, *Soledad Brother*, and publishers were anticipating equal success for *Blood in My Eye*. Contractual records show that in 1971 Random House agreed to pay $100,000 in advance royalties for the book to the party, which also controlled the rights to Jackson's other work and was actively negotiating for the Spanish and Norwegian rights to *Soledad Brother*.[20]

Members of the Black Panther Party have long been portrayed as "media star revolutionaries," but facts like these that attest to the extent to which the party actively, successfully sought and controlled media attention as a means to spread its message are often ignored. During the most active years of the Black Panther Party, Huey P. Newton and Bobby Seale authored texts that would be as widely circulated as *Blood in My Eye*. The party was also involved in several attempts to document the ideology on film, in *Black Panther* and *May Day Panther*, which were created by the Third World Newsreel Collective. The party was also involved with American Documentary Films in the creation and distribution of the films *Stagolee: A Conversation with Bobby Seale in Prison* and *Huey!* and it participated in the creation of a documentary on the 17 February 1968 "Free Huey" Rally by Agnes Varda, an important director of the French New Wave film movement. In this same period, the critically renowned San Francisco Mime Troupe produced a piece with the cooperation of the party that centered on the court trials of Newton and Seale.[21] Collaborative book and film deals were just one means by which the party increased visibility, controlled and circulated its image, and generated income to further and continue its efforts.

Brian Ward records the significant inability of civil rights organizations to successfully utilize recording culture to either translate their message musically or to profitably produce and distribute recordings of various movement events, such as the 1963 March on Washington (268–75).[22] The Black Panther Party, with far fewer connections to established cultural venues, was able to do this and much more, authorizing recordings of various party members and events and producing (among others) *Huey! / Listen Whitey!* an album that placed a recitation of the Ten-Point Platform next to reactions to the murder of Martin Luther King Jr. recorded during a live radio call-in show. The party also successfully promoted benefit concerts at which their own band, the Lumpen, or other progressive, more established groups, such as the Grateful Dead, might perform.[23] Members of the Black Panther Party had a notorious run-in with Ike and Tina Turner at one such event, which culminated in a series of threats and lawsuits.

Reflecting their deep investment in and understanding of American popular culture, the party created a series of greeting cards featuring the images of the more prominent members of the party; they also at one time planned to market an official "Seize the Time" Panther watch featuring a picture of Eldridge Cleaver with arms outstretched, pointing time with a raised gun as one watch hand and an upraised finger as the other.[24] Like the slogan "Black is Beautiful," these items reflect a complex understanding of the deep influence of lived, everyday culture on people's political, social, and cultural perceptions and represent the party's attempts to insinuate itself successfully into popular consumer culture.

Such participation in the commodified arena of American popular culture, as Angela Davis has pointed out, would facilitate the Panthers' work against the state but also its absorption by it. Recent attempts by former Panthers to market everything from a cookbook to hot sauce seem to mock the party's countercultural stance and legacy, but complicated issues around an item such as the "Seize the Time" watch existed from the earliest days of the party as it attempted to negotiate both contesting and flourishing in U.S. aesthetic and political culture.[25] Does it matter that Bell Time, the company that proposed to make the watch, offered similar watches with the face of Moshe Dayan, Israel's minister of defense, while the Black Panther Party staunchly supported the efforts of the Palestine Liberation Organization? Or that the company also offered a P.I.G. watch featuring the image of a pig in a police uniform that the party had popularized along with the slogan *P* for Pride, *I* for Integrity, and *G* for Guts, which was advertised as being "endorsed and worn by law enforcement agencies throughout the USA"?[26] Did the commodification of such images as an armed and belligerent Cleaver cheapen the complexity of his writings even as those images simplified and promoted certain party stances? Whether such a strategy of commodification of its ideology best served the interests of the Panthers or the forces that brought down the party is disputable. What is not in question, however, is the fact that through carefully crafting and circulating its image, the Black Panther Party enabled its critique of the criminal justice system to live and grow long after the demise of the party itself, ultimately allowing it to continue to serve the teaching function that Newton had originally intended as its primary role.

2
Radical Chic

AFFILIATION, IDENTIFICATION, AND
THE BLACK PANTHER PARTY

> I could only place myself among the oppressed people
> of color and among the oppressed revolting against
> whites. Perhaps I'm a black whose color is white or
> pink, but a black. I don't know my family.
>
> —Jean Genet, on his involvement with the Black
> Panther Party

Prisoners of Love Understanding White Affiliation for
Radical African American Causes

In 1970, Tom Wolfe published two short accounts of the exchange between
black radical politics and its white supporters that would become foundational to the ways in which that interaction would come to be defined. The
cover of *Radical Chic and Mau-Mauing the Flak Catchers* sports a satirical
photograph of a well-coifed white woman on the lap of an African American man in an army fatigue jacket, both with black-gloved fists upraised.
The caption is "BLACK RAGE AND WHITE GUILT." Both essays in the
book, "Radical Chic" and "Mau-Mauing the Flak Catchers," traded on and
helped create the popular representation of the Black Panthers as scheming, cynical manipulators of post–civil rights racial politics who willingly
and shamelessly traded in white stereotypes and guilt for selfish economic
gain. "Radical Chic," the first essay, purports to tell the story of a fund-
raising party held in honor of the New York chapter of the Black Panther
Party in the Manhattan home of the conductor Leonard Bernstein, while
the second, "Mau-Mauing the Flak Catchers," concerns the attempts by
individual action groups to get funding from federal Poverty Program
agencies. *Radical Chic* stands not only as a hallmark of the New Journal-

ism movement but was also foundational for the understanding it provided of the cultural politics of radical black activism and the way it came to be understood in mainstream U.S. culture. Michael E. Staub argues, "Its contents arguably shaped the historical memory of the Panthers and their white supporters—and indeed the memory of the sixties generally—more than any other single journalistic piece from the era."[1]

While "Mau-Mauing the Flak Catchers" does not specifically name the Black Panther Party in its indictment of white funding of black radical causes, the entire text of "Radical Chic" revolves around the awkward interactions supposedly occurring between wealthy, status-conscious socialites and members of the Black Panther Party, who are portrayed as uncomfortably out of place, rigid, uncreative, and dogmatic. In characterizing the guests at the event, Wolfe claims that their motivation for supporting Black radicalism stems mainly from the fact that "most of the people in this room have had a problem being unwanted," a quote he directly attributes to Leonard Bernstein. Wolfe also quoted in its entirety a *New York Times* editorial characterizing the Bernstein event as "group therapy plus fundraising," "guilt-relieving fun spiked with social consciousness," and "elegant slumming that degrades patrons and patronized alike" (95).

Most of "Radical Chic" focuses on the confrontation that supposedly occurred between the party member Donald Cox, the party's host, Leonard Bernstein, and the filmmaker Otto Preminger as they argued about the efficacy of armed struggle and the possibility of positive social reform in the United States. Though Wolfe was critical of the Black Panther Party for claiming to represent the disenfranchised while actively courting the cultural elite, he also argued that the party presented the perfect model for political change among not only African Americans but mainstream whites as well. He labeled this interaction between advocates for the disenfranchised and the elite "radical chic" and wrote: "If there was ever a group that embodied the romance and excitement of which Radical Chic is made, it was the Panthers" (63).

Though Wolfe's notion of radical chic is removed from the Black Panthers' concept of vanguardism by its reliance on primitivism and its preoccupation with white subjectivity, it uses a similar model of the group as a vector for intense identification and affiliation. In *Do It! Scenarios of the Revolution*, Jerry Rubin would claim: "The Man tried to execute Huey. But millions of people—black people, white people, liberals, radicals, revolutionaries, housewives, doctors, students, professors—identified with Huey.

They said black people should arm themselves against the violence of the pigs. Huey's action redefined the situation for all of us" (142). Like vanguardism, white affiliation with radical African American causes had the power to change the apolitical and uninformed into supporters of radical causes. However, while the Panthers' model of vanguardism relied heavily on the transformative possibilities of radical politics, Wolfe's notion of "radical chic" revolved around the idea that affiliations between the Panthers and their supporters were marked by a fateful combination of personality failings, sexual deviance, and the rising popularity of radical politics in mainstream U.S. culture.

The Panthers' ability to "redefine the situation for all of us" had already had a transformative effect, not only on the New Left, as Rubin documents in *Do It*, but also on political culture globally. Consequently, when on 4 April 1969 the Black Panther Party member Connie Mathews approached Jean Genet—one of the leading European intellectuals of his time—for support, Genet identified so deeply and so immediately with the Panther cause that he left Paris almost at once for a fund-raising tour of the United States.[2] He spent two months in the United States—travelling illegally as he had been unable to obtain a visa—speaking on university campuses and often drawing crowds that numbered in the thousands. He would characterize himself as "a prisoner of love" when speaking of the years he spent as a spokesperson and fund-raiser for the Black Panther Party and living among the Palestinian Liberation Organization in Jordan and Lebanon (*Prisoner of Love*, 216–17).

Prisoner of Love, Genet's 1986 political memoir of his involvement with radical liberation movements, written years after his actual association with either group and shortly before his death, both celebrates and criticizes the intellectual elite's impulse toward affiliation. Acknowledging the ambivalence of those who chose to affiliate with radical causes for which others were risking their lives, he wrote: "If you can dream, calculate, feel pity at the thought of dead or dying heroes, if you can identify with them, it's because you've got time and are comfortable enough to do so. 'Delight me with the sacred cause for which someone else will die'" (144). At the same time, Genet acknowledged that the commitment of those who affiliated with radical causes could extend far beyond superficial identification with an unambiguous, if differentiated, commitment echoing that of the original martyrs: "When I was writing this book, out there among the fedayeen, I was always on the other side of the boundary . . . I didn't belong to, never really identified with, their nation or their movement. My heart was in it; my body was in it; my spirit was in it. Everything was in it at one point or another; but never my total belief, never the whole of myself" (105).

It was no accident that Genet used the language of a passionate and committed, yet compromised, love affair to characterize his involvement with radicalism and struggle. In its incarnation as a song, "Prisoner of Love" was popularized by James Brown, Billy Eckstine, and Etta James and speaks obviously and poignantly in the way that only pop songs can to the ambiguities of the experience of love as an experience of possession and transformation: "too weak to break these chains that bind me / I need no shackles to remind me, I'm just a prisoner of love." Like the pop song with the same title, Genet's work dwelt insistently within the ambiguity that exists in the interstices between love, possession, desire, hatred, and identification.

The notion of radical chic as popularized by Tom Wolfe takes little notice of the nuances of affiliation, identification, and desire provoked by cross-racial identification as they appear in Genet's work. "Radical Chic" also only briefly mentions the fact that many of the guests present at the party Wolfe lampoons, including both Bernstein and Preminger, were importantly involved in the production of African American images throughout the 1950s and 1960s in ways that had been groundbreaking (84). Rather than being either the shallow socialites or the social misfits that Wolfe described them as, the attendees at Bernstein's party represented a liberal cultural elite with a demonstrated interest in racial politics and social justice. Otto Preminger pushed to get the influential Black-cast film *Carmen Jones* made in 1954 despite warnings from studio executives that "people will not go to see a film with an all-Black cast" (Marcel, 56). Preminger directed the film, which made the African American actors Harry Belafonte and Dorothy Dandridge into recognizable visual icons, and then followed it in 1959 with the Black-cast film *Porgy and Bess*, starring Dandridge and Sidney Poitier, who would go on to become the most successful African American actor throughout the 1960s and 1970s. In 1966 Leonard Bernstein scored the music for the highly successful and controversial *West Side Story*, which used the motif of an interracial Romeo and Juliet–style romance to critique contemporary racial politics in the United States. Wolfe's *Radical Chic* also trivialized the style and cultural politics of the Black Panther Party, reducing them to what he called "pet primitives" who become the unthinking pawns of an upper-class elite who were eager, at the apex of this counterculture revolution, to co-opt unthinkingly passive radicals into a cult of tragically mundane hipness (63).

In reality, the Bernstein event represented a moment of radical confrontation between the burgeoning Black Power culture and the political and narrative limitations of the Civil Rights Movement. In both their production practices and their narrative conventions, *West Side Story, Carmen Jones,* and *Porgy and Bess* celebrated a popular politics and rhetoric of integration that the Black Panther Party was challenging both implicitly and explicitly. Rather than examining the complexities of such an event, Wolfe raised the specter of "radical chic" to make the interaction between Black Panther Party members and their potential supporters look like a sort of style politics of the wealthy. This ultimately ridiculed and deflated the possibilities for meaningful cultural and political exchange between a liberal or civil rights elite and new discourses of empowerment. Since, as Wolfe writes, "Radical Chic, after all, is only radical in style, in its heart it is society and its traditions," *Radical Chic* can never ask why it is "chic" to be radical in this way at this moment or answer the question of how the Black Panthers became a model powerful enough for identification to interest mainstream filmmakers and artists and even corporation heads. In the end, the term "radical chic" disavowed the possibility of vanguardism as a strategy of cross-identification that could potentially cut across class, cultural, and racial lines. White actors, artists, and intellectuals, such as Jean Seberg, Marlon Brando, Bert Schneider, Agnes Varda, Jean-Paul Sartre, and Romain Gary, and political activists such as Ulrike Meinhof of Germany's Red Army Faction, Abbie Hoffman and Jerry Rubin of the Yippies, and Bernardine Dohrn of the Weather Underground, all proclaimed an affinity for and affiliation with the Black Panther Party, which was seen as providing important models not only for political and social change but also for a deeply personal transformation.

The "Feelings of Others" The Possibilities for Racial Cross-Identification

When Genet claimed, "I could only place myself among the oppressed people of color and among the oppressed revolting against whites. Perhaps I'm a black whose color is white," was his statement politically progressive, as the Panthers would suggest, or politically retrogressive, as the work of

Tom Wolfe and others would seem to suggest? (126). The Panthers' ability to create an iconography that seemed to translate their ideology so effectively for cross-racial identification raised important questions about the possibility of a radical politics of alterity. It also brought into sharp focus more general questions about the possibilities for progressive cross-racial identification.

In her *Scenes of Subjection: Terror, Slavery, and Self-Making in Nineteenth-Century America*, Saidiya V. Hartman maintains that the complicated play between sufferance, sentience, and spectacle that is at the root of the African American image in the United States has its foundations in the experience of slavery. Her work on the spectacle of slavery and the way it helped to create the subjectivity of both the abolitionist and the slave owner at the expense of the enslaved demonstrates that the problem of progressive cross-racial identification is deeply rooted in American racial formations. Hartman argues that "the desire to don, occupy, or possess blackness or the black body as a sentimental resource and/or locus of excess enjoyment is both founded upon and enabled by the material relations of chattel slavery" (21). Noting the spectacular nature of the performance of African American suffering during slavery in the "the obscene theatricality of the slave trade," Hartman also recognizes the omission of the material reality of African American suffering from that spectacle (33). She explores the exclusion of African American sentience from narratives of racial suffering in the writings of the abolitionist John Rankin, labeling it "the violence of identification" (20):

> Properly speaking, empathy is a projection of oneself into another in order to better understand the other or the projection of one's own personality into an object, with the attribution to the object of one's own emotions. Yet empathy in important respects confounds Rankin's efforts to identify with the enslaved because in making the slaves' suffering his own, Rankin begins to feel for himself rather than for those whom this exercise in imagination is designed to reach. Moreover, by exploiting the captive body as a vessel for the uses, thoughts, feelings of others, the humanity extended to the slave inadvertently confirms the expectations and desires definitive of the relations of chattel slavery. (19)

In an indictment of the ease with which Rankin transferred the suffering of the enslaved onto himself, Hartman goes on to ask:

By making the suffering of others his own, has Rankin ameliorated indifference or only confirmed the difficulty of understanding the suffering of the enslaved? Can the white witness of the spectacle of suffering affirm the materiality of black sentience only by feeling for himself? Does this not only exacerbate the idea that black sentience is inconceivable and unimaginable but, in the very ease of possessing the abased and enslaved body, ultimately elide an understanding and acknowledgement of the slave's pain? (19)

Hartman's questions suggest the ways in which a problematic cross-racial identification that erases the material reality of African American suffering is endemic to subject formation in the U.S. context. A similar skepticism of radical cross-identification that emanates from personal experience but also extends beyond it to political and cultural expression is reflected in Frantz Fanon's assertion in *Black Skins, White Masks* that race is ultimately an experience of shock, visuality, and fractured subject formation epitomized by the child's simple declaration "Look, a Negro!" (111). Describing "the fact of blackness" as the condition of being constantly "overdetermined from without," Fanon links the shock of racial recognition to the limits of self and cross-identification, declaring that "the black soul is a white man's artifact" and "the black man . . . must be black in relation to the white man" (116, 14, 110).

Elizabeth Alexander, in "Can You Be Black and Look at This? Reading the Rodney King Video(s)," similarly maintains the primacy of the visual in creating the relationship between Black and white subject formation, noting, "Black bodies in pain for public consumption have been an American spectacle for centuries. This history moves from public rapes, beatings, and lynchings to the gladiatorial arenas of basketball and boxing" (92). Like Hartman and Fanon, Alexander sees moments of spectacularized racial terror as constitutive of both African American and white subject formation; however, she sees the experience of racialized terror as the unique property of African American identity formation because of its ability to visually codify a history of African American suffering in the United States into "a collective historical memory": "In each of these traumatic instances, black bodies and their attendant dramas are publicly 'consumed' by the larger populace. White men have been the primary stagers and consumers of the historical spectacles I have mentioned, but in one way or another, black people have been looking, too, forging a traumatized collective historical memory which is reinvoked, I believe, at contemporary sites of conflict"

(92–93). Alexander hopes to rescue the possibility of a progressive politics of intraracial identification from a critique of "identity politics" that sees racial identification as politically dangerous and critically unsophisticated while also asserting the primacy of "collective historical memory" in the quotidian political culture of African American people.

Alexander's work is dismissed as a "polite neonationalist polemic" in Paul Gilroy's *Against Race: Imagining Political Culture beyond the Color Line,* which explores the relationship between fascist politics and aesthetics and contemporary political and cultural formations (262). Motivated by a deep skepticism of the politics of solidarity, affiliation, and identification in identity-based political and cultural organizing, *Against Race* understands the space of affiliative identification and communitarian politics as inherently dangerous precisely because of its power to level political, cultural, and social difference and to replace them instead with "the tyrannies of unanimism" (207). Since Gilroy's book equates black nationalist politics with fascism, it could be seen as the logical culmination of the critique of identity politics that emerged in the 1990s with scholars such as Kwame Anthony Appiah, Henry Louis Gates, and Gayatri Spivak. Gilroy concludes: "The institution of innocent identity makes the difficult work of judgment and negotiation irrelevant. Fascism will flourish where that innocence is inflated by the romances of 'race,' nation, and ethnic brotherhood" (231). For Gilroy, the possibility of fascist identification is created by a visual culture haunted by the specter of iconic identification that created the contemporary possibility of a "logo-solidarity" extending across political and aesthetic and into consumer culture (160). A similar doubt of collective processes of identification shapes Joseph Heath and Andrew Potter's *The Rebel Sell: How the Counterculture Became Consumer Culture,* in which they argue that the ascendancy of "counterculture" as a commodity that exists in the place of a genuine Leftist politics came about precisely because the political culture of the 1960s and 1970s motivated an identification with revolutionary culture rather than revolutionary action itself.

In "Radical Chic," Wolfe depicts the Bernstein event as a fundamentally chaotic encounter motivated almost solely by the identification of various individuals with a set of taboo desires whose racialized erotic charge comes at least partially from the fundamental incompatibility of the positions of those represented. The essay opens with Leonard Bernstein wondering "what the Panthers eat here on the hors d'oeuvre trail? Do the Panthers like little Roquefort cheese morsels" (5). Wolfe describes the Panthers in relation to the libidinal energy with which he invests them, portraying their sexuality as so charged that it "runs through Lenny's duplex like a rogue hormone" (7). He repeatedly contrasts the "Park Avenue matrons" and the "*cultivated* persons" with the "real men" of the Black Panther Party, who represent what Wolfe labels a "superego Negro" for the consciousness of the group (8, 13, 4). The relationship between sexual desire and political action with regard to white affiliation for Black radical causes was a major source of tension and ambivalence for those involved in such affiliations, as well as those critical of them. Jean Genet unambiguously acknowledged the underlying passion and tension of his commitment to the Black Panther Party in his 1975 interview with Hubert Fichte, declaring, "The Panthers are Black Americans, the Palestinians are Arabs. It would be difficult for me to explain why things are like this, but these two groups of people have a very intense erotic charge" (132).

In *Make Believe: A True Story,* Diana Athill writes with an almost shocking candor about the relationship between white women and African American men involved in radical causes in the 1960s and 1970s. She herself became involved on various levels with Black radicals when she worked as an editor at a British publishing house that published their work. These included Michael X, a British West Indian who would be executed in Trinidad for murders that occurred when he attempted to found a Black nationalist commune, and Hakim Jamal, a cofounder of the US Organization who was the African American lover of the film star Jean Seberg. In her memoir, Athill, who would also become Hakim Jamal's lover for a short time, as well as offering him editorial and financial support, writes about the nature of Jamal's relationship to Seberg, a relationship that was one of the factors contributing to Seberg's divorce from the French writer Romain Gary (who would also write a fictionalized account of his encounters with black radical politics). Athill speculates about the nature of Seberg's attachment to Jamal after reading a series of letters between them:

> For all the naturalness of her letters to him, she could at some level have been using him as experience and as fuel for her need to demonstrate her lack of racism; to exercise virtue and to acquire merit. (What white can plead total innocence of exploiting relationships with blacks in this way at least at some point?) And this Hollywood conditioned girl might be extra self-deceiving. Such merit was fashionable in her circle at the time; hard to resist no doubt.

To be the one who really knew about what went on in the ghettoes, the one who really understood what black people feel—she may have wanted that pre-eminence. (106)

Although Seberg's relationship to Jamal could be labeled exploitative, her commitment to him cannot simply be reduced to a sort of radical chic, and she cannot be characterized as a sort of "armchair revolutionary," as Jean Genet does in *Prisoner of Love* (144). Neither term, "radical chic" or "armchair revolutionary," sufficiently accounts for the extreme risks to which people like Seberg subjected themselves in having interracial relationships and supporting Black radical causes: such people lost social standing, marriages, jobs, and even occasionally their lives. The terms are also insufficient to explain the extreme repression to which people like Seberg were subjected by the general public and by government agencies.

Athill notes that although both guilt and a tendency to romanticize danger play a role in white identification with Black radical causes, "only a tiny part of the British public cares two pins about black people in America or anywhere else, and even that part easily becomes fatigued at the prospect of being made to feel more guilty than it already feels" (106). Her account focuses on Gale Benson, the daughter of a conservative member of the British Parliament, who adopted an Africanized name and devoted herself totally to black radical causes before she was murdered during Michael X's failed commune experiment in the West Indies. For people such as Benson, Seberg, and Bernstein, affiliation with Black radical causes seemed to come at greater cost than simple models of identification such as "radical chic" can account for. Rather than merely rearticulating traditional models of cross-racial affiliation and identification that occlude the materiality of African American suffering, as Hartman claims the abolitionists had done, Jean Seberg, Gale Benson, and Leonard and Felicia Bernstein were affiliated with Black radical causes to a degree of physical intimacy that threatened, on a variety of levels, the status quo of racial and gender relations.

In his biography of Seberg, *Played Out*, David Richards charted Seberg's fall from being invited to dinners at the White House with the Kennedys and enjoying life as a fashionable expatriate in Paris to her institutionalization in mental hospitals and her eventual suicide, basing the narrative on her failed attempts to articulate new understandings of race and gender through radical projects and personal relationships. He documents how

FBI surveillance continuously focused on her sexuality, characterizing her as "a sex pervert" (231), and he quotes an FBI agent who opposed the tone with which the other agents discussed Seberg's involvement with the Black Panther Party: "The giving of her white body to a black man was an unbearable thought for many of the white agents. An agent whose name I will not mention, for obvious reasons, was overheard to say a few days after I arrived in Los Angeles from New York, 'I wonder how she'd like to gobble my dick while I shove my .38 up that black bastard's ass?' I was shocked at the licentious talk in the squad room area about the Panthers, Seberg, and Jane Fonda" (237).

The FBI circulated damaging rumors of Seberg's sexual involvement with various Black Panther Party members, even going so far as to send memoranda to gossip columnists urging them to publicly question the paternity of her unborn child in order to "cause her embarrassment and serve to cheapen her image with the general public" (238). As an actress, Seberg had been able to translate her success on-screen with films like *Breathless* (1960) and her public persona as a supporter of radical politics into status as an icon of the French New Wave film movement and of transgressive femininity.[3] But while she was able to challenge and create new parameters for style and fashion on film with her pageboy haircut and avant-garde performance of femininity, she was consistently unable to dictate new parameters for the performance of racial affiliation off-screen. Caught between society's old expectations regarding race and gender and the new possibilities created by radical social movements, Seberg was eventually scapegoated into psychosis and, finally, suicide.[4]

In 1975, the Trinidadian author V. S. Naipaul, whom the Swedish Academy recognized with a Nobel Prize for creating "works that compel us to see the presence of suppressed histories," fictionalized an account of Gale Benson's murder in the novel *Guerillas*. Naipaul struggles in the novel to maintain a consistent narrative voice in the telling of the event, which he characterizes as a failure to create and maintain effective coalitions across race, gender, and nation. A large part of *Guerillas* is constituted by a novel that the character based on Michael X is attempting to write, in which he assumes the narrative voice of Jane, the character based on Gale Benson. In Naipaul's novel, the character of Jane remains mostly voiceless, even as she is slowly raped and murdered with machetes over a prolonged period of time. She cries out, but only briefly, and not in any way that makes the novel's events more comprehensible. So even for a Nobel Prize–winning author like Naipaul, the motivations for the affiliative behavior of Benson or Seberg was beyond understanding or representation except through the exploitative eyes of others for whom they were little more than an "easy mark."

This sort of characterization flies in the face of the actual depth of the affiliations in question and the depth of the repression that faced those who engaged in them. It would be easy to reduce the affiliation to black radical causes sought by people like Gale Benson, Leonard Bernstein, Jean Genet, and Jean Seberg to the kind of counterculture affiliation that Norman Mailer identified as "the war of the Hip and the Square" in "The White Negro: Superficial Reflections on the Hipster," an influential 1957 article exploring white affinity for jazz culture. Like the concept of "radical chic," however, Mailer's "war of the Hip and the Square" was never actually meant to extend beyond cultural politics, while the confrontation between Black Power and the status quo at many points resembled an actual war. Many of the supporters of Black radical causes were invested in and planning on creating revolutionary change across a broad spectrum of the social, political, cultural, and even military terrain.

Wolfe's characterization of the events in "Radical Chic" stands in marked contrast to archival material that suggests the careful consideration and preparation that went into Black Panther Party fund-raising events precisely as opportunities to consolidate what appeared on the surface to be divergent interests around identification with an image of revolution that could convert Wolfe's "Park Avenue Matron" into someone who imagined herself in direct relationship to the aesthetics and ideology of the Black Panther Party. A memo from Judy West, proprietor of Seize the Time Bookstore in New York City, detailed plans for such a fund-raising event to be held at her apartment.[5] The potential guests, who were obviously chosen both for their ability and their willingness to contribute financially to radical causes, as well as for their cultural and political influence, ranged from the African American actor and activist Ossie Davis to Livingstone Wingate, the executive secretary of the Urban League, and Stan Kohlenberg, the president of Cheesebrough Ponds. All of the participants had a demonstrated ability to effect social, political, and cultural change in relation to African Americans. Livingstone Wingate, for example, was the director of the antipoverty summer arts program Operation Boot Strap, which provided funding in 1965 for the establishment of the Black Arts Repertory Theater School in Harlem, a major catalyst for the start of the Black Arts Movement.[6]

Dirty Tricks The Cost of Radical Affiliation

Ten years after the gathering at his home that was parodied in "Radical Chic," Leonard Bernstein would come forward to publicly accuse the FBI of having engaged in a campaign of systematic harassment—which he characterized as "dirty tricks"—aimed at him and his wife, Felicity, as a result of their having hosted the event.[7] His claims were substantiated in 1980 by the release of FBI documents to the attorneys attempting to get a new trial for the former New York Panther Richard "Dhoruba" Moore. According to Gerald C. Fraser in the *New York Times,* the documents demonstrated the FBI's concerted effort "to counter support for the Panthers among the Jews": "In January 1970 Mr. Hoover authorized agents in New York to send letters critical of the group to guests at a Black Panther fundraising party at the home of Leonard Bernstein, the composer and conductor. 'It is recommended,' said Mr. Hoover in a memorandum to the special agent in charge, 'that New York sign this letter with an anonymous name with additional phraseology such as "A Concerned and Loyal Jew" or some other phraseology.' The letters were mailed Feb. 27, 1970" (1).

Bernstein's position as a wealthy, socially conscious Jew with a desire for affiliation with radical African American causes is parodied by Wolfe in "Radical Chic." Although Wolfe acknowledges the complications in crossracial identification, at the same time, he ridicules the Bernsteins' ability to negotiate these complexities: "One of the ironies of the history of the Jews in America was that their long championship of black civil liberties had begun to backfire so badly in the late 1960s . . . Lenny and Felicia could hardly have been expected to comprehend a complex matter like the latterday friction between blacks and Jews" (99, 102). Though Wolfe ridicules the Bernsteins' ability to form coalitions with groups like the Black Panther Party, the FBI's response implicitly recognized the powerful possibilities of cross-racial identification as dangerous, hence the necessity of disrupting those possibilities, including the demand in "a Feb. 25 1970 memorandum to the New York field office from Mr. Hoover [that] correspondence to Mr. Bernstein's guests should outline 'the B.P.P.'s anti-Semitic posture'" (Fraser, 1).[8]

The FBI's interest in and use of the Bernstein's guest list for the purposes of disruption and surveillance begs the following question: If the connections the Black Panther Party made through meetings like the Bernstein event were as frivolous as the nomenclature "radical chic" would have us believe, why did a government agency invest them with such importance? Although there was undoubtedly some status in associating with members of the Black Panther Party because at that point they were widely held to be the vanguard of radical political activism, to characterize these guests simply as status-seeking socialites does a disservice to their potentially radical intentions as well as to the level of cultural intervention that the Black Panther Party was fairly adept at carrying out by this time. It was precisely in being able to draw the connections that made elite members of society imagine themselves as standing in a positive relationship to a culture that was urban, lower class, and African American that the party had managed to craft an international movement that was actually able to "Free Huey."

While Bernstein would claim that "none of these machinations has adversely affected my life or work, but did cause a good deal of bitter unpleasantness, especially to my wife, who was particularly vulnerable to smear tactics," other participants in "radical chic" could claim to have been destroyed by the political and social consequences of their association with the Black Panther Party.[9] Both Seberg, in her suicide note, and her former husband Romain Gary, in a press conference held following her suicide, linked her suicide, the death of her stillborn child, and the destruction of their marriage to persistent harassment by the F.B.I. in retaliation for her support of radical Black causes as personified by her involvement with the Black Panther Party.[10]

Seberg, who thought of herself as "the Panthers' honky representative in Europe," had been deeply involved in financing Black radical politics since she had joined the local branch of the NAACP as a fourteen-year-old child in her small hometown of Marshaltown, Iowa (see Richards). She was defined from the start of her film career at the age of seventeen with a radical politics and aesthetics when the director Otto Preminger cast her in the politically controversial Saint Joan (1957). Shortly thereafter, she became deeply associated with the most politically radical director of the French New Wave, Jean Luc Godard, through her starring role in the avant-garde classic Breathless (1960). Seberg's tragic spiral from celebrated status as a distinguished "American in Paris" to her lonely miscarriage and suicide was marked by the risk and actual consequences of the sort of cross-racial identification provoked by the Panthers.

In his exploration of the events surrounding her death shortly after she died, the *New York Times* theater critic Mel Gussow would label Seberg "the archetypal victim," while Elaine Brown would insist in her autobiography that "there was nothing radically chic about Jean Seberg . . . I felt her genuineness and decency. She really wanted to know about black people, about the nature of our oppression and the price of our freedom" (210). Whether they were victims or saints, to reduce the commitment of politically radical but privileged whites such as Seberg to "radical chic" is to paint a cynical and extremely reductive picture of the possibility and the cost of cross-racial identification in the 1960s and 1970s.

Shadow of the Panther   The Ambiguity of Identification

Wolfe paints an equally cynical picture of the Panthers' symbolic use of particular styles of clothing, hair, and deportment, confusing a simplified style politics with the complicated politics of style through which the Panthers had managed to seize the imagination of U.S. culture by utilizing everything from Huey Newton's movie-star good looks to the sartorial style of the average recruit to suggest the possibility and power of radical change. Wolfe lampoons the possible responses "the Panther look" evoked in the public sphere:

> Then a contingent of twelve or thirteen Black Panthers arrived. The Panthers had no choice but to assemble in the dining room and stand up—in their leather pieces, Afros, and shades—facing the whites in the living room. As a result, whenever anyone got up in the living room to speak, the audience was looking not only at the speaker but into the faces of a hard line of Black Panthers in the dining room. Quite a tableau it was. It was at this point that a Park Avenue matron first articulated the great recurrent emotion of Radical Chic: "These are no civil-rights Negroes wearing gray suits three sizes too big—these are real men!" ("Radical Chic," 64–65)

Wolfe's portrait of the Panthers' appearance at the party and its effect on their audience, both trivializing and hysterical, stands in severe contrast to other first-person accounts of the effect of seeing members of the Black Panther Party for the first time. In *Picking Up the Gun: A Report on the Black*

Panthers, Earl Anthony, who would eventually become the Black Panther Party's Deputy Minister of Education, wrote of his initial encounters with party members in their early days of organizing at San Francisco's Black House:

> As I walked in that night my attention was drawn instantly to two young
> Panther brothers, in black leather jackets, and black pants with black berets
> pulled down on their heads at a slant, each holding a carbine. Whenever I saw
> the Panthers during those early days with their weapons held expertly and
> with that confident air that they had, my heart used to skip a few beats. Other
> people used to tell me they had the same reaction. (26)

Various other accounts of first encounters with the Black Panther Party attest to the overwhelming power of the visual statement created by the Panthers' carefully calculated appearance. Eldridge Cleaver characterized his initial sighting of the Panther Party as "love at first sight . . . the most beautiful sight I had ever seen," giving credence to Anthony's claim that the Panthers' visual presentation could make hearts skip a beat (Cleaver, *Post-Prison Writings*, 19, 29). Contrasting these accounts with Wolfe's in "Radical Chic" illustrates that rather than being "the romanticizing of primitive souls" as Wolfe labels it, to the Black Panther Party, style was a complex and carefully crafted visual statement that more often than not elicited an intense identification with the party from those who encountered it (38). Wolfe's satirical trivialization of the meaning and motivation for the "Panther look" disguises the intense contestation that look represented to contemporaneous stylizations and ideologies of African American progress and empowerment, particularly the civil rights doctrine of nonviolence, whose primary enunciations were decidedly Southern, rural, and clerical.

The failure of the Civil Rights Act of 1965 to translate into widespread material gain led African Americans to doubt that future victories would emerge at the hands of traditional civil rights leadership and organizations. The neatly conservative suits and ties of the Southern Christian Leadership Conference and the "down-homey" overalls that were the uniform for Student Nonviolent Coordinating Committee organizers served to reinforce the notion of nonviolence and the Civil Rights Movement itself as a nonurban, nonghetto, outdated Southern articulation of black empowerment. In contrast, the Black Panther Party went to great lengths to utilize a dress code that consciously restated their affinity with the young, hip, urban "brother on the block." In *Do It! Scenarios of the Revolution* Jerry Rubin stated concretely the vanguardist notion that the Panther dress code provided not only a condensed language of revolution, but revolution itself: "The Panther uniform—beret, black leather jacket, gun—helps create the Panther legend. Three Panthers on the street are an army of thousands" (142). Earl Anthony continues in his account to evaluate the challenge—as articulated by the Panther look—that the Black Panther Party presented to other active Black organizations: "As I listened to Bobby speak that night, I realized that when I first saw the Panthers on the scene—armed—I had felt that they had upstaged everybody. But now as the reality of their presence began to painfully expose the truth of what we who believed ourselves committed to the struggle were about—I analyzed their impact upon me and my contemporaries again. Unlike any other organization in the area, they were making a conscious attempt to bridge the gap between rhetoric and action" (*Picking Up the Gun*, 27).

In actuality, rather than "bridg[ing] the gap between rhetoric and action," more often than not, the Panthers simply created a more dynamic and effective visual rhetoric. In the popular political tract "Huey Newton Talks to the Movement about the Black Panther Party, Cultural Nationalism, SNCC, Liberals, and White Revolutionaries," Newton quoted Regis Debray's maxim from *Revolution in the Revolution?*: "Poor the pen without the guns, poor the gun without the pen" (60). In the context of the Panther look, the gun served a more important purpose than its obvious practical function as an instrument of self-defense; in fact, often in the early years, the Panthers' guns either were not even loaded or at least not enough for any real gun battle. Like the leather jackets, black berets, and black pants, the guns served a stylized, symbolic, visual notice that some African Americans rejected the doctrines of nonviolence and were prepared to organize themselves in a disciplined, military fashion for the defense of their communities.

The problem with "the Panther look" and the Panthers' overall incursion into visual culture was not that it somehow ended up compromising the radical potentiality of the Panther ideology by opening it up for the trivializing of "radical chic," as Wolfe's critique would seem to suggest. The problem with the Panther incursion into visual culture was that it actually worked too well. It successfully raised the specter of radical change and offered an opportunity for deep identification with that possibility without ultimately being able to keep the attendant promise of victory through armed struggle, especially as the party was increasingly subjected to police and government repression following the public relations success of the "Free Huey" campaign. On 28 September 1968, the eve of Newton's sentencing for a reduced charge of manslaughter, Oakland police officers shot out the windows of the Panther headquarters in protest of what they viewed as relatively light sentencing (two to fifteen years with time served). The moment was chillingly prophetic of the repression that would follow. J. Edgar Hoover, the head of the FBI, who would later label the group "without question . . . the greatest threat to internal security," unleashed a campaign of harassment, arrests, disinformation, and internal chaos and violence perpetrated by paid informants that would lead to the party's eventual demise.

The pattern of police harassment and infiltration of the Southern California chapter of the Black Panther Party after 1968 was typical of that faced by many chapters. The Southern California chapter would effectively be destroyed, not only by the killing of Alprentice Carter and John Huggins on the UCLA campus in a COINTELPRO-inspired confrontation with Maulana Karenga's US Organization, but also through a series of violent confrontations with the Los Angeles Police Department, beginning with a police shoot-out on 5 August 1968 and ending with a massive shoot-out following an early morning raid on 9 December 1969 that left the majority of the Panther leaders either on the run or incarcerated. It would subsequently be revealed during the trial proceedings of the remaining Southern California Panthers that one of the key members of the organization, Melvin "Cotton" Smith, had been a longtime police informant.[11]

From 1968 into 1970, police and FBI violence around Black Panther Party chapters escalated so much that many branches were effectively shut down. On 2 April 1968, the New York chapter of the Black Panther Party, one of the strongest chapters outside the Bay Area, was effectively neutralized by the arrest of twenty-one of its most prominent members. It would take over two years for all of them to be exonerated from the spurious charges.[12] On 4 December 1968, the Chicago chapter of the Panthers would be decimated by the death of chapter leaders Mark Clark and Fred Hampton, the latter of whom was particularly noted for his ability to organize among Chicago's poor black community. The early morning police raid had all the marks of a political assassination since a paid informer had provided detailed plans as to exactly where Clark and Hampton would be sleeping on the night of the raid. A later investigation found that the sleeping Panthers scarcely had time to return police fire, with Panther members firing only one shot—to the police department's eighty-two shots—before being killed.[13] On 22 May 1969, Panther cofounder Bobby Seale and the prominent Bay Area organizer Erika Huggins were arrested while attempting to organize in New Haven, Connecticut, along with eight other New Haven chapter members, for the murder of Alex Rackley, who they feared was a police informer. On 25 July 1970, the Panther office in Omaha, Nebraska, was closed after being firebombed.[14]

Harassment arrests would be a significant obstacle for the national party leadership as well during this period as it fought an escalating cycle of arrests and trials. Huey Newton continued to be incarcerated from his October 1968 arrest until 5 August 1970. Bobby Seale, who had been arrested in New Haven, would also stand trial for his role in the rioting that had occurred at the Democratic National Convention in August of 1968. Though eventually exonerated of all charges, Seale would famously be bound and gagged during the trial proceedings. David Hilliard would be arrested on 3 December 1969 for declaring "We will kill Richard Nixon" in a speech. Though acquitted of charges stemming from that incident, he would later be convicted of carrying a loaded firearm in public and given a six-month sentence. Eldridge Cleaver would flee the United States with his wife, the important Panther organizer Kathleen Neal Cleaver, to avoid standing trial for a parole violation. James Carr, a close friend of Black Panther field marshal George Jackson, a personal bodyguard for Huey P. Newton, and an important link between the Panther party and incarcerated activists, would be arrested and threatened with return to prison if he refused to cooperate with the police (see Carr).

On 7 August 1970, sixteen-year-old Jonathan Jackson would seek to liberate by force his incarcerated older brother, Black Panther field marshal George Jackson, who has become particularly well known through the publication of his political memoir *Soledad Brother.* Jonathan Jackson commandeered a courtroom and managed to get weapons to three other prisoners before he was shot and killed by police alongside a federal judge and two other prisoners, William Christmas and James McClain. Later that same year, on 21 August, George Jackson himself would be murdered by guards during an alleged escape attempt at the Soledad Prison. The case would create one of the most high-profile manhunts of the era as the FBI sought to capture Angela Davis, a young radical African American professor and cochair of the Soledad Brothers Solidarity Committee, for her role in the escape attempt.[15]

These events constitute only the most prominent of government and police actions during this time, which Huey P. Newton labeled "a war against the Panthers"[16]; significantly, the party was scarcely able to deal with this war, although their visual rhetoric would have suggested otherwise. Part of the power of the Panther imagery to create fantasies of affiliation was its ability to convince participants, no matter how peripheral their affiliation, of their eventual victory. The power of the Panther imagery to condense Panther ideology into a convincing visual vocabulary allowed them not only to seduce everyone from "Mr. and Mrs. Wealthy Dentist from New Rochelle" and "Park Avenue matrons," as Wolfe claimed, but also to be regarded by J. Edgar Hoover as "the single greatest threat to the internal security of the United States" when by military or strategic terms they were obviously far from it.

The powerful promise of the Black Panther imagery is at least partly responsible for the "disappointment narratives" that have emerged; they are now so numerous that they almost constitute a subgenre of the literature about the Black Panther Party. For example, Earl Anthony's 1971 *Picking Up the Gun* bills itself as "The Book the Black Panther Party Tried to Suppress," and Gail Sheehy's *Panthermania: The Clash of Black against Black in One American City,* also published in 1971, is a sensationalized account of the murder of the suspected police informer Alex Rackley and the demise of the New Haven Black Panther Party chapter.[17] More contemporary "disappointment narratives" include most prominently *The Shadow of the Panther: Huey Newton and the Price of Black Power in America,* a negative evaluation by Hugh Pearson of Huey Newton and the Black Panther Party legacy, and the former Black Panther Party chairman Elaine Brown's *A Taste of Power: A Black Woman's Story,* which provides an account of the events that led Brown to flee Oakland and the party during its last days in the early eighties. The Black Panther Party was prescient in recognizing the increasing power of the image to define popular culture and thus popular political opinion, and the visual culture surrounding the Black Panther Party, including "the Panther look," was particularly adept at promising revolution without necessarily stipulating how, why, or which revolution.

Both Earl Anthony and Eldridge Cleaver, who had been so seduced by the aura of revolution intrinsic to "the Panther look," also ended up having significant ideological conflicts with the party, and both would play an important role in the eventual downfall of the party itself. Cleaver clashed bitterly with Newton about whether the direction of the party was reformist or revolutionary, about leadership and its structures, and about the party's role nationally and internationally. In many ways, the conflict between Newton and Cleaver symbolized the fundamental ideological conflicts that had existed in the party's mission almost from its inception. Though Cleaver was not one of the early members of the Oakland group that had included Bobby Seale and David Hilliard, he had been active in Bay Area politics after his release from prison and the success of his best-selling prison memoir *Soul On Ice* through the formation of Black House, a Black nationalist cultural and political venue.[18] Cleaver was greatly influenced by the revolutionary Black nationalism of the time that valorized armed liberation struggles, particularly those occurring in Africa and Asia. Though Newton would later espouse a global theory of "intercommunalism," his politics grew much more organically out of the localized situation of the Oakland and East Bay Area Black communities and were much more focused on the immediate concerns of those who lived in them.

The conflict between Cleaver and Newton, often erroneously reduced to a simple struggle between two strong personalities over the power and leadership of the party, is best epitomized by considering Newton's decision to name the organization the Black Panther Party for Self-Defense and to focus its efforts on the localized issues of policing, survival programs, and electoral politics, as opposed to Cleaver's continuously conflicting desire to move the party away from self-defense goals and toward an armed, internationally focused liberation struggle, which included the creation of overseas branches of the party. Conflicts about whether to operate from a localized nationalist or an internationalist perspective were exacerbated when Cleaver, who had fled overseas to avoid being reincarcerated as a parole violator, began in 1970 to call for armed insurrection from newly formed party bases in Algiers. In *Who Killed George Jackson? Fantasies, Paranoia, and the Revolution*, Jo Durden-Smith concludes that the Cleaver-Newton split exacerbated conflicts not only between individual members of the party along ideological lines but between chapters as well, mostly significantly bringing the Los Angeles and later the New York chapters in conflict with the Oakland headquarters (143–44). These conflicts were further intensified by the decision of Elaine Brown and Bobby Seale in April 1973 to run, respectively, for a spot on the Oakland city council and for the mayorship of Oakland on a Peace and Freedom Party ticket.[19] The question of whether the Black Panther Party would exist as a vanguard political party, a focoist-style guerilla army, or an armed self-defense unit was never effectively or conclusively answered during its existence.

Earl Anthony represented a different but no-less-debilitating threat to the Black Panther Party. He was a law student and UCLA graduate from a solidly middle-class background when he became drawn to the Panthers' militancy through their visual rhetoric of revolution. Though he enjoyed many of the privileges typical of middle-class African Americans, Anthony felt thwarted by the racism of early postsegregationist U.S. culture and saw the Panthers as a forceful answer to that problem. He was, however, staunchly anticommunist and, by his own account, so frightened by the organization's leftist sympathies and leanings once he became heavily involved in it that he agreed to become the FBI's first informant within the Panthers (*Spitting in the Wind*, 26). Clearly, Anthony, like Cleaver, understood and identified with the Black Panthers' call to revolution, but what exactly that call meant was left ambiguously open, not only by the Panthers' compelling visual rhetoric, but also by the vagueness of identification evoked by the model of "focoism" and the vanguardism adopted by the Black Panther Party.

Panther Iconography A Victory in Defeat?

In *Revolution in the Revolution?* Regis Debray quoted the prologue that Che Guevara had written to Vo Nguyen Giap's *People's War, People's Army* arguing for the primacy of armed struggle over political struggle and postulating victory in armed struggle as the most vibrant of political propaganda tools: "Propaganda is simply the presence of liberation forces in certain places where they demonstrate their power and combat ability, moving among the people as easily as fish in water" (*Che: Selected Works*, 152). The notion that the Panthers should present a model of revolutionary behavior was central to the their articulation of themselves, whether it was as the vanguard of armed struggle, as the Cleaver faction believed, or as the vanguard of a revolutionary political party, as Newton and those involved in the Oakland Branch of the Black Panther Party increasingly seemed to believe.

But did the emphasis on the vanguardist model of inciting revolution by literally embodying its possibility for the field of imaginative identification simply open up "the revolution" to the potential ambiguities that exist within the terrain of representation? Did the Panthers' desire to seize the apparatus of dominant media set it up for later co-option by that media? Furthermore, were there inherent problems in vanguardism as an organizing practice, especially when it came to image culture? Did its emphasis on the iconography of revolution end up validating a sort of idol worship that emphasized the icon over the political explanation? Did the approach validate the creation of models of revolution over the creation of actual widespread support for the revolution, thereby sacrificing not only tactile bases of support but an ideological basis as well? Contemporary responses to the Black Panther Party are telling in regard to how the legacy of the Black radical 1960s was shaped by the particular confluence of the Panther ideology of vanguardism and its practical application throughout the culture of the late 1960s and 1970s.

The ongoing popularity of the Panthers' complicated visual legacy all speaks to Hugh Pearson's question in *The Shadow of the Panther* about why the Panthers live on more vividly in the imagination of young African Americans than do the images of those in such groups as SNCC. In *Power to the People* Jim Haskins correctly notes:

> The legacy of Huey Newton in his prime, and of the Black Panther Party, are primarily symbolic: The image of defiant black men (and women) facing down racist law enforcement authorities resonates in the souls of inner-city African Americans, and many other African Americans, as strongly now as it did thirty years ago. It is a romantic image for the very reason that it is a doomed image. Huey Newton, Bobby Seale, Eldridge Cleaver, and other Black Panther leaders did what ordinary black people were too frightened or too law-abiding to do, and were cheered in the effort by those same ordinary black people. (119)

That the Black Panther Party images and ideology remain so widely circulated, easily identified, and recognizable, while similar contributions of organizations such as SNCC, the Revolutionary Action Movement, and the American Indian Movement are largely forgotten in popular American memory, speaks to the Black Panther Party's understanding of the complexity of American popular culture, a complexity that is often missing from discussions of the party.[20] The ability of SNCC to mobilize masses of African Americans might have been greater and their understanding of electoral politics more sophisticated, but ultimately, it was the Black Panther Party's complex understanding of the workings of American popular culture that left its image and its message—as well as its image minus its message—indelibly burned into the American popular consciousness.

Though the Black Panthers succumbed to a dangerous mix of infighting and police and governmental repression in the late 1970s, in winning popular support for the notion of armed struggle, they had undoubtedly achieved at least one of Guevara's mandates: "One does not necessarily have to wait for a revolutionary situation to arise; it can be created" (*Guerilla Warfare*, 111). It would in some ways be a cruel irony for a group that had managed to gain such widespread popular support that Che Guevara had himself failed to incite revolution in Bolivia, where he was killed, largely because he had failed to fulfill another of his mandates: "For the individual guerilla warrior, then, wholehearted help from the local population is the basis from which to start. Popular support is indispensable" (113).

The Black Panther Party attracted widespread popular support because its visual iconography and discourse of revolution inspired deep identification among audiences with widely divergent aims and interests. However, the Panthers' iconography and revolutionary discourse did not necessarily inspire armed struggle in the manner suggested by Che Guevara or propounded in their own embrace of vanguardist tactics. But could a focus on creating a powerful visual and discursive vision of revolution, however educational, actually be blamed for the Panthers' failure to incite armed struggle? William Van Deburg's *New Day in Babylon* typifies contemporary understandings of the party's imagery and ideology: "In the long run, the Panthers' utilization of the gun as a recruiting device and 'political tool' worked to their disadvantage, inflaming public opinion, skewing news coverage, and spurring a deadly response to their presence in law enforcement personnel" (159). Such claims not only tend to blame the party for its own victimization, they also downplay the deliberateness with which decisions about the Black Panther Party style and image were made. *New Day in Babylon*, which remains the most extensive exploration of the relationship between Black Power and American popular culture, devotes fewer than twenty pages to a discussion of the party's transformative role in American culture, and an examination of the party's direct and indirect ventures into the arena of popular consumer culture—including, most importantly, the creation of Stronghold Incorporated, which oversaw the party's business ventures—has yet to be undertaken. In the end, how much of the way in which the Panther legacy and the legacy of individual Panthers has been received as the legacy of failed or fallen heroes can be blamed on the Guevarist formulations of revolution and ideology?

In *Shadow of the Panther*, Hugh Pearson promises to reveal the unadorned truth about a group that has "legendary appeal to many young blacks who were either infants or toddlers in the party's heyday" (336). His account of the demise of the Black Panther Party, which is highly critical of Newton and the party in general, is an unintended study of the identificatory power of Panther iconography even for those with very different political leanings and concerns and is strongly similar to Earl Anthony's earlier account of his enchantment and eventual disillusionment with the party in *Picking Up the Gun*. Pearson possibly even drew his title from the sensationalistic opening page of Anthony's book: "The Shadow of the Panthers. Today the Black Panther Party has cast its shadow over America. But what is the truth about the Panthers? What are their methods and goals? Above all, what kind of men are their leaders, and what kind of Black man joins the Party? Now for the first time in print here is a full, honest, and intimate account of the Panthers by a man who was in the Party's innermost circles" (2). Pearson mimics Anthony's stylistic attempt to give an account that is "full, honest, and intimate," both implying and stating that earlier accounts of the Panthers were guided by idolatry and misinformation. Though the fact figures only briefly in *Shadow of the Panther*, Pearson notes that Anthony, "known inside the party as the bourgeois Panther," was "COINTELPRO's first recruit inside the party" (181). This startling pronouncement hardly colors Pearson's account of the rise and fall of the Black Panther Party at all; paradoxically, the book skips over governmental structures like COINTELPRO that hounded the party into self-destruction to focus more on the various personality failures and individual struggles for personal fulfillment within the party.

Pearson's stated interest in the Black Panther Party derived from his desire to identify with other African Americans even though he claims to have "felt the sting of rejection by other blacks because my family was successful" (341). His family "had been solidly middle class virtually since the end of slavery," and as he saw it, "confused notions of elitism mixed with a determination to 'remain black'" characterized his identity struggle (340). Pearson's early interest in Black Power emanated from an intense identification with Huey P. Newton based on the fact that they shared the same difficult first name:

My elementary years were also characterized by something else—the sting of rejection I felt because my birth name was Huey. I had been named after my father. Like Huey Newton, I was ridiculed because of that name. But when I reached the seventh grade, I discovered the book *Free Huey!*. It was the first time I had seen the handsome face of Huey Newton. I read the book and became elated that someone named Huey could be such a hero to so many people. (342)

It is both interesting and curious that Pearson's identification with Newton arose from a very individualized sense of oppression—stemming from a shared birth name—instead of from the more common identification of Newton as an antipolice agitator, which is of course the image with which he is more typically associated. What struck Pearson about *Free Huey!* was not that it portrayed the figure of a resistant Black man armed against police violence but rather its depiction of the personal success of someone who had by then been elevated to the level of a matinee idol/genuine folk hero within American popular culture. This is especially striking since *Free Huey!* is Edward M. Keating's meticulously detailed account of the events of the night the police officer John Frey died, allegedly at the hands of Newton himself. Pearson focuses on Newton's heroic qualities, with only the most cursory rendering of the ideological challenges that his image could be said to represent. This allows Pearson to conflate and consequently deflate the Panthers' claims to solutions for racist oppression as easily as he conflated and then deflated his boyhood hero.

Pearson's *Shadow of the Panther* trades in much of the conventional wisdom about the party and its legacy within American popular culture created by people like Tom Wolfe, though it is certainly a more thoroughly researched and ultimately more carefully nuanced account of the party. Accounts like Wolfe's mark the Black Panther Party's genius as accidental, its challenges as poorly thought out and atavistically violent, and its popularity as largely the result of its individual members' "star power." In keeping with his theme of failed or self-actualized personalities, Pearson regards Huey Newton, who died addicted to drugs at the hands of an African American drug dealer, as the ultimate tragic symbol of the party's failures. While carefully painting Newton as little more than a thug and drug addict, Pearson lionizes such former Black Panther Party members as Landon Williams, who went on to college and participation in mainstream struggles for social justice, playing up Newton's "sins" while downplaying Williams's suspected role in the highly publicized death by torture of the New Haven party member and suspected police informer Alex Rackley.

With such barely disguised class interests, Pearson seems to have been un-impressed by Earl Anthony's claim in *Picking Up the Gun* that "none of us, especially those of us who are black, should forget the contribution which the Black Panther Party has made, and I'm sure is continuing to make, in the struggle for survival of black people in America. They picked up the gun to show America, so vain and unconcerned in her power over people's lives, that when she decided to take another black life she would have to bring ass to get ass. That in itself should be enough to warrant the Black Panther Party the undying respect of black people" (xi).

For Pearson, identification with Newton's persona does not require identification with the most fundamental precept of the Black Panther Party: the necessity of revolutionary action for social change. Newton's en-counter with the police officer John Frey on the night of 28 October 1967, which led to Frey's death, Newton's incarceration, and the epic struggle to "Free Huey," was not, for Pearson, a microcosm of the forces of oppression that determine the destiny of Black lives in the United States, which is how the party had painted it. Even though Newton was never convicted of mur-der in a court of law—and there is now overwhelming evidence to suggest that John Frey and the Oakland Police Department were, in fact, engaged in the systematic harassment of Newton and other Black Panther Party members—for Pearson, this moment becomes just one more instance of how the "thuggish" Newton "got over" on the system. At one point Pearson even goes so far as to characterize the shooting of Frey as coming from Newton's need to "release steam" (*Shadow,* 15).

Pearson recognizes and seems confounded by the continuing popularity of the Black Panther Party within American popular culture. He attributes this primarily to a strange mixture of naive idolatry among Blacks and the continuing malevolence of mass-media stereotyping. He searches for an explanation for "the fact that the Black Panthers are far more indelibly stamped in [young African Americans'] imaginations than are, for example, the images of SNCC members such as John Lewis, Bob Moses, and their cohorts" (*Shadow,* 336). Rather than finding his answer in any identifica-tion with the Black Panther Party ideology, Pearson locates it in a "Left and left-liberal media" that, he claims, would continue to play "a major role in elevating the rudest, most outlaw elements of black America as the true keepers of the flame of what it means to be black" (339). He also finds it in young African Americans who, in lacking self-esteem, create iconic figures based on the Black Panther Party's "defiant, uniformed imagery" (336).[21] Pearson contrasts the "constructive, noncriminal behavior" of post-1970s former SNCC leaders such as Lewis and Moses with the post-1970s lives of former Panther party leaders, suggesting that such information represents a final damning indictment of the party and its ideology (339).

Pearson's analysis willfully renders the foundational platform of the party, opposition to oppressive policing, irrelevant, despite the fact that much of what the party called for, including such practices as community policing and citizen-review boards, have become widely accepted in many urban areas throughout the United States. Pearson also refuses to acknowledge that it is precisely the objection to policing for which the party is primarily remembered in the African American cultural imagination, particularly among those too young to have lived through the party's heyday. From the beginning of his project, Pearson refuses to acknowledge the political or cultural efficacy of attempts to reform policing as having as lasting or legitimate an import as SNCC's attempts to reform electoral politics. Presenting the Black Panther Party's influential "Ten-Point Program," he writes: "The platform points about prison and the police clearly reflect a Newton obsession. He acted as though being brutalized by the police and unjustly imprisoned were principal problems most black people faced daily" (112).

In formulating the emphasis on policing as nothing more than "a Newton obsession," Pearson obviously ignores the fact that for many young urban African Americans—especially those whose families have not been "solidly middle class since the end of slavery," as had Pearson's—interaction with the police has increasingly been the determining factor in the shape of their daily existence since the late 1960s.[22] This is particularly true in California, the state that is primarily responsible for creating and perpetuating "law-and-order" oppression of nonwhites. In some senses, experience with the criminal justice system has become the rule rather than the exception for California's African American population. In *City of Quartz: Excavating the Future in Los Angeles*, Mike Davis writes, "California is creating a time-bomb of multiple Attica potential" regarding the fact that the California justice system "since 1974 has arrested *two thirds* of all young Black males in California" (288, emphasis in original). Pearson's *Shadow of the Panther* insists on seeing the experience of African Americans in the American justice system and the increasing criminalization of African American youth as determined more by the content of their character than by either class or circumstance. Consequently, he cannot see, let alone acknowledge, the ways in which Huey P. Newton and the Black Panther Party were on the cutting edge of the antiprison, antipolice discourse that has gained currency within popular culture in the years since the party's demise. This allows Pearson ultimately to reduce the Black Panther Party's enduring legacy within American popular culture to little more than "images of defiant posturing over substance" (340).

Though *Shadow of the Panther* employs a sort of frank, "true-crime" exposé style, the book is ultimately most dependent ideologically on certain individualizing "uplift" strategies in its portrayal of the relationship between African Americans, the party, and crime. Because of Pearson's desire to demonstrate that African Americans can lift themselves out of criminalizing ghetto environments through sheer strength of character, *Shadow of the Panther* misses the Black Panther Party's most enduring legacy: its sophistication in its understanding of the criminalization of African Americans, particularly African American youth. Pearson's otherwise meticulously detailed account of the rise and fall of the Black Panther Party simply misses the point of it entirely and is consequently unable to grasp its true import within either African American or American popular culture. Unfortunately, *Shadow of the Panther* has shaped the way in which the Black Panther Party legacy has come to be re-evaluated by intellectuals on the Left, who have too often been seduced into understanding party members as macho media stars with a naive rhetoric of revolution who happened to "luck into" a dangerous imagery with a curiously widespread and lasting appeal.

Guevara's *Guerilla Warfare* stresses the importance of maintaining the status of the revolution as "a people's revolution": "For the individual guerilla warrior, then, wholehearted help from the local population is the basis from which to start. Popular support is indispensable" (113). Long on military strategy, *Guerilla Warfare* tended to be vague and even contradictory on how exactly support for the revolution should be established with "the people." Che Guevara could claim that "wholehearted help from the local population is the basis from which to start" the revolution at the same time he urged isolationism as a necessary precautionary strategy:

> Trust no one beyond the nucleus, especially not women. The enemy will undoubtedly try to use women for espionage. The revolutionary secretly preparing for war must be an ascetic and perfectly disciplined. Anyone who defies the orders of his superiors and makes contact with women and other outsiders, however innocuous, must be expelled immediately for violation of revolutionary discipline. (146)

More often than not, *Guerilla Warfare* simply regarded popular support as a foregone conclusion. However, when Guevara died in the jungles of Bolivia, he had failed to recruit a single person to the struggle there. Rooted in a sexism that the Black Panther Party would largely refuse as a revolutionary praxis, Guevara's call for isolationism would also be rejected by the Panthers, who actively sought to establish modes of strategic identification as a primary organizing practice. In *Revolution in the Revolution,* Regis Debray urged revolutionaries to remember that "warfare should not be confused with propaganda" (48). The Black Panther Party had undoubtedly triumphed in the propaganda war, but such victories failed to create the desired parallel success on the tactical military front. When the Black Panther Party officially folded in the 1980s, almost all the structures it had created during its nearly two decades of existence were gone.

In the end, the Panther organization's genius lay less in its tactical abilities as a fighting force with a potential to create a mass revolution than in its ability to evoke concrete identification through multiple forms of media with images of revolution that cut widely across divergent constituencies. In creating spectacular images of revolution that tied notions of individual empowerment, independence, and justice together with Black "street" subjectivity, the Black Panther Party helped create the blueprint for notions of Black subjectivity that continue to guide our understanding of race in the United States. The power of this legacy lies not only in its ability to negotiate U.S. cultural politics regarding race, but also in its creation of a group that operated in the symbolic economy primarily as symbols of cultural, moral, and intellectual empowerment and is still a powerful model for identification among the politically disadvantaged. The Civil Rights Movement had won the high ground from the white majority through a powerful negative moral suasion, persuading the white majority not to be the kind of people that racists would be. The Black Panthers, on the other hand, offered up the African American urban underclass culture as powerful and beautiful, the potential object for a powerful identification. The pervasiveness of notions of Black culture that rose out of the image culture of the Black Power era, and the rise of Black culture as the penultimate expression of American popular culture, is something that neither Guevara's nor Debray's accounts of social change could explain or predict. Ultimately, the Black Panther Party created so formidable a cultural legacy that it will most likely endure long after the oppression that necessitated its creation.

3

"We Waitin' on You"

BLACK POWER, BLACK INTELLECTUALS, AND THE
SEARCH TO DEFINE A BLACK AESTHETIC

Dutchman, the Black Arts Repertory Theater, and the
Birth of the Black Arts Movement

On 24 March 1964, LeRoi Jones's *Dutchman* opened at the Cherry Lane Theater, an off-Broadway stage. The play, which was both groundbreaking and controversial, would go on to win an Obie Award. Langston Hughes would characterize 1964 as "The Jones Year," noting that Jones's plays were so controversial that of the five staged in New York in 1964, two were shut down by order of the police (*Black Magic*, 251). Less than a year later, Jones would join up with a group of artists and activists to form the Black Arts Repertory Theater School in Harlem, which would stage a number of his plays, including *Dutchman*. In his 1968 manifesto "The Black Arts Movement," Larry Neal claims that the Black Arts Repertory Theater "represented the most advanced tendencies in the movement" and presented work of "excellent artistic quality" (261). *Dutchman* was typical of the Black Arts Repertory Theater's performances in its polemical narrative and its experimental, highly stylized content. Centered on the seductive interplay between a black male and a white female subway rider, an interplay that culminates in the murder of the man by the woman, the play performs what Phillip Brian Harper terms the "anxious identities and divisional logic" that would come to mark the Black Arts polemical "call" for the unification of the race against the white oppressor.[1]

In Larry Neal's account of the Black Arts Repertory Theater, which lies at the heart of his call for the formation of a Black Arts Movement, the theater opened, like *Dutchman*, to almost immediate controversy and widespread acclaim. The theater's organizers and participants included some of the most important artists, activists, and cultural workers of the day, from Sonia Sanchez, Harold Cruse, John Coltrane, and Sun Ra to LeRoi Jones himself. The confluence of cultural, political, and intellectual events that led to the Black Arts Repertory Theater's production of *Dutchman* would be replicated across the country as debates concerning the relationship between aesthetics, politics, and representation resulted in a vibrant burst of cultural production. By the summer of its opening year, however, the Black Arts Repertory Theater had ceased operations, having survived for less than three months. During its short life, the Black Arts Repertory Theater was rife with the ideological, aesthetic, and monetary crises and critical questions that would create, shape, and ultimately lead to the demise of the Black Arts Movement as a whole.

In its attempt to produce "art that speaks directly to Black people," the Black Arts Repertory Theater created a vibrant alternative to dominant Western culture that continues to be the primary way through which African American culture and identity are created and understood (Neal, "Black Arts Movement" 258). The notion of African American cultural production as "race memory . . . art consciously committed, art addressed primarily to Black and Third World people," as Larry Neal declared in "Reflections on the Black Aesthetic," as well as the notion that African American identity is born out of a struggle with racism, urbanity, and the consequences of slavery, are both a direct legacy of the Black Arts Movement's struggle to redefine African American cultural production (14).

In this chapter, I examine the failures and successes of the Black Arts Movement through its theorization of a "Black aesthetic" and its continuing legacy in order to challenge the commonly held assertion that this movement—with its spectacular successes and failures—offered little more than racial essentialism, a hyperbolically divisive ideology, and a formalistic and essentially flawed aesthetic theorization. I look beyond dismissive evaluations of the Black Arts Movement to argue that the historical moment of both the Black Power and the Black Arts Movements was *the* formative moment, not only for contemporary understanding of African American identity, but also for ideas of blackness in African American cultural production, characterized by artists and intellectuals of the era as "the new thing" but naturalized into contemporary African American culture as "authentic" Blackness. Don L. Lee noted in 1971: "The decade of the sixties, especially that of the mid-sixties, brought us a new conscious-ness, a perception that has come to be known as a *black consciousness*. . . . Along with the new awareness, we get a form that on the surface speaks of newness" (226). I explore the shape and implications of that "new aware-ness" and the new forms it enabled, as well as the continued importance of the death of civil rights–era symbolism for the form, discourse, and ideol-ogy created and shaped in the Black Arts/Black Power moment.

By 1968 the Black Arts Movement and the Black Power Movement had successfully seized the cultural arena as the primary site of political action. The African American freedom struggle in the United States would begin to be represented and debated in virtually *every* artistic and cultural for-mat in the terms defined by the Black Arts Movement: from the politically progressive experiments of free jazz musicians such as Ornette Coleman, Albert Ayler, and Pharoah Sanders to Black popular music, in which James Brown sang "Say It Loud, I'm Black and Proud" as the Impressions urged African Americans to "Keep on Pushing"; from the Black Arts drama of Ben Caldwell, LeRoi Jones, and Ed Bullins to the poetry of Sonia Sanchez, Don L. Lee, Larry Neal, and Jayne Cortez; and in the unprecedented boom in film productions chronicling the African American experience.

In 1971 Larry Neal issued the cry for "an art that speaks directly to the needs and aspirations of Black America" from the pages of *The Black Aes-thetic,* a collection of essays on theory, music, poetry, drama, and fiction edited by Addison Gayle (257). In this chapter, I explore the Black Arts Movement's theorization of a Black aesthetic through a discussion of one of its seminal texts, *Black Fire! An Anthology of Afro-American Writing,* coed-ited in 1968 by LeRoi Jones and Larry Neal. *Black Fire!* collected work by some of the most significant artists, musicians, and theoreticians of the Black Arts Movement, including Sun Ra, Victor Hernandez Cruz, Henry Dumas, John Henrik Clark, Stanley Crouch, Calvin Hernton, Stokely Car-michael, A. B. Spellman, David Henderson, and Sonia Sanchez. In the process of defining a diverse artistic practice, *Black Fire!* participants also created definitions of community, identity, and authenticity that continue to be central to African American cultural production.

"Ethnic Propaganda"   The Black Arts Movement and Its Detractors

In its own time the movement was criticized by everyone from Ralph El-lison (who claimed LeRoi Jones's *Blues People,* when "taken as a theory of

Negro American culture," could "only contribute more confusion than clarity"), to J. Saunders Redding (who, as Houston Baker has noted, labeled the movement "an intellectually unsound discourse of 'hate,' a naive racism in reverse").[2] Like the Black Power Movement itself, which was criticized as reactionary, racist, and theoretically unsound by the civil rights orthodoxy it was attempting to displace, the Black Arts Movement's detractors viewed it as dangerous and critically untenable, in particular its demand that "the cultural values inherent in Western history must be radicalized or destroyed," as well as the observation that "the only way out of this dilemma is through revolution."[3] Many critics of the movement refused to engage with the Black Arts Movement's call for racial unity even as a self-conscious political strategy or as a rhetorical stance that reacted to the perceived failures of the Civil Rights Movement. This fostered a climate in which Black Arts creations were more likely to be dismissed as "ethnic propaganda," as Stanley Crouch says in "The Incomplete Turn of Larry Neal" (5), than seriously critically and examined. Crouch's reductive description of Neal's contributions during the Black Arts period is typical in this regard:

> One encounters the philosophical attacks on the systems of the Western
> world, romantic celebrations of African purity, denunciations of the purported
> Uncle Toms who didn't embrace separatist and violent "solutions" to the
> American race problem, and the demand that all serious young black artists
> commit themselves to a particular vision of political change. Such writing is
> now more important in terms of the thought processes that underlay the work
> of a generation that produced nothing close to a masterpiece, that failed, as all
> propaganda—however well intentioned—inevitably fails. (4)

Crouch's subsequent declaration that the Black Arts Movement "exists more as evidence of a peculiar aspect of social history than any kind of aesthetic achievement" represents the general disregard in which the work of the period is held in many scholarly accounts. This disregard stands in stark contrast to the actual continuing importance of the Black Arts legacy to African American cultural production.

In fact, the Black Arts Movement continues to be one of the most influential and yet least studied moments of African American literary and cultural production. In a 1991 review of the period for *American Literary History*, David Lionel Smith writes of "the paucity of scholarly literature on this body of work":

> A review of the *MLA Bibliography* for the past 10 years gives the clearest pic-
> ture of this dearth . . . one seldom finds more than three or four listings in any
> given year . . . in most years there are only a couple of articles under these
> headings that one can easily obtain through normal channels. Furthermore,
> many of the movement's basic documents . . . are now out of print. (93)

Smith's statement is borne out by a 1985 special issue of *Callaloo* devoted
to honoring Larry Neal, which represents one of the most extensive scholarly treatments to date of Neal and the movement he helped engineer. The
guest editor Kimberly W. Benston begins his introduction by noting, "We
do not yet have a coherent history of the great Afro-American cultural
movement that began in the mid-1960s" (5).[4] Smith attributes the lack of
scholarship on the Black Arts Movement to the fact that "the extremes
of this writing are so egregious that we may come to equate all the work
of the movement with its worst tendencies" (93). Lorenzo Thomas's 1978
exploration of the influence of the Umbra Writers' Workshop on the Black
Arts Movement, "The Shadow World," concludes simply: "It is much too
soon to say what ultimate results this movement might produce, just as it
is not yet time to evaluate all the works of its principal participants" (70).

The sense that African American critical theory has necessarily "moved
on" from the politically charged moment of the 1960s and 1970s that
birthed the Black Arts Movement predominates, perpetuating an understanding of the movement as simply a politically didactic but critically
unimportant moment in African American intellectual and cultural history. However, the effects of Black Arts Movement, especially the critical
assumptions that underpin the notion of the Black aesthetic, continue to
lurk in often unacknowledged ways in the shadows of accepted African
American critical thinking and artistic production.

"Real" and "Out Loud"   The Influence of the Black Arts
Movement on Contemporary African American Cultural Identity

Though the movement was already beginning to dissipate soon after the
publication of *The Black Aesthetic* in 1971, its discourse, along with other
of the Black Power–era discourses—on Blackness, the arts, politics, and
culture—continue to be formative influences on contemporary understanding of race in America. For everything from hip-hop culture to contemporary urban fiction and contemporary cultural assertions about what

constitutes African American identity, the Black Arts Movement's notion of authentic Blackness continues to be the predominant mode for understanding African American identity and culture. Its investment in urban vernacular culture resulted not only in the cultivation of "street" poetry and poetics but also in a positioning of urban vernacular at the center of African American aesthetics.

The impact of the Black Arts Movement on urban American vernacular poetry can simply not be overstated. In an almost verbatim echoing of Larry Neal's statements on the Black Arts Movement and the Black aesthetic, Miguel Algarin writes in *Aloud: Voices from the Nuyorican Poets Cafe*, "The poet of the nineties is involved in the politics of the movement. There need be no separation between politics and poetry. The aesthetic that informs the poet is of necessity involved in the social conditions the people of the world are in" (11). Though Algarin is speaking of the vibrant, multiethnic Slam poetry movement and the poetry of the Nuyorican Poets Cafe, with its ties to the hip-hop culture and its roots in Puerto Rican and African American oral traditions, his constitutive aesthetic values are the same as those first defined by Neal and the Black Arts Movement. Written in 1971 for *The Black Aesthetic*, the categorical analysis of "the black poets of the sixties" produced by Don L. Lee (Haki Madhubuti) could easily be read as a description of the elements of contemporary spoken word poetry:

1. polyrhythmic, uneven, short explosive lines
2. intensity; depth, yet simplicity; spirituality, yet flexibility
3. irony; humor; signifying
4. sarcasm—a new comedy
5. direction; positive movement; teaching, nation-building
6. subject matter—concrete; reflects a collective and personal lifestyle
7. music: the unique use of vowels and consonants with the developed rap demands that the poetry be real, and read out loud. (226)

Black Arts' influence is evidenced by the Slam poetry aesthetic, particularly in Lee's demand that poetry "be real, and read out loud." It is not surprising that *Aloud: Voices from the Nuyorican Poets Cafe* opens with a quote from the *Black Fire!* contributor Sun Ra, or that poems by the contributors Victor Hernandez Cruz and David Henderson appear in its "founding poems" and "poems of the 1990s" sections, respectively. The influence of the Black Arts Movement runs consistently not only through the Slam poetry and the spoken word movements, which prides themselves on orality, vibrancy, and populism, but also within a hip-hop culture that positions urban vernacular traditions at the core of its aesthetic.

The influence of the Black Arts Movement extends far beyond the formal elements of African American poetry to the ways in which African American culture is defined and produced. In the introduction to *The LeRoi Jones/Amiri Baraka Reader,* William J. Harris summarizes the importance of the Black Arts Movement for a variety of emergent literary traditions:

> The Black Arts Era, both in terms of creative and theoretical writing, is the most important one in black literature since the Harlem Renaissance. No post-Black Arts artist thinks of himself or herself as simply a human being who happens to be black; blackness is central to his or her experience and art. Furthermore, Black Arts had its impact on other ethnic groups primarily through the person of Baraka . . . He opened tightly guarded doors for not only Blacks but poor whites as well and, of course, Native Americans, Latinos, and Asian-Americans. We'd all still be waiting for an invitation from *The New Yorker* without him. He taught us all how to claim it and take it. (xxvi)

Harris highlights the importance of the Black Arts Movement challenge as a critical practice as well as an aesthetic demand. Jones, Neal, and other Black Arts practitioners and critics positioned social change and identity struggle at the center of an aesthetic agenda for an entire emergent African American literary tradition and intellectual class. Their demand to clarify the aesthetic dimensions of "Black Art" in relation to the political demand for the creation of discrete spaces in which to articulate that aesthetic shaped the way in which an entire generation of critics and practitioners would define their role within culture and society.

Though Black Arts Movement practitioners were most deeply invested in creating an alternative to mainstream culture, contemporary popular culture remains the domain in which the Black Arts Movement's influence continues to be most openly celebrated. The African American presence in U.S. popular culture continues consistently to pay homage to the Black Arts Movement's cultural politics through actual allusion and in the way an African American cultural aesthetic is articulated and authenticated. While political groups like the Black Panther Party successfully incited a lexical revolution through the popularization of slogans such as "Black is Beautiful!" that were meant to transform the American Negro into a powerful Black revolutionary, it was within the arena of popular, rather than political, culture that notions of authentic blackness as soulful, urban street life, and ghetto-fabulous masculinity were popularized and defined and continue to have an acknowledged resilience today.

Like the Black Arts and Black Power movements themselves, popular culture's tributes to these movements continue to locate the essence of African American culture in the street-savvy urban dweller rather than within the African American folklife of the South celebrated by earlier African American literary and cultural movements. From Snoop Doggy Dogg's warning that he can "clock a grip like my name was Dolemite" and Tupac Shakur's tributory Black Panther Party tattoos, to the name of Notorious B.I.G./Biggie Smalls, which is drawn from Hiawatha "Biggie" Smalls, the ill-fated gangster from the 1975 Blaxploitation film *Let's Do It Again* (1975), the urban poor, yet occasionally ghetto-fabulous, "brother on the block" constructed during the Black Arts Movement as a representational standard continues to provide the most pervasive assumption of essential Blackness in contemporary understandings of race and racial politics. "The Corner," from Common's 2005 album *Be*, is typical in that it proclaims the contemporary urban ghetto landscape to be marked by, as well as to mark, the spiritual and psychic dimensions of African American identity, in addition to configuring the spatial parameters and configurations of racialized urban poverty. The video for "The Corner" trades on the Black Arts Movement's focus on art as a concrete documentation of African American life and its belief that African American identity is profoundly urban by proclaiming itself to be shot on location in the artist's hometown of Chicago. The video not only explicitly references Black Power culture through raised fists and self-conscious markers of ghetto identity, it also includes an appearance by the Black Power–era spoken-word artists The Last Poets, who proclaim the corner to be "our Rock of Gibraltar, our Stonehenge, our Taj Mahal." In keeping with the Black Arts Movement's belief that the free articulation of African American expressive culture would create spontaneous articulations of both political and cultural value, The Last Poets declare: "The corner was our magic, our music, our politics / Power to the people, black power, black is beautiful."

Some of the other more self-conscious tributes to the Black Arts/Black Power Movements in hip-hop include the 1995 compilation album *Pump Ya Fist: Hip Hop Inspired by the Black Panther Party*, which includes contributions from some of the most respected artists in hip-hop, including KRS-

ONE, Grand Puba, Jeru the Damaja, Yo-Yo, The Fugees, and Tupac Shakur; Talib Kweli's 2004 album *The Beautiful Struggle,* on which he asserts that he is "from a place where real is real;" and Ras Kass's 1998 album *Soul on Ice,* which references the title of Eldridge Cleaver's 1968 book. Direct and indirect tributes to the Black Power/Black Arts era represent far more than a nostalgic yearning for the panache of 1960s and 1970s street culture; they reveal the unheralded and pervasive ascendancy of the very aesthetic championed by the Black Arts Movement.

Hip-hop culture has continued to draw extensively on African American culture of the 1960s and 1970s and to reenvision the era's cultural politics as its most extensive legacy. In *Soul Babies: Black Popular Culture and the Post-Soul Aesthetic,* Mark Anthony Neal notes the way in which a pivotal line from the popular 1970s sitcom *Good Times* becomes the important re-frain for a song by Outkast on their cutting-edge 1998 hip-hop album *Aque-mini.* According to Neal, the repetition of the phrase "damn, damn, damn, James" is a lament both for the loss of the traditional African American family structure and for the lost opportunity and broken promises that ac-companied African American migration from the South to northern cities (62–64). Thus, *Aquemini* not only directly recycles the culture of the 1960s and the 1970s, it continues its debates on community, family, and "home."

In "Stakes Is High: Conscious Rap and the Hip Hop Generation," Jeff Chang argues that though "political rap" was more prevalent in the 1980s, "conscious rap" artists, such as Talib Kweli and Dead Prez, as well as "gang-sta rap" acts, such as Scarface, Trick Daddy, and DMX, continue to negoti-ate the cultural politics of the 1960s and 1970s. And in 2004, Dead Prez attempted to explicitly mix the "gangsta rap" genre with "political rap" on the album *RGB: Revolutionary but Gangster.* Its track "I Have a Dream, Too" articulates a desire to "turn drive-bys revolutionary" and ends with the invocation of the names of such Black Power–era activists as Assata Shakur, Geronimo Pratt, Bunchy Carter, George Jackson, and Ruchell Mc-Gee. Rather than offer a critique of capitalist structures that create crimi-nality, as the Panthers sought to do, the album's single "Hell Yeah (Pimp the System)" describes a number of criminal scenarios and ends by com-manding its audience to "Get that paper till we get our freedom / We got to get over." The album's powerful call to action and its seeming inability to resolve the relationship between revolutionary action, capitalism, and cul-tural production comes as a direct result of debates in the 1960s and 1970s on aesthetics, community, and culture.

The Black Aesthetic, the Death of the Civil Rights Movement, and the Black Arts Movement's Search to Define a Black Community

The search for a Black aesthetic began and was inextricably tied, according to Larry Neal, Addison Gayle, Hoyt W. Fuller, and Don L. Lee in *The Black Aesthetic*, to the advent of the Black Power Movement. The Black Arts Movement considered itself the academic and cultural branch of what was intended to be an armed revolutionary political struggle. As such, the Black Arts Movement's search to define and codify a Black aesthetic became a search for the trace elements of community as a necessary means to lay representational claims to that community. If Stokely Carmichael and members of the Student Nonviolent Coordinating Committee, the Congress of Racial Equality, the Black Panther Party, and other participants in the Black Power Movement were busy creating and defending the Black community, the task of defining it fell to the artists and intellectuals of the movement. Had the movement failed to provide an answer to the question K. William Kgositsile emphatically posed in the *Black Fire!* anthology—"Who are we? Who are we?" (228)—or to provide evidence to "let Black people understand / that they are the lovers and sons / of lovers and warriors and sons / of warriors," as Amiri Baraka declared in "The Black Arts Movement," the political claims of the Black Power Movement to represent the community would have been without validity.

The Black Arts Movement asserted its definition of "Black community" as an open contestation to the Civil Rights Movement's utopian vision of community based on racial inclusion, integration, and cultural harmony. A poem by Clarence Franklin from *Black Fire!* offers "Two Dreams (for m.l.k.'s one)" (364). As the poem imagines "the cosmic pistol" held by "a million black hands / linked like chain, surrounding the world," a discourse connecting African American identity with violent African American resistance emerges in contrast to Martin Luther King's famous vision of a nonviolent utopia as articulated in his "I Have a Dream" speech. Franklin's vision lacks the symbolic force of grand oratory, a historic location, or a mass audience, but—characteristically for the Black Arts Movement— what it lacks in symbolic capital, it makes up for in boldness, irreverence, and attention to the plain-speaking bravado of the streets, in which "the cosmic pistol was cocked and the / finger was squeezing . . . squeezing . . . and suddenly." Franklin's rhetorical celebration of violent action mirrored the hyperbolic language of groups like the Black Panther Party, who defended their use of such rhetoric in speeches as the rhetoric of the Black ghettoes. The Panther David Hilliard was arrested by federal agents for making terroristic threats against Nixon two weeks after he said, in an antiwar rally in San Francisco, "Fuck that motherfucking man! . . . We will kill Richard Nixon" (265). Hilliard and the Panthers seemed genuinely surprised by the arrest. Hilliard writes in his autobiography: "The whole thing is absurd. Any number of tapes will prove I spoke the words. But it's equally clear I'm not about to kill the President. What do they imagine— I'm going to order some ICBMs to bomb the White House?" (65). Hilliard and the Panthers defended the use of hyperbolic language as typical of the urban street aesthetic that they wished to embody (272).

Franklin's suggestive terseness complements the hyperbolic action in a manner disallowed by the lyrical traditions of African American oratory to which King subscribed. Franklin's poem continues: "and a million liquid bullets were shot into the heart of / the city and everything was wet and running, / like open wounds." It is hard to imagine Franklin's vision of destruction emanating from King, not only because of its confrontational and aggressive narrative point of view, but also because its equally confrontational and aggressive vernacular "street" poetic style clashes with the tradition of African American oratory that King's performance of Blackness embodied and was so much in evidence at the March on Washington. In developing the African American urban vernacular as an aesthetic, the Black Arts Movement attempted to reclaim the artistic merit of the poetics of a people for whom, as Don L. Lee put it, "poetry on the written page . . . was almost as strange as money" (223).

The twin guiding precepts of the Civil Rights Movement, nonviolence and a vision of an integrated "beloved community," were the ones most contested by the Black Arts and Black Power movements. This contestation is epitomized by the Student Nonviolent Coordinating Committee's (SNCC) shift away from its early orientation as the student wing of the Civil Rights Movement to its later attempts to re-create itself as a radical advocate of Black Power. In his *In Struggle: SNCC and the Black Awakening of the 1960s,* Clayborne Carson documents the process by which the group's shift resulted in the controversial expulsion of all of its white members and the eventual dissolution of the organization. Martin Luther King Jr. would remark on the challenges to civil rights ideology from "various black nationalist groups" as early as 1963 in "A Letter from the Birmingham Jail": "I am further convinced that if our white brothers dismiss as 'rabble-rousers'

and 'outside agitators' those of us who are working through the channels
of nonviolent direct action and refuse to support our nonviolent action,
millions of Negroes will . . . seek solace and security in black nationalist
ideology."

King devoted the entire opening chapter of his final book, *Where Do
We Go from Here: Chaos or Community*, to contesting Black Power ideology.
For King, Black Power represented a distinct move away from the ideals of community he wished to enshrine as the core values of the Civil
Rights Movement, and toward disorder, violence, and chaos. King begins
the chapter with an anecdote about the announcement of the shooting of
James Meredith to a group of young civil rights workers who subsequently
refused to sing the song "We Shall Overcome," which had become the
movement's anthem. Instead, they suggested "We Shall Overrun" as an appropriate substitute (King, *Where Do We Go from Here* 26).

The year in which the *Black Fire!* anthology was initially published,
1968, marked several key moments in the destruction of symbolic markers of the civil rights era, especially in the transition away from a mass-
movement politics and nonviolent struggle and to a post–civil rights era of
vanguardism and violent repression. On 3 April 1968, members of J. Edgar
Hoover's counterintelligence program who were based in San Francisco
first expressed grave concern in a report to Hoover about Oakland's Black
Panther Party; this would eventually lead Hoover to declare the party "a
major threat to U.S. internal security of the country" and to initiate a campaign of state-sanctioned violence against it and other organizations like
it (Haskins, 122). Exactly one day after the report was filed, on 4 April
1968, Martin Luther King was assassinated on the balcony of a Memphis
hotel in circumstances so suspicious that decades later, historians, activists, and conspiracy theorists alike continue to speculate about the exact
nature of and political motivation for the killing.[5] However, of even greater
significance than the ambiguity surrounding the circumstances of King's
violent death is what his assassination would come to represent in terms
of a definitive, symbolic end to the popularity of nonviolence as a cultural
phenomenon in African American social protest, thus marking the beginning of the end of the civil rights era.

Two days after the assassination, Eldridge Cleaver composed a scathing
condemnation of King's legacy of nonviolence titled "The Death of Martin
Luther King: Requiem for Nonviolence," in which he declared: "The assassin's bullet not only killed Dr. King, it killed a period of history. It killed a
hope, and it killed a dream" (*Post-Prison Writings*, 74). In Cleaver's account

of King's assassination, King's philosophy and rhetoric of nonviolence are what render him "dead"—as much from the symbolism as from the social forces at work in his actual assassination. Cleaver connected the literal violence of the King assassination to a symbolic violence in a time when "words are no longer relevant" (78):

> In the last few months, while Dr. King was trying to build support for his projected poor people's march on Washington, he already resembled something of a dead man. Of a dead symbol, one might say more correctly. Hated on both sides, denounced on both sides—yet he persisted. And now his blood has been spilled. The death of Dr. King signals the end of an era and the beginning of a terrible and bloody chapter that may remain unwritten, because there may be no scribe left to capture on paper the holocaust to come. (74)

Cleaver ends the essay by declaring 1968 "the Year of the Black Panther," a year in which "action is all that counts," and presumably an era in which "action" would replace "dead symbols" (78).

The King assassination did indeed trigger violent unrest across the country, with major outbreaks of rioting in 131 U.S. cities as African Americans struggled both physically and intellectually with the civil rights legacy of nonviolent protest (Allen, 106). By the early summer of 1968, the brief, tenuous alliance between SNCC—the organization that had made a radical break with the Civil Rights Movement when its members coined the phrase "Black Power"—and the Black Panther Party had fallen apart. The schism that had grown between SNCC and the Panthers was symptomatic of the altered political and cultural terrain of the post–civil rights era as African Americans searched for meaning, direction, and leadership in the wake of the King assassination and the unrest that followed. Intellectuals, artists, and activists alike struggled to come to grips with the fallout from the Civil Rights Movement and the new "Black Power" in articulating a cultural agenda appropriate to the events that preceded and followed 1968.

The End of Beloved Community Larry Neal and the Beginning of a "Black World"

The stirrings of a post–civil rights cultural revolution as represented by the Black Arts Movement were brought to fruition with the 1968 publication of *Black Fire! An Anthology of Afro-American Writing*, edited by Larry Neal and LeRoi Jones, the two most prominent proponents and spokespersons for the Black Arts Movement. They attempted, in anthologizing African American literature at this point, to perform an intervention that was as much political as it was cultural. In "The Black Arts Movement" Neal claimed, "Poetry is a concrete function, an action. No more abstractions. Poems are physical entities: fists, daggers, airplane poems, and poems that shoot guns" (260). Appearing first in a 1968 issue of *Drama Review*, Neal's essay was to become the movement's manifesto, and it remains the definitive statement of its goals and ideas, especially when taken together with Jones's famous exhortation in "Black Art," "We want 'poems that kill' / Assassin poems, Poems that shoot . . . / We want a black poem. And a / Black World." The claim that poetry is "an action" speaks to the Black Arts Movement's profound belief in the positive transformative effects of cultural change.

According to James Smethurst in "Poetry and Sympathy," as a staff writer and later the arts editor for New York's important Black radical arts and news venue the *Liberator*, Larry Neal helped shift African American discourse away from leftist politics toward nationalism (270). In "Reply to Bayard Rustin," Neal criticized civil rights leaders, labeling critics of the Black Power Movement "'civil rites' intellectuals" and further criticizing "Black intellectuals of previous generations for failing to ask" questions such as "whose vision of the world is finally more meaningful, ours or [that of] the white oppressors? . . . whose truth shall we express, that of the oppressed or of the oppressors?" ("Reply to Bayard Rustin," 7). From the pages of the *Liberator*, Neal used every opportunity to declare the necessity of African American artistic self-determination and celebrated the earliest impulses of those participating in the Black Arts Movement.[6] In a 1965 discussion of the controversial rejection by the Pulitzer Prize Advisory Board of a music jury citation for Duke Ellington, Neal wrote: "I am proposing that what we understand is the necessity of establishing *our own* norms, our own values; and if there must be standards, let them be our own. Recognition of Duke Ellington's genius lies not with white society that has exploited him and his fellow musicians. It lies *with us*, the Black public, Black musicians and artists. Essentially, recognition of that sort, from a society that hates us and has no real way of evaluating our artistic accomplishments, is the meanest kind of intrusion upon the territory of Black people" ("Genius and the Prize," 11).

The major dilemma of the post–civil rights era was how to face the two-fold problem that integration and desegregation presented: What would be the consequences for African American intellectuals and the African American middle class of their entry into the majority institutions and are-nas of the United States? And would programs for desegregation and inte-gration result in the destruction of the very African American community and traditions that had birthed the African American freedom struggle in the first place? In 1995, Manning Marable described the crisis facing the African American community in the 1990s as being rooted in the racial, cultural, and social politics of the 1960s. Noting that sharp disjunctions in African American class advancement since the 1960s, when coupled with the significant changes in the social composition of the African American community, make it almost impossible to speak today of shared "black ex-perience," Marable states:

> One cannot really speak about a "common racial experience" which parallels the universal opposition blacks felt when confronted by legal racial segrega-tion. Moreover, contemporary black experience can no longer be defined by a single set of socioeconomic, political and/or cultural characteristics. For roughly the upper third of the African American population the post-1960s era has represented real advancement in the quality of education, income, po-litical representation and social status. Social scientists estimate that the size of the black middle class, for example, has increased more than 400 per cent in the past three decades. The recent experience of the middle third of the African-American population, in terms of income, has been a gradual deterio-ration in its material, educational and social conditions. For example, between 1974 and 1990, the median income of black Americans compared to that of white Americans declined 63 per cent to 57 percent. However, it is the bottom one-third of the black community which in this past quarter of a century has experienced the most devastating social consequences: the lack of health care, widespread unemployment, inadequate housing, and an absence of opportu-nity . . . The resultant divisions within the black community . . . contributed to a profound social and economic crisis within black households and neigh-borhoods. (128–29)

By focusing on African American cultural expression as creating a sort of unifying continuity, the "Black Aesthetic" as articulated by Neal implic-itly asserted that the "devastating social consequences" that make up "the Black experience" for the bottom one-third of the African American com-munity would have symbolic, spiritual, and real material consequences for the upper third of the African American community who were situated to reap the benefits of desegregation.[7]

It is no accident that Marable's discussion of a post–civil rights African American community in crisis in the late 1990s comes at the end of the contemporary debate about African American studies and multicultural-ism in the university, a primary and ongoing site of struggle in the battle for desegregation. Marable locates a shift in the political and social condi-tions of what he terms "the post-1960s era" specifically in the failed project of integration and the attendant "ghettoization" within African American studies departments of a social-change agenda in U.S. universities. While he does not directly relate the early post–civil rights era intellectual strug-gles to the questions he lays out for contemporary African American stud-ies, his emphasis on post–civil rights shifts in notions of "black experience" and the possibility for "black community" reflect the fact that contempo-rary debates on African American identity have their foundational mo-ments in the early post–civil rights intellectual struggles and questions of community and culture as exemplified by the Black Arts Movement.

The Black Arts Movement began its negotiations around class, inclu-sion, and cultural production precisely when changes created by the Civil Rights Movement and the end of legalized segregation fostered opportuni-ties for economic advancement and inclusion. The Black Arts Movement would try to negotiate the economic opportunities and the class rifts such changes would create by posing the question of how the artist and intel-lectual would be accountable to the masses of African American people and, conversely, how the masses of African American people were to be included in dominant culture. The creation of African American studies departments during the Black Arts Movement was one means by which the problem of inclusion within U.S. institutions was addressed. The Black Arts Movement attempted ultimately to provide a model for African Amer-ican advancement that would avoid the pitfalls of mainstream institutional inclusion, including the disintegration of African American culture and community that was believed to have been produced by the Civil Rights Movement.

"Black Theater Go Home!" Conceptualizing the Black Aesthetic and the Black Experience

The search by Larry Neal, Addison Gayle, and LeRoi Jones to define a Black aesthetic was related to attempts to determine what constituted "Black

community" and "the Black experience." *The Black Aesthetic,* edited by
Gayle in 1971, is divided into five major sections: theory, music, poetry,
drama, and fiction. Most of the text is given over to music, poetry, and
drama, forms that are not only primarily communal but also have their
foundations in the African American oral folk cultures. In "The Black Arts
Movement," an essay in *The Black Aesthetic,* Larry Neal explained the relationship between Black Arts drama and African American people as rooted
in the give-and-take between creator and audience that is made possible by
the performative nature of the genre: "Theatre is potentially the most social of all of the arts. It is an integral part of the socializing process. It exists
in direct relationship to the audience it claims to serve" (263).

For Neal, it was the theater's imagined populist ability to communicate
aurally and orally directly for and to African American people that was
at the heart of the Black Arts Movement's embrace of it as an efficacious
form. Neal and the other writers on theater in *The Black Aesthetic* concep-
tualize it as freely available in a variety of ways to the masses of African
American people still by definition anchored in the extreme specificity of
an African American identity born of the struggle against racism. Ronald
Milner writes in "Black Theater—Go Home!":

> If a new black theater is to be born, sustain itself, and justify its own being,
> it must go home. Go home psychically, mentally, aesthetically, and, I think,
> physically. First off, what do I, myself, mean by a new *black* theater? I mean
> the ritualized reflection and projection of a new and particular way of being,
> born of the unique and particular conditioning of black people leasing time
> on this planet controlled by white men. A theater emerging from artists who
> realize that grinding sense of being what we once called the blues but now
> just term: *blackness.* (288)

In "The Black Arts Movement," Neal writes succinctly of what he presumes
to be the natural and inextricable relationship between African American
people and African American poetry: "The poem comes to stand in for the
collective conscious and unconscious of Black America—the real impulse
in the back of the Black Power movement" (261).

Neal and Milner both articulated a desire to create a cultural and artistic
tradition that would feed rather than feed off of African American people
and the traditions they had created in their struggle to survive America's
repressive social and economic order. For this reason, Richard Wright's

"Blueprint for Negro Writing," with its demands that "Negro writers . . . stand shoulder to shoulder with Negro workers in mood and outlook," is one of the only works by the previous generation of African American writers or artists to be included in *The Black Aesthetic*. The Black Arts Movement dreamed of creating an artistic tradition that not only celebrated the cultural impulses of the African American community but also became a natural part of constructing and maintaining that community.

In *The Autobiography of LeRoi Jones*, Baraka recounts how the concept of a Black Arts Movement arose from the Black Arts Theater after a discussion between Baraka, Neal, and the Revolutionary Action Movement organizer Max Stanford in which Baraka "felt particularly whipped and beaten" by his inability to define the relationship between his role as an artist and his role within the African American community (197). Baraka had previously wondered in discussions with Neal "what was going on in the world, who were we in it, what was the role of the black artist" (197). Baraka notes that not only had Stanford "had communications with exiled Rob Williams," he "was actually distributing his newsletter, *The Crusader*" (197). Stanford's ability to marry radical political action, community organizing, and cultural work created an imperative that Baraka felt he could not ignore. Baraka wrote: "To me, the young tireless revolutionary I saw in Max was what I felt I could never be" (197). For Baraka, the conversation with Stanford became the catalyst for reimagining a relationship between artist and community with radical political activism at its center. It also became the genesis for the creation of the Black Arts Theater. Baraka writes: "One evening when a large group of us were together in my study talking earnestly about black revolution and what should be done, I got the idea that we should form an organization" (197).

The search to define a black aesthetic that arose directly out of a shared community-building racial episteme termed "the Black experience," and the attempt to convert the vernacular rhythms and behavior of everyday African American life into a viable poetics and powerful praxis formed the central cultural and aesthetic agenda of the Black Arts Movement. The Black Arts agenda manifested itself in the desire to directly convert the rhetoric and poetics of the movement into the creation of active, independent African American–owned venues for African American artistic and cultural production, not as an extension of the movement, but as the foundation for further cultural development. For the Black Arts Movement the conditions of African American artistic production were obviously and inextricably linked to the aesthetic concerns of its product. Ekkehard Jost writes of the impact of social conditions on the creation of "free jazz":

> Free jazz shows precisely how tight the links between social *and* musical factors are, and how one cannot be completely grasped without the other. Several of the initiators of free jazz, for instance, had to contend for a long time with systemic obstruction on the part of the record industry and the owners of jazz clubs (who continue to control the economic base of jazz). This circumstance is by no means void of significance for the music of the men concerned. Being without steady work means not only personal and financial difficulties; it also means that groups may not stay together long enough to grow into real ensembles, that is, to evolve and stabilize a concept of group improvisation— an absolute necessity in a kind of music which is independent of pre-set patterns. (9)

According to Jost, free jazz, like other forms born out of the social conditions of the era, was foundationally shaped, both aesthetically and socially, by its attempts to combat systematic exclusion while maintaining a productive cultural and aesthetic integrity. The presumption that free jazz was forged out of the linkages between repression, cultural production, and resistance, as Jost claimed, helped to enshrine it in the lexicon of the Black Arts Movement as a barometer of "all the hurt, pain, and good times which black people share through their daily experience," as Peter Labrie declared in "The New Breed" (64).

When Robert Williams began broadcasting from exile in Cuba a radio program directed at the United States, jazz, particularly the jazz experiments of Max Roach and Ornette Coleman, formed a significant part of the musical selection. Williams claimed free jazz enabled his efforts to create "a new psychological concept of propaganda" by providing "the type of music people could feel, that would motivate them" (Tyson, 288). The free jazz aesthetic celebrated by Robert Williams and the Black Arts Movement was, according to them, a direct consequence of the process by which an independent African American musical style was created and articulated under the duress of exclusion and partial inclusion. The Black Arts Movement struggled to create the venues that would allow for the free articulation of a Black aesthetic fully supported by the people whose ideas it articulated.

As was the case with the Black Arts Repertory Theater, many of the attempts to establish institutions that reflected the Black Arts agenda were short-lived. But as with the free jazz movement, the attempts and attendant critical shifts and ruptures that they caused often resulted in major shifts in the cultural and aesthetic agendas of the various media in which they participated. It is as impossible to imagine contemporary jazz without the influence of Ornette Coleman, for example, as it is to imagine the creation of contemporary African American poetry without the presence of Amiri Baraka, whose every challenge ultimately aided African American poetry's institution in mainstream anthologies and classrooms.

Black Fire! Anthology Production, Historical Trauma, and Cultural Production

Black Fire! An Anthology of Afro-American Writing, edited by Larry Neal and LeRoi Jones and published in 1968, raised important questions about the shape a viable African American poetics might take in a postsegregation African American context. It also highlighted questions about the function of artistic and intellectual work in the formation of notions of "the Black community" in the postdesegregation period. Reexamining *Black Fire!* provides the opportunity to challenge or to acquiesce in Larry Neal's final statement in the anthology that "the artist and the political activist are one" within African American cultural production (656). The Black Arts Movement revolutionized African American literary and intellectual life with its insistence that artists and intellectuals be directly accountable to the masses of Black people and vice versa. It also revolutionized African American life by politicizing the aesthetics of popular music and film, as well as the culture of everyday African American life as reflected in clothing, food, speech, and expressive or "soul" styles. Manning Marable claims: "The politics of soul in the 1960s was the personal and collective decision to fight for freedom" (*Beyond Black and White*, 95). The Black Arts Movement successfully rescripted the challenges of African American inclusion and exclusion in American culture as a cultural imperative in a historical moment in which not only were the political goals of the Civil Rights Movement increasingly at risk, but the very project of Black emancipation seemed to come under fire.

By late 1968, the Civil Rights Movement was mourning the highly publicized deaths of the four little girls killed in a Birmingham church bombing, and also those of Medgar Evers, Malcolm X, James Earl Chaney, Jimmy

Lee Jackson, Sammy Young Jr., and countless others who had given their lives to the struggle for civil rights. It was not only vulnerable African American bodies, however, but also newly formed African American institutions that came under siege. The early post–civil rights period is most frequently characterized not by the destruction of nascent cultural ventures, such as the Black Arts Repertory Theater, but rather through the much more brutal and high-profile disruption of African American radical political organizing as epitomized by the destruction of the Black Panther Party and the Revolutionary Action Movement by law enforcement and the federal government, and by the deaths of civil rights leaders. However, the destruction of political organizations was also a direct attack on the civil rights symbolism of "beloved community," which served as the key organizing principle for much of the civil rights and early post–civil rights culture. Thus, the civil rights period can be characterized as a period of intense, systemic repression and historical trauma as well as one of intensely positive social change and transformation. This resulted in a tremendous anxiety regarding the future not only of African American institutions but of African American culture itself.

Larry Neal had been in the auditorium of the Audubon Ballroom selling *Black America*, the newspaper for the Revolutionary Action Movement, on the day that Malcolm X was assassinated. The moment of Malcolm X's assassination, according to Neal, "was an awesome psychological setback to the nationalist and civil rights radicals" ("On Malcolm X," 128). He characterized the moment as one that traumatized individuals as well as a movement, writing, "Malcolm's death—the manner of it—emotionally fractured young Black radicals," and he went on to speculate about how the fracturing of young African American radicals extended to a breakdown in collective organizing:

> Some of us did not survive the assassination. Strain set in. Radical black organizations came under more and more official scrutiny, as the saying goes. The situation made everyone paranoid, and there were often good reasons for being so. People were being set up, framed on all kinds of conspiracy charges. There was a great deal of self-criticism, attempts to lock arms against the beast we knew lurked outside. Some people dropped out, rejecting organizational struggle altogether. Some ended up in the hippie cults of the East Village. Some started shooting smack again. Some joined the poverty programs; some did serious work there, while others, disillusioned, and for now, weak, be-

came corrupt poverticians. Malcolm's organization, the Organization of Afro-American Unity (OAAU), after being taken over briefly by Sister Ella Collins, Malcolm's sister, soon faded. But the ideas promulgated by Malcolm did not. ("On Malcolm X," 129)

According to Neal, Malcolm X's death led to a fragmentation and then a flowering of African American radical culture based on Malcolm X's ideas that led directly to the founding of the Black Arts Repertory Theater School of Harlem.

Neal claimed in "On Malcolm X" that "what was happening in Harlem was being repeated all over the United States" (129). But just as Malcolm X's death was both traumatic and productive for an African American radical culture, the Black Arts Repertory Theater School of Harlem would prove a consistently contested and productive site for cultural production. Neal pointed to the systematic defunding of the Black Arts Repertory Theater School of Harlem by government arts agencies as a symbolic starting point in the destruction of African American radical culture by the government. LeRoi Jones would flee the Black Arts Repertory Theater collective in Harlem to organize in Newark, New Jersey, when infighting turned ugly, and Neal himself would be shot when leaving the theater one night.[8] The destruction of the Black Arts Theater, like the death of Malcolm X, would not result in the defeat of the movement but would rather signal the need for the rebirth of such ventures in African American communities throughout the country, or, as Neal claimed: "The Black Arts group proved that the community could be served by a valid and dynamic art. It also proved that there was a definite need for a cultural revolution in the black community" (257).

Since anthology production is almost inherently a collective venture, anthologies such as *Black Fire!* and the collections that followed it provided one way of preserving and transmitting the notion of cultural collectivity that had developed out of the Civil Rights Movement and was very much under siege by 1968. The publication of *Black Fire!* set off a virtual explosion of African American anthology production: more than thirty new African American literary anthologies were published in the years between 1967 and 1973 alone. Structured around categories of genre or identity, these anthologies were as varied in shape and tone as their titles indicate: Toni Cade's *The Black Woman*, Dudley Randall's influential *The Black Poets*, Etheridge Knight's *Voices from Prison*, and Arthur P. Davis and Saunders

Redding's popular classroom text *Cavalcade: Negro American Writing from 1760 to the Present.* Many of the anthologies consciously identified with the Black Arts Movement or were edited by the key figures of the movement themselves, from Sonia Sanchez's *We Be Word Sorcerers: 25 Stories by Black Americans,* to Dudley Randall's *Black Poetry: A Supplement to Anthologies which Exclude Black Poets,* Ed Bullins's *New Plays from the Black Theatre,* Ahmed Alhamisi and Harun Kofi Wangara's *Black Arts: An Anthology of Black Creations,* Gwendolyn Brooks's *A Broadside Treasury,* and Addison Gayle's *The Black Aesthetic.*[9]

Black Fire! created the climate for the later anthologies, not only in its multigeneric format and its powerful drive to document African American art and culture, but also in its strident political and aesthetic challenges to the preexisting codes and canons of American literature. Bullins, Sanchez, and Alhamisi—who would all later edit anthologies that challenged the parameters of established generic codes in theater, the short story, and "the arts"—published their own work initially in *Black Fire!* The opening essay of *Black Fire,* "The Development of the Black Revolutionary Artist," by James T. Stewart, reiterates the need for a separate aesthetic: "The black artist must construct models to correspond to his own reality" (3). The essay section also contains work by some of the key intellectual and political figures of the Black Power era, including Stokely Carmichael, Harold Cruse, John Henrik Clarke, and Nathan Hare. In placing Stewart's essay at the beginning of the anthology, Neal and Jones obviously hope to posit a model for artistic construction that is "Black" and "revolutionary," but one that is, above all, *communal:* the anthology represents a radical call to create a community of revolutionary artists and cultural workers in the face of a fractured African American community and an increasingly fractured Black liberation movement.

Several of the writers in *Black Fire,* including Lorenzo Thomas, Henry Dumas, A. B. Spellman, Lance Jeffers, Calvin Hernton, David Henderson, Joe Goncalves, and Ronald Snellings, had been involved with the influential artistic collectives that were clustered around small magazines such as *Umbra* and *Dasein* and around radical journals such as the *Liberator.*[10] In general, journals and magazines of this type had relatively limited circulation and often enjoyed only short life spans. Nonetheless, the collectives that formed around these projects provided a forum for intellectual exchange and collectivity around African American poetics that was unmatched and helped create a climate in which anthology publication would later flourish.

The beginning of the Black Arts Movement was rooted in the spirit of collectivity as evidenced by the establishment of the Black Arts Repertory Theater, which was founded the day after the assassination of Malcolm X through the efforts of an artists' collective that included LeRoi Jones, Charles Patterson, William Patterson, Clarence Reed, and Johnny Moore and was instituted by a fund-raising concert that featured John Coltrane, Betty Carter, Albert Ayler, McCoy Tyner, and Archie Shepp, among others (Neal, "Black Arts Movement" 261). Once established, the Black Arts Repertory Theater School became a meeting place for such black artists and intellectuals as Harold Cruse, Sonia Sanchez, and Stokely Carmichael to meet and to teach others. Efforts like the repertory theater school meant not only to showcase the Black Arts creations of the influential collective that had participated in its birth but also to provide an arts and cultural education to black youth in the area, who would then go on to form its repertory company (Riley, 21). While the Black Arts Repertory Theater was unable to survive the pressures created by government interference and repression and group infighting, the anthologies provided a permanent place of exchange and challenge to consolidate the ideas of a movement that was increasingly under fire.

The Beautiful Day   Transforming a Western Cultural Aesthetic

The Black Arts project was not only about transforming the notion of the black community as the spirit of a new politicized collectivity, it was also about preserving old notions of community as they came under siege in the late 1960s. James T. Stewart's essay in *Black Fire*, "The Development of the Black Revolutionary Artist," declares, "Revolution is fluidity" (4). The collection of writers anthologized in *Black Fire!* became a revolutionary African American community through their determination to articulate African American culture and community as a cohesive experience, and through their insistence on discarding old models, old markers, old forms, and old conventions in their search to declare a new Black aesthetic. For these writers, the dismantling of corrupt social and political structures would necessarily go hand in hand with the destruction of the culture that underpinned that structure. This revolution went far beyond the simple social-protest formula made famous by Black writers like Richard Wright. As Larry Neal would write in *Black Fire:* "The West is dying and offers little promise of rebirth . . . The West is dying, as it must, as it should. However, the approach of this death merely makes the power mad Magogs of the West more vicious, more dangerous like McNamara with his computing machines, scientifically figuring out how to kill more people. We must address ourselves to this reality in the sharpest terms possible. Primarily, it is an address to black people. And that is not protest, as such" (64). The critical re-evaluation of Western culture and African American people's place in it would not be accomplished through the simple, formulaic "mau-mauing" to which later evaluations of the period would reduce it.[11] Rather than simply protesting Western norms, the Black Arts Movement sought to provide new paradigms for understanding experience that shed light on the destructive nature of existing paradigms.

In "The Beautiful Day #9," a poem dedicated to the U.S. Secretary of Defense Robert McNamara, A. B. Spellman reenacts the bitter ambivalence that characterized the post–civil rights era's attitude toward social change, a mindset that by the poem's publication in 1965 had become an awesome apocalyptic possibility:

> stateside shades
> watching the beast in his jungle
> biting blackness from the sides of
> ibo, shinto, navajo, say
> no mo, charlie
>
> by biting i mean standing before
> all that is human
> ripping the shadow from a man's back
> throwing it in his face
> & calling it him.
>
> but what if the shadow was the beast
> gray as the grave and hanging on?
> what if his mirror was blackness
> the knife was the shadow
> the thaw of the times?

With his chant of "ibo, shinto, navajo, say / no mo, charlie," Spellman invokes the genocidal politics of the U.S. government in relation to the indigenous peoples of Africa and the Americas and the historical resistance to those practices as epitomized by the Viet Cong saying "no mo, charlie." However, the line also invokes the complicated complicity of nonwhite people in the U.S. war machine through its invocation of the Navajo "code talkers" of World War II. When Spellman rejects the possibility of "ripping the shadow from a man's back / throwing it in his face / & calling it him," he is exploring the Black Arts ambivalence toward contemporary human experience that would seem to lock injustice and human suffering into everyday practices as a quiet inevitability.

Though now largely forgotten, Spellman was a major figure in New York City's Black Arts scene and a close associate of LeRoi Jones; he was also involved with the Umbra group.[12] While a student at Howard University, Spellman had studied with Sterling Brown, and his poems, according to Aldon Nielsen, "mark a site of convergence for all the tendencies linking the various black practitioners of the newer poetics who formed the generation that first began publishing after World War II and established the formal structures that would subsequently be taken up as a vocabulary of aesthetics during the Black Arts Movement" (98). The Black Arts Movement represented both a continuation of and a notable break with the poetics of a Sterling Brown or a Langston Hughes, whose jazz poetics, as Nielsen notes, continued to exert considerable influence over the jazz-inspired poetry of Spellman and other Black Arts practitioners.

"The Beautiful Day #9" continues Brown's investment in African American vernacular English and Hughes's interest in descriptive, rhythmic wordplay, but it is equally shaped by its stern confrontation with the vicious, cold mechanization of state repression and the difficulty of tearing that repression from the fabric of everyday experience. Spellman asks of his metaphoric "beast, sexless & fragile, frail / as machine, his energy made, whiter / than air, strength leaking from every / hole, & richer than god, what do you do with him?" The contradictions of the "fragile, frail / as machine" beast who nonetheless has "strength leaking from every / hole, & richer than god" and the stanza's ambivalent spacing, which leaves every descriptor in the stanza hanging half-declared, create a feeling of tepid, unresolvable instability for the reader. This is only reinforced by the stanza's last question: "what do you do with him?"

It is no accident that Spellman's series of "Beautiful [Vietnam era] Days" poems are as numerically categorized and itemized as Hills 881s, 861, 861a, 558, 950, and 1015, the names given to the hills that surrounded the decisive battle at Khe Sanh. In 1964, in his infamous "An End to History" speech delivered at the University of California, Berkeley, Mario Savio, one of the leaders of the Berkeley Free Speech Movement, pronounced, "The most crucial problems facing the United States today are the problem of automation and the problem of racial injustice" (194). While the grouping of "automation" with "racial injustice" may seem arbitrary in a contemporary context, Savio's hyperbolic fear of technological culture would seem to be borne out by the mechanized horror of the Vietnam War. Spellman's "sexless & fragile, frail / as machine" beast is realized in the impotent war machine that prepared to defend Khe Sanh during the Tet Offensive of 1968:

> Circling the skies above Khe Sanh for thirty miles in every direction, aircraft took high-resolution photographs, scanned the ground with radar for evidence of enemy movement, and recorded the findings of an array of complex, highly classified gadgets designed to locate enemy positions and movements: acoustic sensors that picked up voices; seismic sensors that registered vibrations from marching soldiers, trucks, and armored vehicles; infrared heat sensors that could identify cooking fires; and electrochemical analyzers that could detect high concentrations of human urine. Technicians in an airborne electronic laboratory read, collated, and interpreted the data. (Dougan and Weiss, 42)

For Spellman and for other *Black Fire!* poets, most notably David Henderson, Joe Goncalves, and LeRoi Jones, the wanton destruction that characterized the post–civil rights era produced texts in which the destruction and re-creation of language and language forms were an inherent part of the composition. Nielsen concludes, "Spellman was willing to advance into the shadowy text of the world's future, but he could not know what he would find there" (*Black Chants*, 105).

Black Fire! pieces like Jones's "Three Movements and a Coda," Henderson's "Neon Diaspora," and the technopaegniac experiments of Joe Goncalves preserve a wordplay tradition rooted in African American oral and musical traditions at the same time that they suggest that the new forms and formulas of expression are necessitated by the social instability of the times. The challenging street language of urban rebellion is matched in Jones's "Three Movements and a Coda" by a challenge to create poetry as "the music" that matches the destruction and reconstruction of meaning inherent in such events. *Burn, Baby, Burn: The Los Angeles Race Riot, August 1965*, Jerry Cohen and William S. Murphy's sensationalist account of the Watts rebellion, offers an intriguing account of the way a popular radio deejay's trademark tagline ("burn, baby, burn") was transformed into a powerful rebellion invective with a life of its own: "Not once during the rioting did Montague mention the violence on his three-hour program, and he immediately ceased using the expression. His station's news reports covered developments closely as a public service, and one of its mobile units was stoned. But unintentionally Magnificent Montague had given rioters a rallying cry. The first night a few teenagers shouted it in jest, then defiantly, and finally, with fire in their eyes and rocks in their fists. Young adults seized on it later. Then so did their elders. As mobs shrieked 'Burn, baby, burn,' large parts of Los Angeles would do just that" (76–77).

Black Arts poets wished to harness the transformative power of language as epitomized by the call "burn, baby, burn" to new forms worthy of the radical new possibilities that revolutionary change would bring. Joe Goncalves's experiments in concrete poetry "Now the Time Is Ripe to Be" and "Sister Brother" swirl hopeful statements about the spiritual possibilities for Black people around the single exclamatory statement "OH!"[13] Because they appear on the page in the form of a circle, the poems force the reader to perform a repetitive cyclical motion to read them. This motion literally suggests the cycles of change and transformation that the poems' simple declarative statements of hope, such as "Our kingdom was not of this world but it has come now," and "your hand is here and I know we are on our way," wish to enact. These statements are also enclosed within illustrations of a pyramid and a star of David, symbols that evoke mystical connections between the Black struggle in the United States and the history of ancient Israel and Egypt.

Converting the political "action" of urban unrest and the rhetoric of Black Power into a workable cultural aesthetic became the focus of the Black Arts Movement, which demanded that "the black artist must link his work to the struggle for his liberation and the liberation of his brothers and sisters," as Larry Neal declared in "Shine Swam On," the afterword to the *Black Fire!* anthology (655). Politically and socially, the book was meant to function as more than just a simple showcase for African American literary production. Despite Eldridge Cleaver's pronouncements that 1968 was a year in which "words are no longer relevant" and "action is all that counts," the contributors to *Black Fire!* believed in the power of their intellectual efforts to, as Neal put it, "make literature move people to a deeper understanding of what this thing is all about, [to] be a kind of priest, a black magician" (655). Sun Ra, already present as an influential innovator of free jazz, contributed several pieces of poetry to the anthology. His "To the Peoples of the Earth" is a succinct testament to the perceived possibilities of language for the Black Arts Movement:

> Proper evaluation of words and letters
> In their phonetic and associated sense
> Can bring the peoples of earth
> Into the clear light of pure Cosmic Wisdom. (217)

As LeRoi Jones, writing under the name Amiri Baraka, states in the foreword to the collection, "Black Fire" represents "the black artist. The black man. The holy holy black man. The man you seek. The climber the striver. The maker of peace . . . We are they whom you seek. Look in. Find yr self . . . We are presenting. Your various selves" (xvii). Like Sun Ra, Jones believed in the power of words to create—not simply describe—social change and community itself.

The Black Arts Movement used language to invoke a cultural and social unity that was increasingly difficult to claim in the face of post–civil rights social changes. The participants in the *Black Fire!* anthology most often grappled with the class dynamics of an emergent intellectual class that had no desire to be anyone's "Talented Tenth" by positioning themselves in the manner that Jones's foreword and as the meaning of Jones's new name— "enlightened prince/spiritual leader/blessed one"—would suggest. The contributors to *Black Fire!* contradictorily imagined themselves as both the leaders ("the climber the striver" and "the holy holy black man") and the incarnations of the "various selves" of the masses of African American people. The vanguardist, yet insistently populist, demand of the Black Arts Movement created a dynamic in which Black Arts poets stood not for what the average African American man or woman *could* strive to be, as in the earlier Du Boisian "Talented Tenth" model, or what they *should* want to be, as in even earlier "uplift" paradigms, but rather what African American people *would* naturally and essentially be if it weren't for their lack of spiritual enlightenment and political consciousness. The poet Edward S. Spriggs's contribution to the volume, "We Waiting on You," begins and ends with the invocation of the title (337), and this could be a summation of the anthology's sometimes contradictory stance on intragroup politics, class or otherwise.

"Anxious Identities and Divisional Logic" Fracturing Communities, Class Divisions, and the Black Arts Movement

Instead of expressing the cultural unity that they sought, the Black Arts Movement's desire to articulate concepts such as Black aesthetic, Black experience, and the Black community created what Phillip Brian Harper has labeled in a discussion of Black Arts poetry "anxious identities and divisional logic" (49). Ironically, the Black Arts Movement's most glaring class-based omission was its failure to acknowledge or critique the increasingly important role African Americans were playing in American popular culture.

For Larry Neal as for most of the Black Arts practitioners and critics, the notion of African American community was so closely linked to the popular and vernacular traditions of African American folk and folklore that he found it difficult to factor in all the elements of urban commodification necessary to form a complex understanding of postmigration African American artistic practice. In *Hoodoo Hollerin' Bebop Ghosts,* Neal lamented the move from the rural South as an authentic and primary site for the articulation of African American culture, while in "Shine Swam On," he struggled to articulate a relationship between the ascendancy of African American popular music culture and the potential for creating a literary aesthetics with a connection to African American mass culture: "The key to where Black people have to go is in the music. Our music has always been the most dominant manifestation of what we are and what we feel, literature was just an afterthought, the step taken by the Negro bourgeoisie who desired acceptance on the white man's terms. And that is precisely why the literature has failed" (654).

Much of the tension in the Black Arts Movement's reception of popular culture resulted from the fact that the Black Arts Movement expressed a desire for separate spheres of articulation at the precise moment when African American culture saw increasing inclusion in the mainstream. It was difficult enough for Neal to imagine an African American community constituted as a market; it would ultimately be impossible for him to understand the market value of African American culture within mainstream American popular culture. The Black Arts Movement's failure to provide complete intellectual guidance for the radical political movements of the time was ultimately linked to an inability to define or find significance in the relationship of African American culture to American popular culture in general and the wider dissemination of African American culture throughout American popular culture. In *The Crisis of the Negro Intellectual*, Harold Cruse asserts: "The Black Arts was not a failure in achievement, so much as a failure in its inability to deal with what has been achieved" (539). Though Cruse does not address the specific developments in postwar culture that Jones and the Black Arts Movement were unable to relate, he correctly identifies ambivalences in their role as intellectuals in a developing cultural movement that negotiated changing class, cultural, and political positionings for African Americans.

Phillip Brian Harper locates what he labels the "divisional logic" of the Black Arts Movement in the need to be *"heard by whites and overheard by blacks"* (*Are We Not Men*, 53, emphasis in original). He discusses how this "divisional logic" invokes a fantasy of African American unity in order to both create and negotiate intragroup hierarchies: "For according to this fantasy, not only would to be *heard* be to annihilate one's oppressors, but to be *overheard* would be to indicate to one's peers just how righteous, how nationalistic, how potently Black one is, in contradistinction to those very peers, who are figured as the direct addressee of the Black Arts works" (53).

The "insistent use of the second-person pronoun," which Harper characterizes as the address convention of Black Arts poetry, is very much in evidence in *Black Fire*, from Sonia Sanchez's "to all sisters" and Reginald Lockett's "Die Black Pervert," to Bobb Hamilton's "Poem to a Nigger Cop" and "Brother Harlem Bedford Watts Tells Mr. Charlie Where It's At" (47). Harper indicates that the "anxious identities and divisional logic" of Black Arts poetry are rooted in phallocentric, homophobic gender politics, which the Black Arts Movement is often also reduced to in contemporary rememberings of the period:[14]

The Black Aestheticians' development of such potent gender-political rhetoric through which to condemn perceived failures of Black consciousness is significant . . . for at least two reasons: First, it can clearly be seen as establishing a circular dynamic whereby Black Arts writers' own need not to be deemed racially effeminate fueled the ever-spiraling intensity of their repudiative formulations, including the divisional *I-you* constructions . . . second, it indicates the Black Aestheticians' preexistent anxiety regarding their own possible estrangement from the very demands of everyday black life that were repeatedly invoked as founding their practice. If the routine figuration of such estrangement as a voluntary and shameful effeminization was a powerful signal practice in Black Arts poetics, this may well be because the estrangement itself was experienced as the unavoidable effect of inexorable social processes—specifically, the attenuation of the Black Aestheticians' organic connection to the life of the folk (to invoke the Gramscian concept) by virtue of their increasing engagement with the *traditional* (Euro-American) categories of intellectual endeavor, through which they largely and inevitably developed their public profiles in the first place. (*Are We Not Men*, 51)

As Harper indicates, what is most central to the Black Arts project and its strongest point of tension and contention is the question of inclusion: How exactly were the masses of African American people and the rich traditions of the African American culture to be included and maintained within the decentralizing project of integration? How would the intragroup politics of the African American community be negotiated as it increasingly fractured?

Although heteronormative hypermasculinity is widely on display throughout *Black Fire*, as is "anti-white" performativity, it is definitely tension over intragroup class divisions and the possibilities for class ascendancy that most consistently permeates the anthology and much of Black Arts writing. It is also that which gets the least critical attention in scholarly studies of the period. In one of the opening essays in *Black Fire*, "The Screens," C. E. Wilson writes, "The changing world often makes some terms obsolete and requires new names and concepts in order that men can communicate with one another" (133). Wilson hopes to elucidate a term that describes those for whom "'Uncle Tom' is no longer apt." He claims that "'Uncle Toms,' 'Handkerchief Heads' or 'Aunt Jemimas'" are a thing of the past, since increasingly, "whites have had to recruit willing, middle-class Negroes to do their dirty work for them" (133). His subsequent labeling of this group as "the screens" is dependent on a class politics that would have the readers of *Black Fire!* define themselves against a group he variously labels "the have-resume-will-travel professionals" and "the poverticians" (136). Similarly, David Llorens in "The Fellah, The Chosen One, The Guardian," borrows terms from the political struggle for independence in Northern Africa to castigate those whom it labels traitors to the "Fellah" class of African Americans.

Marvin E. Jackmon's (Marvin X's) one-act play *Flowers for the Trashman* is exemplary of Black Arts attempts to negotiate the role of the intellectual among characters who represent standards within the Black Arts vision of Black community. In the play, Joe, an African American college student, spends an unexpected night in jail with his hip, "hoodlum friend" contemplating his relationship to his family, especially his brother, who is in prison, and his father, who owns and operates the community's flower shop and whom he views as having impotent "establishment" values. Joe's anxiety over his inability to communicate with or to understand either his jailed brother or his broken father ends when he connects action for social change with the potential end of his alienation, declaring, "That's why I gotta start doin' somethin'—I wanna talk to ma sons" (*Black Fire*, 558). *Flowers for the Trashman* suggests that action for social change as a sort of community-building project will alter the dynamic that has caused Joe, the representative intellectual, to be estranged from those to whom in an ideal world he would logically be close, his incarcerated brother and streetwise friend, who are both representatives of the African American lower classes. The "race as family" model that is the premise of the play allows elision of trickier questions concerning the unifying social action to be taken, but it also wishes away the myriad conflicts that created the African American establishment father, the hip outlaw, and "the brother on the block" as representational figures for Black Arts literature in the first place.[15]

In "le roi jones talking," a 1964 essay that appeared in *Home*, a collection of his essays published in 1966, Jones writes about the agonies of writing: "I write now, full of trepidation because I know the death society intends for me. I see Jimmy Baldwin almost unable to write about himself anymore. I've seen Du Bois, Wright, Himes driven away—Ellison silenced and fidgeting in some college" (179). It is noteworthy that even as early as 1964, Jones conflated Baldwin's silence and Du Bois's, Wright's, and Himes's exile with Ellison's employment at "some college" as potential forms of death facing the African American writer. For Jones, the college campus, the site of so many contentious and ultimately at least partly victorious civil rights battles, is clearly not a desirable location for the racially conscious African American to inhabit according to the Black Arts Movement, which wanted to "keep it all in the community." A large portion of the Black Arts impulse, as evidenced by Jones's title, *Home,* comes from an anxiety to claim an appropriate "home" site for an emergent intellectual class. Larry Neal's "Ghost Poem #1," which appeared after the publication of *Black Fire,* invokes similar conflicts about "home"; it is a moving meditation on rural to urban migration and what Cornel West labeled "black nihilism" (*Black Popular Culture,* 271):

> You would never shoot smack
> or lay in one of these Harlem
> doorways pissing on yourself
> that is not your way not the
> way of Alabama boys groomed slick
> for these wicked cities momma
> warned us of
>
> You were always swifter than that:
> the fast money was the Murphy game
> or the main supply before the cutting—
> so now you lean with the shadows
> (at the dark end of Turk's bar)
> aware that the hitman is on your ass
>
> You know that something is inevitable
> about it
> You know that he will come as sure as shit
> snorting blow for courage
> and he will burn you at the peak of your peacocking
> glory
> And when momma gets the news
> she will shudder over the evening meal
> and moan: "Is that my Junie Boy runnin
> with that fast crowd?" (7–8)

Here Neal attempts more than simply to document, discover, or revive what is valuable about African American folk and mass culture in two of its most mythic locations, Harlem and Alabama. The tension of the poem, as indicated by its irregular line breaks and spacing and its fluid, understated narrative, is the sum total of a culture that is in the midst of an intense transition. Like the liminal figure of the ghost who is caught between the worlds of the living and the dead, Neal's "Ghost Poem #1" is an attempt to maintain a cohesive culture in the midst of intense social, economic, and political transformation while marking the inevitability of its eventual change. The character who "lean[s] with the shadows / (at the dark end of Turk's bar)" is saturated with the fatalism and precariousness of the social forces that are about to do him in, and the poem anticipates the problems of the urban underclass as clearly as it signifies Neal's inevitable estrangement from that class.

The Black Arts Movement's critics and practitioners responded to the question of "Black Art" and the postsegregation problematic of African American artists and intellectuals by calling for an art that would, as Larry Neal writes, "speak directly to the needs and aspirations of Black America" ("Black Arts Movement," 257). The desire to articulate a collective identity as the basis for the form and function that is designated the Black aesthetic necessitated that the Black Arts Movement be, as Neal writes, "radically opposed to any concept of the artist that separates him from his community" (257). The notion of community that the Black Arts Movement constructs is constituted around oppositional struggle, and the function of "art" within that struggle is the primary criterion for judging it through the Black aesthetic. As Ron Karenga writes in "Black Cultural Nationalism," which appears in *The Black Aesthetic*, "all African art has at least three characteristics: that is, it is functional, collective, and committing or committed," and, "Black art, like everything else, must respond positively to the reality of revolution" (32, 31). This, according to Karenga, is in marked contrast to the African American cultural and critical practices of other eras. Neal, Karenga, Jones, and other Black Arts practitioners desired to create an aesthetic that was, in the words of Etheridge Knight, "accountable . . . only to the Black people" (*The Black Aesthetic*, 259).

While Karenga, Jones, and Neal would agree for the need for a revolutionary Black aesthetic, the question of exactly how that aesthetic would be constituted was very much up for debate. Whereas Neal and Jones struggled to define a revolutionary cultural practice within existing African American practices, Karenga's US Organization and its philosophy of "kawaida" called for the complete overthrow of existing cultural norms and practices and the instilling of new practices based in a direct reclamation of African culture. The US Organization based its entire doctrine of nationalist change deeply within the transformation of culture. According to Karenga, "Kawaidists are essentially the new nationalists, spiritual and theoretical heirs of Garvey and Malcolm and the immediate products of the fire, feelings, and formations engendered by a decade of Black revolts," and while their imperative for change was political, their mechanism would largely come through a reorganizing of culture ("Kawaida and Its Critics," 126). While Larry Neal saw radical possibilities especially in existing musical forms such as gospel and the blues, Karenga as US's spokesman declared such folkloric practices as the blues "invalid" (*Black Aesthetic,* 36). Baraka was deeply involved in the philosophy of kawaida before he left the US Organization to embrace a more aggressive form of Marxism, but from his earliest writings as LeRoi Jones to his later writings as Imamu Amiri Baraka, he struggled more positively with the place of existing African American practices in the development of a racial aesthetic in a way that kawaida's strict articulation of cultural change would not allow. Though Karenga would dismiss Baraka in 1977 as "essentially a man of arts and letters . . . neither a theorist nor an accomplished organizer," ultimately, the Black Arts Movement's debates about the relationship between cultural and political practice and the everyday lives of African American people would prove to be the major nexus around which Black radical politics would come to be defined (136).

Today, the attempt to realize and define an intellectual endeavor "accountable . . . only to Black people," or accountable *even* to black people, remains as unrealizable as attempts to resolve the dilemmas highlighted by the Black Arts project. As African American intellectuals rapidly enter a post–affirmative action, postsegregation era, the questions raised by the Black Arts Movement take on an even greater urgency, demanding scrutiny more than ever.

4

"People Get Ready!"

MUSIC, REVOLUTIONARY NATIONALISM, AND
THE BLACK ARTS MOVEMENT

A Liberated Aesthetic African American Musical Production,
Politics, and the Black Arts Movement

"Theme music . . . *every* hero needs to have some," says the hero of Keenan
Ivory Wayans's underappreciated spoof of Blaxploitation films, *I'm Gonna
Get You Sucka* (1988). For the African American heroes of the struggle for
social justice, this was undoubtedly true. Historically, African American
culture has regarded musical genres as arbiters of heroic proportions for
Black styles, behaviors, and mores. African American music in turn has
also repeatedly thematized heroism, tying it to collective action for social
change to the extent that the struggle for social change has been reflected
in every genre of every period of African American music. In the Black
Power era, politically inspired aesthetic innovation would cause John Coltrane to record the elegiac "Alabama" as Nina Simone lamented "Mississippi Goddamn!" in a song she proclaimed to be "a show tune whose show
has not yet been written" (*Best of Nina Simone*). The self-consciously political innovations of avant-garde jazz, including pieces like Albert Ayler's
"The Truth Is Marching In," Ornette Coleman's "Free Jazz," Max Roach's
"Garvey's Ghost," Archie Shepp's "Attica Blues," and Pharoah Sanders's "Red,
Black and Green," would help to recreate avant-garde jazz as "the artistic signal of the imminent maturation and self-assertion of the black man
in an oppressive American society," as A. B. Spellman would proclaim in
Black Fire! (160).

Politically inspired aesthetic innovations were not only occurring in the established genres of gospel, blues, and jazz, however. The evolving popular genres of soul, funk, and rhythm and blues synthesized and commodified the older African American musical forms in a manner that posed a significant challenge to every level of African American musical production in the United States, not only in production and consumption, but also in terms of formal and stylistic innovation. The experimentation across genres, blending across categories, and the creation of new categories that occurred during the Black Arts Movement resulted in a musical era that Rickey Vincent has rightfully characterized as "a celebration of the entire spectrum of the black music tradition" (32). This experimentation across genres and categories created a liberated aesthetic that inculcated a reverence for past struggles even while it demanded and created new expressive idioms. According to Vincent, the category-defying nature of the era "was not appreciated by the music industry," since the industry had "made a killing by separating black acts into Motown style soul, pop-jazz, and token rock or pop acts" (24). The very innovations in style and form that the industry resented were enabled by changes in cultural production that were creating the opportunity for African American musicians to have unprecedented creative freedom and control in the creation of popular music. Artists such as Curtis Mayfield, James Brown, Ray Charles, and Sam Cooke were able to pioneer innovative new approaches to the production of traditional African American genres and sounds largely because they did so at labels and studios that they created and owned.

Blues People   Toward an African American Music Criticism

In the same way that musicians were attempting to lay claim to the economic capital of African American music production, an intense battle for the symbolic capital of African American music began to emerge within critical and analytic circles. In 1963 LeRoi Jones published the brilliantly polemical *Blues People: The Negro Experience in White America and the Music that Developed from It* to contest the status quo of Black music criticism. In "Jazz and the White Critic," an essay originally published in the jazz magazine *Down Beat* in 1963, Jones had declared his methodological challenge to established music criticism:

> This is not a plea for narrow sociological analysis of jazz, but rather that this music cannot be completely understood (in critical terms) without some at-

tention to the attitudes that produced it. It is the philosophy of Negro music that is most important, and this philosophy is only partially the result of the sociological disposition of Negroes in America. The blues and jazz aesthetic, to be fully understood, must be seen in as nearly its complete human context as possible. People made bebop. The question the critic must ask is: *Why?* But it is just this *why* of Negro music that has been consistently ignored or mis-understood; and it is a question that cannot be adequately answered without first understanding the necessity of answering it. (*Black Music*, 11, emphasis in original)

Blues People repeats the call of "Jazz and the White Critic" that critics move away from music criticism whose descriptive and analytical thrust was toward decontextualized musical structures and classifications. Instead, Jones proposed a theory of African American musical forms that would not only chart the relationship between structural developments and in-novations in the forms themselves but also theorize these developments as the movement toward a larger cultural functioning of music within African American identity and cultural production. In *Blues People* Jones concluded: "In other words, I am saying that if the music of the Negro in America, in all its permutations, is subjected to a socio-anthropological as well as musical scrutiny, something about the essential nature of the Negro's existence in this society ought to be revealed, as well as something about the essential nature of this country" (x).

Jones's central thesis—that jazz and the blues evolved from the tensions created as enslaved Africans forcefully and creatively transformed them-selves into American Negroes—became a plea for historical acknowledg-ment that would be transformative in charting a new relationship between the critical enterprise and the community from which the music sprang. This relationship would be founded on a fundamental acknowledgment that social and political conditions influenced the creation of African American musical forms and were the determining factors in their even-tual aesthetic constitution: "Blues is the parent of all legitimate jazz, and it is impossible to say exactly how old blues is—certainly no older than the presence of Negroes in the United States. It is a native American music, the product of the black man in this country: or to put it more exactly the way I have come to think about it, blues could not exist if the African captives had not become American captives" (*Blues People*, 17). Though the contem-porary situation figures only briefly in *Blues People* in a chapter called "The

Modern Scene," the transformation of "African captives" to "American captives" became for Jones a metaphor for the processes of assimilation that were beginning to shape cultural production at the end of segregation.

Blues People begins with slavery in order to reinforce the relationship between the conditions of slavery in the past and of the conditions in the United States in the twentieth century, implying that the ongoing process of transforming "African captives" into "American captives" is wrapped up not only in social and political production but in cultural production as well. In situating the historical reality of slavery at the heart of African American cultural production, Jones implies that such creative endeavors involve a symbolic resisting and adjusting on the part of captives against a developing commodity culture that has built its repressive structures on African Americans' status during slavery as a "commodity" and their continuing status as a disposable labor force. Jones's *Blues People* and Albert Murray's *Stomping the Blues* both demonstrate the ways in which African American music's development as a commodity ironically occurred at exactly the same time when enslaved Africans were attempting to shed their unique cultural, economic, and social status as a commodity within American culture. African American music was thus caught, like African American people themselves, within the complex cycle of uneven economic development that both determined and was determined by the music's wider symbolic status as American culture and society struggled to determine an appropriate place for it. *Blues People* is deeply concerned with the impact of oppressive economic conditions on the early formation of African American culture, especially as it relates to the Great Migration and the development and dispersal of the blues. *Blues People* also offers a cautionary note regarding African American cultural production occurring during the early desegregation period of the Black Power era.

Jones's critique of the existing body of music criticism surrounding African American music turns on his primary claim that until *Blues People*, such critical ventures had been far removed culturally, socially, and politically from the social, political, and artistic conditions of musical production itself. In "Jazz and the White Critic" Jones opens by stating bluntly: "Most jazz critics have been white Americans, but most important jazz musicians have not been" (11). Jones's placement of music as the central metaphor for understanding the cultural development of African American people stems from the belief that African American music is central to African American culture as the primal site of African American creative expression, but also that it is a primary site for a profound misrepresentation and misunderstanding of African American culture within wider American culture.

Though Jones's titles would suggest otherwise, one of the primary critical concerns of "Jazz and the White Critic" is how African American culture has been consistently mishandled and undervalued by those to whom it should, he argues, be most easily entrusted. He uses "Jazz and the White Critic" as an opportunity to deride "the Negro middle class": "Jazz was collected among the numerous skeletons the middle-class black man kept locked in the closet of his psyche, along with watermelons and gin, and whose rattling caused him no end of misery and self-hatred. As one Howard University philosophy professor said to me when I was an undergraduate, 'It's fantastic how much bad taste the blues contain!'" (11). As in *Blues People*, where Jones lamented "the beginnings of a 'privileged' class" of "house niggers" in a chapter titled "Enter the Middle Class," the strongest vitriol of "Jazz and the White Critic" is repeatedly aimed at "the Negro middle class" (123). In "The Myth of Negro Literature" Jones created a correlation between the potential dissolution of African American culture, the need for African Americans to assimilate, and the rise of the African American middle class. He concludes: "The abandonment of one's local (i.e. place or group) emotional attachments in favor of the abstract emotional response of what is called 'the general public' (which is notoriously white and middle class) has always been the great dilutor of any Negro culture. 'You're like a nigger,' was the standard disparagement" (*Home*, 108). "The Myth of Negro Literature" and other essays like it ultimately called for African American unity on the basis of race in the face of anxiety that desegregation would cause African Americans to become divided according to other interests, most glaringly class.

Anxiety around the class politics of racial unity was repeated again and again by Jones and by the Black Arts critics whose views he helped shape as they attempted to negotiate and situate the articulation of Black Arts culture within newly created African American spaces and forums. Anxiety in relation to intraracial class politics increased as the community faced potential fracture through the process of desegregation. In Larry Neal's "A Conversation with Archie Shepp," an interview that appeared in the *Liberator*, Archie Shepp, one of the most politically astute and celebrated of the jazz avant-garde, struggles to articulate the relationship between the jazz avant-garde and the African American working-class community that appeared to be rejecting it. Neal asks Shepp, "How can we make the art more meaningful to our people?" to which Shepp replies, "We have to take advantage of a certain overview that we have that others don't have. Other people may have an intuitive working class instinct but it takes the intelligentsia to give that order and to make it meaningful" (24). The struggle to claim an aesthetic of everyday Blackness while at the same time articulating a distinct role for the artist and critic within aesthetic production reflected a general anxiety about the preservation of African American cultural production as a discrete and significant articulation in the face of a desegregation imperative.

Shepp and many of the jazz avant-garde attempted to negotiate the complications of the period immediately following desegregation by organizing in collectives such as the Jazz Composers Guild, Charles Mingus's Jazz Composers Workshop, and the Association for the Advancement of Creative Musicians, out of which they hoped not only to control musical production resources but also to create a broader, community-based popular reception for their avant-garde stylings. In *Four Lives in the BeBop Business*, A. B. Spellman offers the kind of music criticism that LeRoi Jones called for in "Jazz and the White Critic," chronicling the history of jazz culture in relation to its artistic masters and innovators and to the complicated economic politics that, according to Spellman, helped to control its shape and growth. In profiling Cecil Taylor, Ornette Coleman, Herbie Nichols, and Jackie McClean, Spellman creates a picture of jazz in which the aesthetic innovation that each musician contributes to the tradition is inseparable from the conditions of jazz production itself. In *Four Lives in the BeBop Business*, the lives of Coleman, Taylor, Nichols, and McClean create a continuum of musicians and creative outcomes that are based on their refusal to concede their individual aesthetic development to the existing jazz institutions that control the means of jazz's production. Spellman proclaims: "If managers of record companies and club owners appear as villains in these pages, it is because they are; blameless villains, perhaps, but villains nonetheless" (x, 137). The text, though largely consisting of first-person narratives from the musicians themselves, celebrates efforts to establish musician-driven collectives even when those efforts failed, as they did when Ornette Coleman tried to create a nightclub and publishing company.

Spellman believed that the future of jazz innovation hinged on whether jazz musicians would be able to take control of its production. He uses the story of an encounter between Jackie McClean and Charlie Parker to illustrate the ways in which racist economic humiliation and stunted aesthetic growth went hand-in-hand:

> Bird tried to get into the Open Door. For some reason, the owner of the Open Door didn't want to have jazz there anymore . . . Bird asked the owner to please let him play, but the guy didn't want to hear it. So we went to that place on Christopher Street off Seventh Avenue, Arthur's, and he literally had to talk the man into allowing him to play . . . As we were leaving he got outside and told Jackie to kick him in the ass, because he said, "Here I am begging pennies for drinks, begging people to buy drinks for me and putting myself down. And here I am begging people to let me play. I am Charlie Parker, and I have to beg people to let me play. Kick me, Jackie, and don't ever allow this to happen to you." (223–24)

In *Four Lives in the BeBop Business*, Ornette Coleman dismisses as irrelevant discussions of making club owners and music industry executives more responsive to the needs of jazz musicians, declaring simply that "in jazz[,] the Negro is the product" (130).

In the face of crippling humiliations and unevenly recognized cultural production, jazz musicians such as Coleman, Taylor, and McClean struggled to articulate a language of blackness that would negotiate aesthetic production between the demands of commodity and identity. In claiming jazz musicians as the ultimate African American revolutionaries, *Four Lives* and *Black Fire!* ultimately sought to celebrate the articulation of a Black aesthetic in full revolt against the constraints that hindered African American cultural production in the United States. Jones's exhortation in *Blues People* of a new kind of music criticism emulates the vision of African American jazz musicians that led them to unify as a professional class defined by their collective investment in African American music and to protect and advance a discrete aesthetic that rejected the aesthetic conventions and production constraints of mainstream culture.

Say It Loud   Soul Music and the "Popular Avant-Garde"

Jones's call to recontextualize African American music within the context of African American culture and criticism came at a moment when African American cultural nationalism was beginning to make serious inroads into popular culture and was becoming the driving force behind some of the most important music of the soul/funk era. From James Brown's well-known exhortation to "Say It Loud: I'm Black and Proud" and the Impressions' "People Get Ready!" and "We're a Winner," to the more politically diffuse "What's Going On?" or "Inner City Blues" by Marvin Gaye and Parliament's "One Nation under the Groove," a concern with the politics of African American existence in America infused nearly every line and rhyme of the soul era.

Soul music was developing very much in tandem with the Black Arts Movement. The Impressions' "People Get Ready" was released the same year as LeRoi Jones published "STATE/MEANT," his declaration defining the role of the artist in Black liberation struggles as "to band his brothers and sisters together in common understanding of the world (and the nature of America) . . . teach the White eyes their deaths, and teach the black man how to bring these deaths about" (252). Though the Black Arts Movement declared itself "the aesthetic and spiritual sister of the Black Power concept," valorized music as one of the primary forms of African American expression, and was fundamentally rooted in the desire for a cultural populism, it developed an ambivalent relationship to soul, funk, and rhythm and blues, even that music's most overtly political manifestations.[1] Although Baraka and Neal celebrated the rise of Black popular performers such as James Brown, Junior Walker, Booker T and the MGs, and Smokey Robinson, they were also deeply ambivalent about whether it was possible for African Americans to produce revolutionary art forms while remaining implicated in American systems of thought and cultural production. This conflict is best epitomized by Maulana Karenga's rejection of the blues as "invalid" because "they teach resignation" in his influential essay "Black Art" (9). Though Karenga's position was criticized as "awesomely erroneous" by Larry Neal, Neal and Baraka's own embrace of early forms of African American music such as blues, gospel, and jazz often came at the expense of a more complete attention to such forms of African American popular music as soul and rhythm and blues, which were being created as a result of the changing cultural politics of the postsegregation era. In "Towards a Relevant Black Theatre," Neal would state uncategorically: "A cultural revolution that does not include and absorb blues feelings and modes of sound will surely fail" (14), and he would call for a consideration of the "inner workings of African American urban life-styles," arguing

The Black theatre, it seems to me, must incorporate all of the useable elements that spring from that collective sensibility. If we don't, the white boy will. Dig the imitations of Black sound on the part of Janis Joplin, Cream, Blood, Sweat and Tears, etc. Considering the pervasiveness of Black sound, why is that there are no revolutionary Black musicals? There are only a few plays that work with dance; and where is the poetry? Where is the actual energy? Where is the ritual; the ritual that informs our daily lives, the ritual that moves people in the Apollo theatres of America? Where is the sound of James Brown, Junior Walker, and Smokey Robinson? How can we unify these vectors of Black cultural life and shape a relevant theatre out of them? (14)

Neal's demand for the necessary inclusion of the blues within a revolutionary aesthetic contrasts with the more speculative nature of his discussion of more contemporaneous Black urban styles and popular music. Baraka, similarly, calls for "an art that would reach the people, that would take them higher, ready them for war and victory, as popular as the Impressions or the Miracles or Marvin Gaye" (*Autobiography of LeRoi Jones,* 204), but the musicians he mentions in his next sentence include the avant-garde jazz artists Sun Ra and Albert Ayler rather than the Black popular singers whose popularity he wished to emulate. Baraka identifies Curtis Mayfield's "Keep on Pushing" as "one of our themes" and Mayfield's "We're a Winner" as music that "moved us and spoke, it seemed, directly to our national desire" (210); he also recognizes the work of Black popular musicians such as Mary Welles, Dionne Warwick, and The Supremes as music that "seemed to carry word from the black for me" and identifies Martha and the Vandellas' "Dancing in the Streets" as "our national anthem" (210). Ultimately, however, though Baraka "rhythm-and-bluesed to Ray Charles," it was as "a jazz freak" that he identified, and it is in jazz that he locates the major aspirations of the Black Arts movement, using the Black Arts Theater as a platform for Sun Ra and Ayler as well as avant-garde jazz musicians such as John Coltrane, Archie Shepp, Cecil Taylor, and Pharaoh Sanders.[2] The Black Arts Movement's ambivalent attention to popular forms such as soul, rhythm and blues, and funk reveals uneasiness with an increasingly significant African American popular culture that was taking an unprecedented significance within mainstream American culture. The Black Arts Movement's celebration of avant-garde jazz and its ambivalent relationship to other forms of contemporaneous Black popular music points to the difficulty it experienced in defining the role of popular culture within a truly populist arts practice.

In "'Pat Your Feet and Turn the Corner,'" James Smethurst claims that the Black Arts Movement embodied "a popular avant garde" in its attempts to create an aesthetic that celebrated the esoteric experimentation of free jazz while embracing the popular culture of the masses of Black people. In some instances, the Black Arts Movement attempted to address an audience that loved James Brown and Otis Redding rather than Eric Dolphy and John Coltrane through gestures such as featuring Stevie Wonder on the cover of *The Cricket* and arguing that rhythm and blues represented "the changing same" with regard to black musical forms such as jazz and gospel, as Amiri Baraka would famously do in *Black Music*. However, most of the consideration and praise the Black Arts Movement gave to African American music was directed to the free jazz movement, labeled "The New Thing" by mainstream jazz critics.

The Black Arts Movement critics struggled, as did the politically conscious musicians themselves, to justify supporting a musical style that lacked a widespread popular appeal. Archie Shepp responded to Larry Neal's comment in the *Liberator* that "the Black artist is faced with some serious problems vis-à-vis the Black community" with the observation, "I think it would be very difficult for Cecil or Ornette or myself to just go up to Harlem and expect to be accepted right away—as good as our intentions may be" (24). In a later interview, the saxophonist Billy Harper concurred with Shepp, noting, "I certainly don't think that Archie Shepp could play at the Apollo! The people who go there are programmed for a certain kind of music and that's all that they can hear, that's all they can accept" (Wilmer, 220). In a piece for *The Cricket* called "Respect," Roger Riggins laments the death of Coleman Hawkins, saying: "I've seen this man play to an audience of ten on a shallow bandstand at the Five Spot Café in New York City (and none of those in the audience were spooks!) This should never have been—it must never happen to one of our artists again!" (33). Criticism of free jazz musicians' attempts to negotiate their populist politics and avant-garde styles was not limited to the criticism inherent in the lack of a popular reception. When musicians such as Albert Ayler attempted to experiment with stylistic innovations that were directly aimed at capturing a mass audience, as he did on the album *New Grass* (1968), which blended free jazz with rock and roll, funky soul, and choruses performed by a gospel group, the attempts were mostly either panned or ignored.

Ayler had been widely hailed by Black Arts critics for his innovative ability to blend improvisational techniques with traditional African American forms found in New Orleans Dixieland jazz and gospel on tracks like "Witches and Devils," "Truth Is Marching In," and "Ghosts." Amiri Baraka noted that Ayler's "playing was like some primordial frenzy that the world secretly used for energy," and the poet Ted Joans famously said that Ayler's playing was "like screaming the word 'FUCK' in Saint Patrick's Cathedral on crowded Easter Sunday."[3] Though Ayler became famous with his reinvention of traditional jazz forms, he was also conversant with a number of diverse styles beyond the "Black classical" styles of gospel and jazz. He began his professional career as a teenager in a band called Little Walter's Blues Band, which performed popular African American dance music, and he had also done an extensive stint as a soloist in the U.S. Army band. Ayler quickly became an influential figure in jazz circles and beyond, even influencing pop musicians. In one of the final interviews he gave before his death, Ayler accused the Beatles, Tom Jones, and Frank Sinatra of "copying off" his music.[4] It is hard to dismiss such claims, since even Paul McCartney had attributed some of the sounds of *Sgt. Pepper's Lonely Hearts Club Band* to Ayler's influence in interviews. According to one Beatles biographer, McCartney alternated "flitting around town in his Aston Martin [with] examining avant-garde jazz . . . Paul was most struck by controversial American tenor saxophonist Albert Ayler."[5] In the interview with Neal for the *Liberator*, Archie Shepp states that the single most important move for avant-garde musicians to make is to reconcile themselves to pop music. In answer to Neal's question: "How can we make art more meaningful to our people?" Shepp responds: "I could advocate more musicians listen to rock and roll" (24). Shepp didn't necessarily need to suggest that rock and roll musicians listen to the avant-garde.

Ayler's claims about artistic appropriation are made all the more poignant when one compares the critical and financial success of the Beatles' *Sgt. Pepper* with the failure of Ayler's cross-genre experimentation on *New Grass*. In his final interview, Ayler is preoccupied with the inability of his music to be a reliable source of income. The image of Paul McCartney "flitting around in an Aston-Martin" contrasts with Ayler's prophetic pre-performance observation that "Right now they are going to make a tape of us and hold it until I die [because] people try to get my music for nothing."[6]

Ayler's observation that he would never profit from the recording of the concert that he would play the night of his final interview took place in the middle of a long discussion of exactly how he planned to support himself and his family on the meager seven thousand dollars that he had made that year from a recording date with ABC: "When you only have love in your heart you don't have time to think about how somebody is copying off your music, but if you start seeing it and you don't have food hardly to eat, man, it's something else now and you be fighting not to play in any of these clubs and they want to see how long you're going to last. Yeah, I mean, it becomes ridiculous after a while." There is no doubt that the so-called British invasion did much to displace any possibility of a rising position of jazz within popular music and that the exchange between pop music and jazz, when it did occur, was decidedly unequal. At the same time, scholars such as Brian Ward, Gerald Early, and Craig Werner have documented the ways in which African American music was profoundly affected by its increasing inclusion in postwar mainstream American popular music culture.

On *New Grass,* Ayler continued the practice of utilizing an eclectic mix of sounds, grounding the album in the work of the gospel group The Soul Singers while also consciously seeking to expand into contemporary commercially successful popular musical forms. Larry Neal's acerbic response to Ayler's *New Grass* in *The Cricket,* in which he labels the album "a failure," has been cited as one of many factors in Ayler's eventual undoing and demise and is instructive in understanding the Black Arts Movement's relationship to popular music production and aesthetics (Review of *New Grass,* 37).

In recognizing Ayler as "one of the driving geniuses of the Music," Neal argues that "lately Albert's music seems to be motivated by forces that are not at all compatible with his genius" (37). Though Neal concedes that the pressure to be commercially successful may have affected the construction of *New Grass,* he ultimately refuses to explore those pressures or the possibilities that popular success might have created for a musician like Ayler, and he shifts the blame for this failure onto Ayler himself, almost as if it is a sort of character failing. According to Neal, "There is even a strong hint that the brother is manipulated by Impulse records[,] or is it merely the selfish desire for popularity in the American sense?" (38). While the Black Arts critics celebrated the innovations that allowed Ayler to recreate traditional New Orleans funeral marches and gospel songs as highly experimental, discordant, and otherworldly ballads, they were unable to see anything at all positive in his similar forays into contemporary popular music.

Class Conflict and Postwar African American Cultural Development

LeRoi Jones's *Blues People* attempted to account for the development of African American music production in relation to the historical and cultural development of African American people and thus to provide a blueprint for a new type of jazz music criticism. This account reflected Jones's ambivalence about class structures within the African American community, which were undergoing significant shifts in the postwar period. Jones's account of African American culture explains class divisions along two simple political lines: (1) the African American middle class follows an assimilationist cultural politics; and (2) the African American lower and working classes, who are for the most part newly urban, follow separatist cultural politics and practices that promote and preserve an "authentic" African American culture.

This methodological and critical stance ignored the ways in which jazz and the blues developed as a consequence of changing social and political conditions that situated African Americans within reach of postwar technologies of cultural production precisely because they had a more immediate access to wealth. For example, W. C. Handy, Duke Ellington, and Miles Davis, all undeniably significant innovators in African American music and in musical production, came from and were supported in their musical endeavors by families that were both socially prominent and relatively wealthy. *Blues People*'s methodological and ideological approach also refused to recognize or account for contradictions within the forms and figures it valorizes, such as Marcus Garvey's United Negro Improvement Association, an undeniably populist, separatist organization that politically followed Jones's model in that it was both separatist and largely supported by an African American urban working class, but oscillated culturally between the use of European concert-hall music and urban blues music for its anthems and events.[7]

One of the more problematic aspects of Jones's refusal of the Black middle class in *Blues People* lies in his failure to acknowledge the role economic development has played in causing certain kinds of formal changes in the very music that Jones valorizes. Jazz would not have developed so seamlessly from the blues had it not been for the commodification and dissemination of the music by people such as W. C. Handy, who published scores for songs that would become jazz standards. Jones fails to ask the provocative questions that arise when consideration is given to the relationship between the development of jazz and the blues and the music's dependency on the commodification and dissemination undertaken by people such as W. C. Handy as they developed a nascent African American recording and publishing industry. Ultimately, Jones's work in *Blues People* refuses to pose or answer the thornier questions regarding the relationship between cultural creation, commodification, and the production of African American music.

Black Fire! is the most comprehensive account of the Black Arts Movement's collective understanding of Black aesthetics. Composed of pieces written by the movement's key figures, the anthology typifies the collective understanding, because music is not only celebrated but becomes the major metaphor through which African American cultural production is articulated. In *Black Fire!* music is referred to more consistently than any other single source, subject, or form. From Richard W. Thomas's "Jazz Vanity," Ted Wilson's "Music of the Other World" and "Count Basie's," Lethonia Gee's "Black Music Man," Ronald Snellings's "Mississippi Concerto," and Sonia Sanchez's "Blues," which are all found in the poetry section of the anthology, to fiction such as "A Love Song for Seven Little Boys Called Sam" and Charlie Cobb's "Ain't That a Groove," to essays such as A. B. Spellman's "Not Just Whistling Dixie," music became the most commonly explored trope for African American creative output by participants within the movement. In addition to situating music as the primary mode and metaphor of African American experience, *Black Fire!* also features poetry and fiction from several musicians, the most notable of these the jazz innovator Sun Ra.

Developments in African American popular music during the Black Arts Movement stand as a test of its supposition that music is capable of modes of expression impossible in other art forms. Unlike jazz, which has come to be regarded and designated as "art" by both mainstream and African American audiences, soul and funk have remained strictly popular music and as such are uniquely positioned to question and test the Black Arts Movement's emphasis on folk culture and its frequent evocation of the power and importance of the culture of "the masses." Since African American popular music of the soul era so often self-consciously addressed itself to the situation of African Americans in the United States, it also worked to challenge the rhetorical and definitional limits of "the Black experience" as a conceptual framework as articulated in the work of LeRoi Jones, Larry Neal, Maulana Karenga, and other Black Arts Movement proponents.

In "Jazz at Home," his contribution to *The Black Aesthetic*, J. A. Rodgers reflects on what he saw as the uniquely American configuration of race, class, and rhythm that created jazz: "The average Negro, particularly of the lower classes, puts rhythm into whatever he does, whether it be shining shoes or carrying a basket on the head to market as the Jamaican women do" (108). "The average Negro" and the assumption of a natural capacity for creation preoccupied much of the Black Arts Movement in its search for a liberating praxis and theory. The Black Arts Movement held that music, unlike the literature and arts of earlier periods and because of its proximity to "the average Negro," was the only African American expressive form almost completely ideologically and formally uncompromised by its situation in U.S. culture. "Black music has been the vanguard reflection of black feeling and continuous repository of black consciousness," declared Ron Welburn in a chapter of *The Black Aesthetic* titled "The Black Aesthetic Imperative" (126). It was the music's imagined link to "the average Negro" and the natural rhythms of his everyday life that prevented it from being compromised in the imagination of the Black Arts Movement. LeRoi Jones states in *Blues People:*

> I think it is not fantastic to say that only in music has there been any significant Negro contribution to a *formal* American culture. For the most part, most of the other contributions made by black Americans in areas of painting, drama, and literature have been essentially undistinguished. The only Negroes who found themselves in a *position* to pursue some art, especially the art of literature, have been members of the Negro middle class. Only Negro music, because, perhaps, it drew its strength and beauty out of the depths of the black man's soul, and because to a large extent its traditions could be carried on by the "lowest classes" of Negroes, has been able to survive the constant and willful dilutions of the black middle class and the persistent calls to oblivion made by the mainstream of the society. (131)

Following Jones's imperative to unlock African American culture from the "constant and willful dilutions of the Black middle class," the project of the Black Arts Movement became one of elucidating and actualizing African

American culture as a culture of everyday struggle. The goal was to retrieve from African American culture the revolutionary "soul" potential embedded within it. Ron Welburn states uncategorically: "Our music is our key to survival" (142).

"Poems That Kill"   African American Cultural Production and Revolution

For LeRoi Jones, Larry Neal, and the commentators on music in Addison Gayle's *The Black Aesthetic,* African American cultural production was often analogous to African American political and social revolution. While Jones's "Black Art" had admonished, "We want 'poems that kill'" (302), and Larry Neal urged, "Poetry is a concrete function, an action. No more abstractions. Poems are physical entities" (260), Don Lee would state in Alhamisi and Wangara's *Black Arts* collection, "We must destroy Faulkner, dick, jane and other perpetuators of evil. . . . As Frantz Fanon points out: destroy the culture and you destroy the people" (96). Maulana Karenga simply concludes in "Black Art": "The real function of art is to make revolution" (33).

Though the majority of artists involved with the Black Arts Movement were poets, Black Arts criticism proclaimed music as the poetry of the people. Rather than existing merely for entertainment value, music, as the highest of the Black art forms, had the potential, the Black Arts Movement believed, not only to chronicle or reflect on revolution, but to actually create and participate in it. According to Hoyt Fuller, music could be a vehicle for the expression of aspects of the Black aesthetic that were otherwise "beyond codifying" (9). Fuller writes of the way in which writers in the important Chicago-based Black Arts group, the Organization of Black American Culture, utilized what Kimberly Benston would label "the ordeal of authority and meaning at the heart of modern black performance" to create beyond categories and genre boundaries (*Performing Blackness,* 117): "In Chicago, the Organization of Black American Culture has moved boldly toward a definition of a black aesthetic. In the writers' workshop sponsored by the group, the writers are deliberately striving to invest their work with the distinctive styles and rhythms and colors of the ghetto, with those peculiar qualities which, for example, characterize the music of a John Coltrane or a Charlie Parker or a Ray Charles" (9). John Coltrane, Sun Ra, Charles Mingus, Bessie Smith, and other jazz and blues musicians functioned, according to Black Arts Movement critics, as revolutionary proponents of social change. When James T. Stewart constructs a "model" for "the development of the Black revolutionary artist," the artists explicitly mentioned by name who personify elements of the Black revolutionary include Ornette Coleman, John Coltrane, Giuseppi Logan, Grachan Moncur, and Milford Graves—all musicians associated with the 1960s jazz avant-garde (*Black Fire!* 8). Though the Black Arts movement was generally critical of the African American church, Neal, Jones, and Spellman also found revolutionary potential in gospel practitioners.

Despite the fact that at this point, jazz had ceased to be a strictly popular African American musical form, it still figured as the pinnacle of African American musical expression for most of the Black Arts critics, at the same time that it operated as a barometer of the experience of "the average Negro." Though the contradictions inherent in the embrace of a form that was no longer widely popular as the ultimate populist expression are occasionally noted, they are rarely directly addressed. For example, in A. B. Spellman's *Black Fire!* essay, "Not Just Whistling Dixie," he notes: "The man standing in line for the Otis Redding show at the Apollo almost certainly never heard of tenor saxophonist Albert Ayler, and wouldn't have the fuzziest idea of what he was doing if he did hear him" (167). Rather than probe what the implications of this observation might be, either for the man in line at the Apollo or for a populist theory of African American music, Spelman opts for a mythos of shared origins. He concludes: "Yet the roots of Ayler's music are largely the same as Otis Redding's" (167). *The Autobiography of Leroi Jones* typifies this tendency in that it acknowledges the importance of popular music in African American public life, to the construction of personal consciousness, and to the individual subjectivity of African American people. Baraka notes that "the Smokey Robinson hit 'Tracks of My Tears' was popular at the time, and for me that summed up what was going on in my own life" (234). However, the bulk of *The Autobiography*'s critical acknowledgement and personal reminiscences of the period is given over to avant-garde jazz music and musicians. When it comes to creating the Black Arts Theater, Baraka and the rest of the organizers privileged jazz over other musical expressions, with the list of performers for its events reading like a roll call of the most prominent avant-garde jazz musicians of the era, from John Coltrane to Archie Shepp and Sun Ra. In *The Autobiography*, Baraka notes that one of the "first official actions" of the Black Arts Theater was "a parade across 125th Street with Sun Ra and his

Myth-Science leading it, Albert [Ayler] and his brother Don blowing and Milford [Graves] wailing his drums" (205). Though the years of the Black Arts Movement were among the most important and productive for a number of African American popular music forms, those performing in areas outside of jazz, gospel, and blues largely escaped serious critical scrutiny by Black Arts Movement critics.

This omission of a prolonged examination of contemporaneous African American popular music is particularly striking when one considers the tremendous outpouring of popular music that directly aligned itself with Black Power cultural politics. The year 1968 saw the release of *Black Fire*, as well as James Brown's "Say It Loud: I'm Black and Proud." In 1971 Addison Gayle's *The Black Aesthetic* was published, and Earth, Wind and Fire debuted with the concept album that was the soundtrack to the film *Sweet Sweetback's Baadasssss Song*. In 1967, a year before LeRoi Jones published *Black Music* as a follow-up to *Blues People*, both black and white radio stations refused to play the Impressions' "We're a Winner," because its "message of black pride might alienate white listeners" (Pruter, 141). Even though African American popular music was explicitly addressing itself in an unprecedented manner to African American social issues, *Black Music*, although its title might suggest otherwise, contains only one chapter devoted to popular music other than jazz and blues. That the chapter again substitutes a mythos of shared origins for a serious critical inquiry is evident in its title, "The Changing Same (R & B and the New Black Music)."

In an essay in *The Black Aesthetic* entitled "Reflections on the Evolution of Post War Jazz," Leslie B. Rout Jr. notes that, as was typical for all African American metropolises in the late sixties, "as of the fall of 1967, there did not exist on the South Side of Chicago a single club that booked nationally established jazz talent on a consistent basis" (151). African American jazz was plagued, as Spellman documents in *Four Lives in the BeBop Business*, by the racist practices of the recording industry and nightclub management, but it also suffered from its own inability to consistently connect with its audience as it evolved. Anxiety about the African American community's rejection of avant-garde jazz haunted almost all the discussions of the music in journals like the *Liberator*, in which, for example, Larry Neal asked the free jazz drummer Milford Graves "why Black people, generally don't seem interested in the 'new thing,'" or in Neal's coverage of the opening of the Black Arts Repertory Theater in June 1965 in which he notes defensively, "The idea behind both this event and the one discussed above is to open a dialogue between the artist and his people, rather than between the artist and dominant white society which is responsible for his alienation in the first place. When one hears the poetry of Ronald Snellings, David Henderson, Calvin Hernton, and other fine poets represented that night, one is certain that soon there will be no need for dialogue, but that the artist and the community will be wedded in an assault on racist America." In *Four Lives,* A. B. Spellman notes: "The mobile avant-garde jazz performances that LeRoi Jones' Black Arts group put on in the streets of Harlem during the summer of 1965 received a generally favorable audience response, but eggs were thrown at one group" (17). Neal's "A Conversation with Archie Shepp" evokes both the tension and the possibility inherent in the Black Arts movement's relationship to "community" (24). In response to Neal's comment that "the Black artist is faced with some serious problems vis-à-vis the Black community," Shepp remarks, "I think it will be a long time before the Black artist and the Black community can really stand next to each other because so much has been done to separate them; and for pure economic reasons, many have moved away from Harlem. Thus, a really vital element of the community was taken away. Systematically, it was made possible for that element to be stolen from the Black community. And so differences have developed" (24). By the time Shepp was noting the distance between "the Black artist" and "the Black community" in 1965, the forces of commodification and urbanity that had enabled the development of free jazz were recombining with immediate postsegregation shifts to create new possibilities for the production of African American popular music, and that music was motivated by the production imperatives and aesthetic concerns of Black Power politics.

Living for the City   Urbanity, Identity, and African American Cultural Production

Starting at the turn of the century during what has come to be known as the Great Migration, African Americans began to leave the rural South to seek freedom from violent oppression and to take advantage of the expanded economic opportunities in the urban centers of the North. Industrialization, spurred by the war effort, contributed to the rapid growth of Black populations in urban centers. For example, the African American population of Oakland, California, the future home of the Black Panther Party and the site of a blossoming wartime industry, was typical in that it grew from 8,462 in 1940 to 37,327 just five years later (Crouchett, 22). The growth spurt continued as labor recruiters from Oakland's shipping industry actively sought new African American laborers with recruitment drives in Arkansas, Louisiana, Texas, Mississippi, and the Carolinas (Crouchett, 46). Urban African American populations grew so much that, by the late 1950s and early 1960s, the cultural milieu and predominant mode of expression for African Americans was an urban one.

Initially, for the early, oppressed African American migrants from the South, the city signaled the possibility for "Jobs, Homes, Dignity," as Jones points out in *Blues People* (96). However, the postwar years increasingly found many of those hopes unfulfilled. While Jones and others from the Black Arts Movement use the rural-to-urban shift to account for a new aesthetic in African American traditional forms of jazz, blues, and gospel that the migrants had carried with them from the South, they fail to explain shifts in cultural production that gave rise to the newer, popular, commercially successful African American musical forms of rhythm and blues, soul, and funk.

Rhythm and blues, far from being more of "the changing same" of gospel, jazz, and blues, actually signaled a radical break in the development of African American expression in its relationship to its tradition and culture. Soul and funk not only articulated the changing relationship of African Americans to processes of urbanization, industrialization, and commodification, they also articulated a significant change in their relationship to the traditional African American expressive forms of gospel, jazz, and the blues. By the time Detroit, the Motor City, became the Motown of popular music legend, something had dramatically changed in how African Americans read and rearticulated their culture, as well as in the ways in which they themselves were read and rearticulated by mainstream culture. That change could be charted in the popular music of the time, particularly within the categories of soul and funk. Although the Black Arts Movement did not devote time to soul and funk, it seems obvious in retrospect that anyone who wanted to understand the African American postslavery experience of industrialization and the city first had to come to terms with soul and funk as African American musical forms.

By the time gospel, blues, and jazz had given way to the more commercially viable medium of rhythm and blues, many urban African Americans were at least a generation removed from the southern rural experience. However, just as previous African American musical forms continued to affect the formation of newer ones in new ways, the southern, rural agrarian experience continued to influence African American urban dwellers. Curtis Mayfield, born in Chicago and raised in the Cabrini-Green public housing projects, formed the Impressions with a vocal ensemble that had moved to Chicago from Chattanooga, Tennessee, specifically to be near a viable recording industry (Pruter, 30). Berry Gordy founded Motown with money borrowed from family funds accumulated in the South (George, *Where Did Our Love Go?* 33). Marvin Gaye was born in Washington, DC, but learned to sing in his father's South-influenced Baptist church (Shaw, 176). However, more than an accident of birth separated these musicians from their predecessors. If gospel expression was naturally located in the church, the blues in the rural fields and factories of the South, and jazz and blues lore echoed with the legends of the rural juke joints and urban clubs that served as its venues, then funk and soul were most at home with the burgeoning technologies of the studio and on the radio.

Motown and Stax Studios (which billed themselves as Hitsville, U.S.A, and Soulsville, U.S.A., respectively) became legendary for their ability to develop and market award-winning gold and platinum classics. When rhythm and blues music of the era was classified, it was almost always in relation to the city that housed its respective recording studio: a "Philadelphia Sound" in relation to Philadelphia International Studios, a "Detroit Sound" in the studios of Motown, and a "Memphis Sound" associated with the studios of Stax Records. They all recognized consumer mediation as deeply involved in musical production in ways that spoke to the newer, complicated relationship African Americans had developed to the consumer culture of the city as they became further and further removed from the reality of rural agrarian existence in the South.

In the cultural transition from southern and rural to northern and urban that marked the Great Migration, African Americans had gradually begun to mark their unhappiness with the unfulfilled promise of the urban space by reconceptualizing "the city," formerly a place of hope and opportunity, as "the ghetto," a place of inescapable despair and a crushing lack of opportunity. The rise of rhythm and blues, soul, and funk as distinct musical categories signaled a change in the functional relationship of African Americans to industrialization as it was manifested in the commodity culture of the cities, and this change is embodied in the creation of "the ghetto" as the key myth and metaphor through which African Americans viewed urbanity.

Ted Vincent links the rise of African American professional musicianship directly to the rise of the cities, stating uncategorically: "The environment of the blues coincided with the growth of the city" (1). Vincent argues that African American migration to the cities offered "one of those rare windows of opportunity for African-Americans that open up when rapid social change creates new situations which the White power structure is slow to control" (1), and he links the growth of a Black urban presence, which increased as much as 400 percent in cities like Detroit between 1910 and 1920, to the development of an entire Black commercial and cultural infrastructure that came into being too quickly to be stifled by the interference of the oppressive forces of white racism. Consequently, newly urbanized African Americans were able to create the idiom of cultural production labeled "the Jazz Age." Vincent writes: "The window opening in this case was the great exodus of Black Americans from the rural South to the urban North around the time of the First World War. Almost overnight there were new Black urban neighborhoods. Within the new neighborhoods there was, initially, little involvement from the White music world or from downtown. Consequently, it was African-Americans working among themselves, or in concert with Whites yet to flee the suburbs, who organized the Jazz Age" (1).

For Vincent, the rapid growth of the cities and the rapid urbanization of the previously rural and southern African American population went hand-in-hand with the creation of a viable commercial culture for African American music. Blues music, which had previously been the strict purview of rural folk culture, became a highly commercialized enterprise with the runaway success among the African American urban population of the first blues recording by Mamie Smith in 1920. No longer driven by the need to merely satisfy an audience by repeating familiar, collective forms of folk culture, music became tied to the individual expressions of a professional class of musicians as they strove to establish an individual signature in order to create themselves as unique and commodifiable objects. According to Vincent, "when musicians first referred to 'jazzing' music, they spoke of a rebellious quality of individualizing a song, phrase, or note" (7). Urbanization in combination with the forces of commodification that created musicians as a professional class all provided for the development of African American music as a product. As music technology developed in tandem with the changes that immediately followed desegregation, African American music would find new possibilities in mainstream popular culture that had previously marginalized its contributions and subjected its producers to extreme artistic and production restraints.

Technology, African American Music, and the Commodification of Cultural Production

In *Stomping the Blues,* the historian and theorist Albert Murray ties the professionalization and refinement of blues as a genre to the rise of recording and publishing technology at the turn of the century. By the time soul music established itself as a genre, the transformation of African American musical production from a performance-based, largely local industry to a recording industry with national scope was more or less complete. The careers of many classic soul musicians testify to the totality of this transition from "musician as folk artist" to "musician as primarily performer" and, finally, to "musician as producer of market commodities." African Americans not only had greater and more immediate access to recording technology in the Black Power era, but they were also beginning to take steps toward a basic ownership of the means of musical production. Jacques Attali notes that the beginning of the commodification of recorded music coincided with the beginning of the jazz and blues eras: "Music did not really become a commodity until a broad market for popular music was created. Such a market did not exist when Edison invented the phonograph; it was produced by the colonization of black music by the American industrial apparatus" (103). The colonization of African American music successfully produced a market for popular music, but it also became a major structuring factor in the production of that music.

As Attali implies, when recorded music became a commodity for the popular market, the effects of this shift were wide-ranging, and had implications for more than just African American music, its creators, and its audience. The colonization and commodification of African American music and the resultant development of a market for popular music had the unintended effect, Attali argues, of symbolically transforming economic relations as a whole by re-creating the manner in which use value is stockpiled. The creation and commodification of African American recorded music could therefore be said to have done no less than redefine the manner in which commodities were conceptualized and circulated within U.S. culture. Such change was, of course, far beyond the original scope or intention of the technology's inventors. Attali notes that recording technology was originally developed to stabilize meaning and fix power as a "word preserver" of the ideas of "great men": "The phonograph was thus conceived as a privileged vector for the dominant speech as a tool reinforcing representative power and entirely of its logic. No one foresaw the mass production of music: The dominant system only desired to preserve a recording of its representation of power to preserve itself" (93, 92).

Attali writes that Thomas Edison specifically opposed using the phonograph for the reproduction and mass distribution of recorded music because "he thought it might make it [the phonograph] 'appear as though it were nothing more than a toy'" (93). Though Edison did not specifically exclude the recording of music as a function of the phonograph, he suggested a long list of other possible uses for the recording of speech, such as recording "letter-writing and all kinds of dictation, without the aid of a stenographer" and keeping a "'Family Record,' a registry of sayings, reminiscences, etc . . . the last words of dying persons" (93). However, once the technology appeared, preserving and instituting the ideas of "great men" took on a secondary role as the unanticipated market for recorded music developed and flourished and as this market transformed American commodity culture. Recording technology introduced repetition as a significant factor of production, thereby allowing consumers to stockpile use value. Attali writes: "Repetition creates an object that lasts beyond its usage" (100). This simple, yet revolutionary, symbolic function enabled by recording technology made it possible to popularize the concept of commodity on a widespread basis. That this popularization occurred through the commodification of African American music would have broad implications for the development of African American culture.

Though Attali recognizes the ways in which "jazz was strategically situated to produce this market," his discussion of the relationship between jazz and commodification actually occupies fewer than three pages of an otherwise significantly detailed study of the political economy of music (103). Attali's short discussion of African American music almost makes it appear as though the role that the colonization of African American music played within the creation of music as a commodity was a minor coincidence. Though he writes that "with the appearance of the phonograph record, the relation between music and money starts to be flaunted, it ceases to be ambiguous and shameful," and, further, that "the emergence of recording and stockpiling revolutionizes both music and power; it overturns all economic relations" (88), he fails to examine thoroughly the connection between the formation of music as a commodity culture and the people unequivocally formed through slavery by commodity culture itself.

If we begin to understand the historical "coincidence" of the emergence of recorded music as popular music in the context of the African American cultural production of the blues and jazz, we begin to understand that the emergence of recorded music is deeply linked to the emergence of classic blues and jazz. Murray's *Stomping the Blues* marks the connection between the emergence of that genre and the emergence of popular recorded culture and shows how it developed as a commodity in direct relationship to music as a product for wider general consumption.

According to Murray, the historical distinction and disjunction between blues as a folk expression and blues as a musical tradition, or what many critics term the distinction between rural and urban blues, is linked to the transformative effects of technological advances in sound recording and production. Calling the transition "a perfectly natural historical development," he writes: "That blues music began as folk expression goes without saying . . . But in point of historical fact, once W. C. Handy had arranged, scored, and published *The Memphis Blues* (1912), *The St. Louis Blues* and *Yellow Dog Blues* (1914), and *Beale Street Blues* (1916), it was no longer possible to restrict blues music to the category of folk expression" (73).

W. C. Handy's codification of the blues into a replicable and easily circulated product as sheet music would in turn create a class of musicians whose own circulation through American culture would be increasingly marked by the complexities of a market-driven professionalization. Murray continues: "Certainly there was nothing provincial about the musicians who were providing the instrumentation for Bessie Smith by the early 1920s when her now classic repertory was being established as a nationwide phenomenon (via phonograph records to a great extent). Clarence Williams, Fletcher Henderson, James P. Johnson, Louis Armstrong, Joe Smith, Buster Bailey, Coleman Hawkins, Charlie Green, and the rest were anything but folk performers. They were professionals with no less talent and authenticity for all the technical facility, range, and control at their command" (73–74).

For Murray, the transition between blues as a rural folk expression and blues as an urban tradition practiced by well-trained and credentialed professional musicians was linked to its development as a commodity as it changed venues from "the street corner and cheap honky-tonk" to the relative stability and prosperity of the vaudeville circuit (70). The transition was greatly furthered by the emergence of a pervasive and available recording culture that not only enabled the development of musicians as a professional class but also helped create a demand for recording technology. Murray identifies blues as "the music that the phonograph records were all about in the first place": "Once they started making phonograph records of it you could hear it almost any time of the day on almost any day of the week and almost anywhere that was far enough away from church. Because not only did there seem to be at least one phonograph in almost every neighborhood from the very outset, but it was also as if that was the music that the phonograph records were all about in the first place" (131).

The blues era is commonly considered the foundational moment of African American music. The work of Murray clearly demonstrates that the production of African American music from the advent of the blues era was inextricably linked to the commodification of that music. This, of course, had multiple implications for African American cultural production. It not only created music production as an increasingly profitable, professional possibility for African Americans but also made African American cultural production a viable, visible, and profitable cultural venture. What the early commodification of African American music did not necessarily do was put the control of that production and commodification into the hands of the newly emergent class of professional African American cultural producers.

Commodity Culture in the Black Power Era

Not unlike the blues era, the Black Power era saw advances in sound recording and radio technology that enabled music to disseminate varied philosophies of Black empowerment widely, unifying African Americans as its intended audience. What made the Black Power era different from the blues era, however, was that for the first time, the artistic producers began on a large scale to try to successfully assert control over the conditions of production of African American music. This is not to say that artists and cultural workers did not attempt to control the means of music production before the Black Power era. Ted Vincent records the efforts of people such as W. C. Handy and Andy Razaf to preserve and create African American music and African American music venues as not only political, but also artistic and financial ventures through the 1930s. What makes the Black Power era different from either the blues era or the Jazz Age is that the

Civil Rights Movement had created a climate in which African American business ventures could exist and flourish in a limited, yet previously unheard of, manner.

Ben Caldwell's 1968 play *The King of Soul (or The Devil and Otis Redding)* dramatizes the conflict between African American musicians and the white-controlled music industry as the mythic conflict between Otis Redding and Satan, who has taken the earthly form of a white manager and record producer. Redding's ill-fated contract with the devil, which he obviously is unable to renegotiate and finally simply walks away from, is terminated only with his premature death at the devil's hands. In reality, as Peter Guralnick mentions in *Sweet Soul Music: Rhythm and Blues and the Southern Dream of Freedom*, Redding was attempting to renegotiate his contract, and there are indications that he was considering leaving his parent label, Stax, when he was killed in 1967 (356). However, Caldwell's play does not really address the nuances of Redding's situation as it developed at Stax. Rather than being a strict racial hierarchy in which the management was white and the staff was African American, as *The King of Soul* suggests, over the period of its existence, Stax had the most multiracial executive staff of any major recording label. The collaborative, multiracial nature of the Stax studio had reached near legendary status during the period in which Redding was associated with the label. Caldwell's play also ignores Redding's own position in a southern culture in which he "was so universally respected . . . that even the local KKK appreciated him" (Guralnick, 147). He was therefore uniquely positioned to negotiate and represent African American culture to wider southern and American cultures, and he did so with success enough throughout his life and work to profitably make his way through the early days of postsegregation American popular culture.

The increasing destabilization of white supremacist culture and institutions brought about by the Civil Rights Movement and the beginnings of the end of segregation began to open up spaces for new articulations of culture and power. The artists who followed Redding were increasingly able to gain artistic freedom and greater levels of control over music and cultural production. Sam Cooke, who, like Redding, died prematurely, achieved far more unambiguous independence by successfully forming his own record label and music publishing company with the manager J. W. Alexander, while also successfully suing to gain greater control over the legal rights to his previously released work. Cooke, who had originally risen to fame performing in the gospel music circuit, even went so far as to declare in a

1963 press release, "My future lies more in creating music and records than in being a nightclub performer" (qtd. in Guralnick, 41).

Peter Guralnick describes the unheard-of success of Alexander and Cooke's entertainment business ventures in *Sweet Soul Music*: "To a lot of people's astonishment the label continued to thrive, or at least put out strong, good-quality releases. Not everyone was prepared to see a black entrepreneur and a popular singing idol show some expertise in the business, and the fact that Alexander was able to get credit from hard-boiled distributors on the strength of his word alone shocked not a few" (40). Like Cooke, James Brown insisted on an unprecedented level of control over the production of his music. He exerted a notorious control over band members' performances and production, even going so far as to scold them on stage in song. On one notorious evening after an argument over working conditions, Brown replaced the entire lineup of his legendary backup band with a group of studio musicians led by William "Bootsy" Collins, who was only eighteen at the time. It was inevitable, perhaps, given Brown's deep investment in the control of his performances, that he should seek to gain control over all other aspects of his music's production. For Brown, this eventually meant not only artistic control of production and the legal rights to his music, but also ownership of production studios and several radio stations.[8]

Other artists followed Brown's lead to varying degrees in ways that had significant results for the production and articulation of Black music. Rickey Vincent writes: "The strongest examples of black music that directly spoke of empowerment and liberation were produced by artists who possessed the greatest degree of independence and control over what they said in their music" (154). In fact, the implications for Black cultural workers of this newly sought independence in music and popular cultural production were profound, allowing for the creation of new forms and genres and the transformation of older forms and genres.

Super Fly The Cultural Politics of Commodification

While the development of earlier African American musical forms has been attributed to the independent economies created by segregation in the "chitlin circuit," musical developments in the Black Power era were clearly linked to postsegregation social forces, which created and even demanded a market for African American cultural production in the mainstream as a means of understanding the dramatic shifts in social and political power that were taking place. Ironically, as these social forces created a need for hymns as central to African American emancipation, the market demanded that African American cultural production be co-opted in the service of the creation of new markets. New musical forms and genres grew directly out of this particular confluence of historical and cultural circumstances.

Curtis Mayfield, one of the most prolific and influential popular musicians of the era, began his career, like many Black artists, with training and performance in the classical traditions of the Black church. Unlike his blues-era predecessors, however, by the age of fourteen, Mayfield had put aside any sacred or scholastic aspirations in order to pursue professionalization as a musician and songwriter. He came of age when the transition of African American music from the rural folk expression of an oppressed class to the commodified expression of a highly specialized, often prosperous class was largely complete. Soul funk or funky soul, the stylistic form he is often credited with creating, also marked a transition from the classical forms of African American music that had birthed rhythm and blues toward more eclectic electronic and urban amalgamations that would give birth to hip-hop generations later.

The hip-hop practice of sampling, for example, has its roots in the controversial "borrowing" practices of rhythm and blues that pirated entire song structures from gospel and the blues, reworking them for a popular music market. Gospel music was so scandalized by the success of such appropriations by Sam Cooke and Ray Charles, for example, that when Sam Cooke was murdered in 1964, many gospel fans viewed it as a sort of divine retribution.[9] Funk and soul standardized this practice of sampling from other forms. The use of electronic guitars and recording equipment also gained a foothold in African American music during this period because of artists like Mayfield, who, while working as producer, manager, and songwriter for himself and other artists on a series of labels he created, would pioneer a number of key musical and production changes, including the transition from soul to funk with the albums *Curtis Live* and *Super Fly*.

Lyrically and conceptually, *Super Fly* is overwrought by the ambivalence of its production. It is, after all, an antidrug album that celebrates the life and times of a drug dealer. The essential problematic it poses, however, is the central problem of the postsegregation era: how to participate in American consumer culture and not be dirtied by it. The album opens with the declaration "Can't reason with the pusherman / Finances all that he understands" in "Little Child Runnin' Wild," a basic analysis of capitalism's most popular ghetto emissary, and then moves directly to exploring the omnipotent presence and mystique of this figure in "Pusherman," an exploration that often borders on celebration: "I'm your momma. I'm your daddy. I'm that nigger in the alley. / I'm your doctor when you need want some coke, have some weed." Mayfield captures the essential quality of a ghetto economy structured around base-level consumption, greed, and need. Indeed, the song is one of the most sampled songs of the era, rewritten by Ice T and reappearing in the work of such artists as T.I., Notorious B.I.G., and the Wu Tang Clan.

In one of the final vocal selections on the album, "No Thing on Me (Cocaine Song)," Mayfield intones, "I'm so glad I got my own. My life's a natural high / The Man can't put nothing on me." Like many other Black political and cultural workers of the era, he offers a simple Black self-determination as the improbably uncomplicated solution to the complexities and ambivalent possibilities of ghetto oppression and the new postsegregation economies. Like "People Get Ready," "We're a Winner," and "Keep on Pushing," compositions of Mayfield's that had become Civil Rights Movement anthems, his later work also gave lyrical articulation to the central problematic of the time. For the Black Power era, this problematic was clearly the inability of Black Power politics to translate into real material gains for urban, disenfranchised populations. But while the articulation of Black self-determination on *Super Fly* might have been overly simplistic, in reality, Mayfield—with Curtom Records, his independent label and production company—was able to claim ownership of all aspects of his music, from form and styling to production and distribution. His success in this regard was largely instrumental in pioneering a new relationship between African American music and its producers.

If the film soundtracks of the era provided the directive and razor-sharp edge of analysis for Blaxploitation film audiences, the music of the Black Power era served even more to provide the direction and analysis of a contemporary culture in flux for a general audience. Over a hundred years after the advent of the phonograph, the Blaxploitation film boom promised to give "all power to the people" in African American cultural production and commodification. The boom caused an outpouring not only of films and related cultural production but especially, though not exclusively, in music production. Numerous critics and fans have pointed out that the soundtracks to Blaxploitation films are often far more compelling then the narrative or visual effects of the films themselves—that it is, in fact, the soundtracks that control the film experience. Truly, some of the most revered musicians of the era—from Curtis Mayfield, Isaac Hayes, and James Brown to Willie Hutch and Earth, Wind and Fire—created film scores that were as much credited with creating and enhancing the film experience as the often sparse narrative and low-budget production qualities for which the films are remembered.

Blaxploitation-era film soundtracks function to direct the viewer's interaction with the film in a manner atypical of other genres of film. In fact, soundtracks are so significant to this body of work that films like *Shaft* (1971), *Super Fly* (1972), and *Black Caesar* (1973) are remembered today more for their soundtracks than for any other typically noted filmic elements, such as narrative, visuals, or cast. For example, in a matter typical of the urban gangster genre, the narrative and visual styling in the opening sequence of *Super Fly* establish a formulaic Hollywood tale of the life of an inner-city gangster, with all its emphasis on ghetto-fabulous excess and masculine empowerment, whereas Curtis Mayfield's ballad "Little Child Runnin' Wild" tells a haunting tale of lost potential and wasted innocence between the lines of the film's seductive narrative and seductive visuals. For young African American urban spectators, the films' intended audience, the soundtracks to Blaxploitation films provided a counternarrative of poverty, loss, and despair disavowed by the standard American visual conventions that governed the gangster genre.

In 1971 Earth, Wind and Fire collaborated with the self-taught filmmaker and musician Melvin Van Peebles on the soundtrack to Van Peebles's film *Sweet Sweetback's Baadasssss Song*. The resulting soundtrack attests to the dramatic social and cultural shifts that had occurred, not only in the function, aesthetic composition, and consumption of African American popular music, but also in relationships between African Americans and their notions of belonging to the city and urban life. *Sweet Sweetback's Baadasssss Song!* is a mixed-media "concept album" that relies on a combination of album-cover art, liner notes, and the film experience in combination with the music to convey what might loosely be termed the film's "message" of struggle and redemption. The film, which was produced and financed independently, attempted to self-consciously actualize the rhetoric of Black Power politics by negotiating African American culture's commodification for the benefit rather than at the expense of that culture's producers. By proving its marketability through its intense popularity, it gave rise to the entire genre of Hollywood-produced Blaxploitation films. However, its innovation was not only economic: *Sweet Sweetback's Baadasssss Song!* was conceived as a mixed-media production from its inception, and as such, the work attempts to negotiate a different relationship between film as medium and other commercialized art forms, such as literature and music. In "He Won't Bleed Me: A Revolutionary Analysis of Sweet Sweetback's Baadasssss Song," his commentary on the film, Huey P. Newton "urge[s] all of you who want to understand the deep meanings of the movie to also buy the record and the book" (114).

The film creates new relationships among soundtrack, film narrative, and spectator. It is the ideas expressed in the soundtrack, rather than the characters themselves or the political dialogues that they engage in, that the characters within the narrative and eventually the spectators themselves should adopt. Furthermore, and most importantly, the album negotiates a new relationship between a black cultural tradition and the emergence of new formulations of that tradition made manifest in soul music. The *Sweet Sweetback* soundtrack opens with the plaintive wail of the gospel standard "Wade in the Water." The soundtrack eclectically combines Melvin Van Peebles's spoken-word performance, gospel standards such as "Wade in the Water" and "This Little Light of Mine," African-style drumming, and syncopation and assorted jazz and blues riffs with the soul and funk rhythms that Earth, Wind and Fire would eventually popularize in the 1970s as top-selling soul artists. The album's hectic sound is at least partly created by its sampling of a range of black musical traditions without an apparent ordering logic or reverence.

Sweet Sweetback and the Changing Structures of African American Music

Albert Murray, LeRoi Jones, and most writers on the jazz and blues tradition emphasize the deliberateness with which artists in traditional black musical genres would deviate from or utilize traditional methodology and styles in their extreme devotion to developing their craft. In "The Development of the Black Revolutionary Artist," which appears in *The Black Aesthetic*, James T. Stewart writes of the ways that knowledge was formulated and contested among jazz practitioners, using as one such example the story of Sonny Rollins's legendary self-imposed recording exile in which he practiced alone on New York's Williamsburg Bridge:

There was a well-defined procedure for qualification as a musician that required that the neophyte musician serve a required period of apprenticeship
by studying the acknowledged masters . . . then the arduous practicing or
"shedding" where he perniciously attempted to emulate his teacher, and then
finally putting all of it to test by applying it with others in the act of making
music . . . This is what all our musicians, in the context of that development
of our music we know by the name of Jazz, were required to pass through . . .
The music literally proliferates with such tales. Even the John Coltrane/Sonny
Rollins encounter, and the self-imposed retirement of Sonny from the music
scene after that encounter, gave credence to those arguments that Trane and
Sonny had indeed participated in a contest of saxophone playing and Sonny
lost and that a new voice in tenor playing was on the scene. (88–89)

The aesthetic of *Sweet Sweetback's Baadasssss Song!* operates quite differ-
ently from the traditional model of mastery in Stewart's account of the
Rollins/Coltrane confrontation. The musical pastiche that creates *Sweet
Sweetback's* sound borrows haphazardly from a variety of other African
American musical traditions without African American music's traditional
reverence for the original referent that indicated the master's knowledge
of its sources.

Soul music as a genre often faced accusations that its musicians irrev-
erently pillaged other traditional African American musical forms. Ray
Charles, Sam Cooke, and James Brown were all accused of stealing from
the gospel music tradition in order to create an entirely new product whose
value lay completely outside of that tradition. In many cases, these accusations of pilfering were well-grounded. James Brown proudly claimed, "I
took gospel and jazz and defied all the laws" (qtd. in R. Vincent, *Funk* 60).
According to Arnold Shaw, Ray Charles simply rewrote the words to the
gospel hymn "My Jesus Is All the World to Me" to create "I Got a Woman."
"This Little Light of Mine" became "This Little Girl of Mine" for Charles's
first album, while Booker T. Jones of Booker T. and the M.G.'s explains,
"The Memphis Sound started in a church . . . We've retained the basic elements of this church music in the Memphis Sound" (qtd. in R. Vincent,
Funk 181). Later funk groups would bastardize the entire concept of the
church service in songs such as Funkadelic's 1970 "Free Your Mind and
Your Ass Will Follow" and "Eulogy and Light."

Sweet Sweetback's soundtrack follows these models in its appropriation
of various gospel and jazz traditions. It allows us to hear "Wade in the Wa-

ter" as background to the prostitute's moans of ecstasy as she initiates the preadolescent Sweetback into sexuality. We hear "This Little Light of Mine" as they climax, and she gives him his nickname. Gospel music is interspersed throughout the album not to suggest possibilities for redemption in an afterlife, which would be in keeping with its tradition, but rather to suggest the profanity of the extended suffering of the characters. Instead of providing complete songs or narration in homage to traditional Black music forms, the album recognizes these traditions by presenting small pieces of sound for all their suggestive power without necessarily contextualizing them. This use of traditional African American musical forms without the establishment of a sustained dialogue with them is emblematic of the new relationship between soul musicians and an African American musical tradition in which the uses to which a piece can be put, rather than reverence for or work within a tradition, is the ultimate determination of value.

Traditionalists had been quick to dismiss the new commodified forms of African American popular music as insignificant in comparison to the traditions of gospel, jazz, and the blues. It is undeniable that the evolving commodification of African American popular music made the creation of certain forms efficacious to their production and consumption. The practices of borrowing and recycling that were endemic to the production of soul music made it more readily available for commodification than other art forms that had the traditional notions of reverence for mastery at their center. However, the pastiche quality and irreverent borrowing of funk and soul also significantly liberated its creators and audience from the conventions, traditions, and burdens of African American music reproduction just as soul and funk era musicians were also managing to free themselves from many of the racist constraints that kept them from participating in recording culture as anything other than performers. Soul and funk's irreverent approach to the African American musical tradition would enable sampling to become a practice much later in hip-hop and contribute to hip-hop's subsequent ascendancy as one of the most important musical developments in contemporary American culture.

Soul and funk's practice of repackaging earlier classic African American musical forms into an easily consumable product helped to create African American music as a product easily circulated to the wider mass markets of American culture. Post-1960s African American music could no longer be consigned to its previous designation as the extremely limited specialty market of "race records." African American music culture increasingly became an integral part of the broader postwar American market, and the African American popular genres of the Black Power eras helped create it as a defining force in American popular music.

Gerard Early describes the ways in which Motown Records willingly translated African American culture so that it could be incorporated into mainstream white American culture as part of its corporate mission. This "Motown effect" created "The Sound of Young America"—as Motown was called—as the sign of a newly miscegenated American culture that incorporated the dreams and aspirations of African American youth culture with white youth culture. African American popular music of the late 1960s and 1970s took the idea of miscegenated cultural forms beyond the simple binary of African American and white and explored the complex interrelationship of African American musical traditions. This created a broader base for innovation that went beyond the basic formulas offered up by Motown and also allowed African American musicians to create as rich a dialogue between themselves and their traditions as with American culture.

5

"You Better Watch This Good Shit!"

BLACK SPECTATORSHIP, BLACK MASCULINITY, AND BLAXPLOITATION FILM

"Resistant" and "Oppositional" Constituting an African American Audience and the Question of African American Spectatorship

In 1965 much of the world watched on television as the Watts section of Los Angeles exploded in what was up until then the largest urban uprising of its kind in U.S. history. Images of African American bodies as active agents of violence in the rioting and as the inescapable victims of the batons and bullets of the Los Angeles Police Department and the National Guard were widely circulated. These images began to compete with the other image of African Americans created in the Hollywood section of Los Angeles through films such as *Hallelujah,* Charles Vidor's celebration of plantation life (1929); *Song of the South,* Walt Disney's celebration of slavery (1946); and more recent "noble Negro" vehicles, such as Sidney Poitier's *Lilies of the Field* (1963). When the historic events in Los Angeles in the late 1960s and 1970s were coupled with the competing images and agendas of mainstream Hollywood, the Black film boom that has come to be known as "Blaxploitation" was born. Between 1966 and 1975 approximately seventy feature-length Black action films were created as part of this genre, either by Hollywood studios making extensive, first-time use of African American production and distribution staff or by newly formed independent African American production companies. The films that fall within the genre category of Blaxploitation are in some senses as varied and uneven as the conditions of their production. They range from slick blockbuster-style studio films to low-budget films with low production values created in B studios such as American International Pictures, which initially came to prominence with the success of teen exploitation films such as *Beach Party* (1963) and *Pajama Party* (1964).[1]

Because the 1960s and 1970s were the first time that African Americans and their desires and concerns became the conscious focus of mainstream U.S. visual culture, Blaxploitation era film production points to the ways in which "a Black audience," a notion that was very much the product of a historically specific moment, was deliberately socially constructed, not only to answer the calls for an aesthetic revolution befitting the social and political revolutions of the time, but also as a marketing niche to fill the specific needs of a Hollywood film industry that was floundering badly in the wake of the rise of television and the failure of the studio system. Consequently, the production of Black-themed films during the Blaxploitation era reveals the ways in which African American film strove to create a visual tradition that specifically negotiated and counteracted a history of African American oppression that had largely been formulated and enacted through visual culture and visual coding. It also reveals the limitations on and possibilities for resistance within the commodification and co-optation of African American popular culture as it was developing in the period immediately following segregation. To determine what is at stake in the production and consumption of Blaxploitation, this chapter examines the following issues: the relationship between black action films, the African American community's rejection of nonviolent protest, and the consumption of popular culture, grounded in a discussion of how visual pleasure was constituted for the audience of Blaxploitation.

The fact that the Black film boom of the 1960s and 1970s constructed an African American audience that actually mattered had broad implications for film production and consumption and also for notions of African American subjectivity. In *Black Looks: Race and Representation*, bell hooks explores what she terms "the oppositional gaze" and the centrality of visual culture to the totality of African American historical experience by describing the ways in which African Americans have been compelled by historical necessity to recognize and participate in the power of the gaze: "The politics of slavery, of racialized power relations, were such that the slaves were denied the right to gaze. I knew that the slaves had looked. That attempts to repress our/Black people's right to gaze had produced in us an overwhelming longing to look, a rebellious desire, an oppositional gaze. By courageously looking, we defiantly declare: 'Not only will I stare. I want my look to change reality'" (116).

According to hooks, an "oppositional gaze" both informs African Americans of the oppressive social field in which they must operate and "opens up the possibility of agency itself" (289). For her, the ways in which African Americans have been conditioned by, and resist subject formation within, visual culture result from the specificity of a historical oppression rooted in a denial of the right to lay claim to either the look or the gaze.[2] In a similar argument—a highly contested discussion of the failure of the director Steven Spielberg to translate Alice Walker's novel *The Color Purple* effectively to film—Manthia Diawara coined the term "resistant spectatorship" to denote what he claims are significant differences in the visual experiences of African Americans and white Americans regarding processes of identification and spectatorship. For Diawara, spectators are "socially and historically as well as psychically constituted" (212).[3] Exploring the ways in which an African American population constitutes a "resistant spectatorship" sheds light, according to Diawara, on processes of identification and spectatorship and unmasks the problems inherent in theorizing visual culture without recourse to a historical and cultural specificity.

The notion that African Americans possess "an oppositional gaze" or enact "a resistant spectatorship" in the act of watching mainstream culture speaks directly to the notion of "witnessing" as a mechanism of social change within African American spectatorial culture. The African American tradition of witnessing to social injustice was at least as old as Frederick Douglass's invocations in *The North Star*, the abolitionist newspaper that he edited from 1847 to 1851, and Ida B. Wells's incendiary 1892 pamphlet *Southern Horrors: Lynch Law in All Its Phases* and *A Red Record* in 1895, reports on lynching that triggered a nationwide antilynching campaign.[4] These printed texts called on African Americans to be active agents in social change by witnessing and documenting racial injustice. With the rise of visual culture in the postwar period, the witness tradition colluded with the historical reality that race in the United States was understood to be easily demarcated through visual markers, creating visual culture as the major negotiator of U.S. cultural politics in relationship to race. This was particularly true in Los Angeles, where the African American participation in visual culture was defined by Hollywood and also by reaction against it.

The visual culture of Los Angeles as it was developing in the period of the Watts rebellion reveals how mechanisms of power were embedded in everyday lived experiences of visuality and hegemony, as well as in the resistance to that power. Los Angeles's history of visual culture was ultimately tied to the city's problematic history of policing, which had historically relied on the visual technique of surveillance as a control in a manner unprecedented in other urban spaces. In his influential study of Los Angeles, *City of Quartz: Excavating the Future in Los Angeles,* Mike Davis cites the cultural importance of the Los Angeles Police Department's pioneering use and development of innovative surveillance technology in the service of policing:

> Technology helped insulate this paranoid *esprit de corps.* In doing so, it virtually established a new epistemology of policing, where technologized surveillance and response supplanted the traditional patrolman's intimate "folk" knowledge of specific communities. Thus back in the 1920s the LAPD had pioneered the replacement of the flatfoot or mounted officer with the radio patrol car—the beginning of dispersed, mechanized policing. Under [William] Parker, ever alert to spinoffs from military technology, the LAPD introduced the first police helicopters for systematic aerial surveillance. After the Watts Rebellion of 1965 this airborne effort became the cornerstone of a policing strategy for the entire inner city. (251–52)

The policing strategies of the Los Angeles Police Department were both causal and symptomatic of the way in which power relations in urban spaces had come to be consciously and unconsciously structured around visuality. This structuring extended far beyond the basic tendency of American state structures to criminalize certain populations solely on the basis of visual cues such as race and ethnicity. The city of Los Angeles instituted and subjected its entire African American population to an oppressive policing regime based on visuality, its structuring principles revolving around visual codes of recognition, surveillance, and identification.

Film theorists have suggested the importance of the look and the gaze as structuring mechanisms not only in the experience of the visual pleasure of film but within the very structuring mechanisms of identity itself. Kaja Silverman posits that "hegemony hinges upon identification; it comes into play when all the members of a collectivity see themselves within the same reflecting surface" (*Male Subjectivity,* 24).

According to Silverman, identity formation is an experience of visuality that involves interiorizing the external through processes of removal that begin at what Jacques Lacan has called the mirror stage. In this stage, the infant first recognizes his or her alterity through recognizing a separation from the mother as symbolized by a first encounter with his or her own *whole* image as reflected in the mirror: "It is only at a second remove that the subject might be said to assume responsibility for 'operating' the gaze by 'seeing' itself being seen even when no pair of eyes are trained upon it—by taking not so much the gaze as its effects within the self. However, consciousness as it is redefined by Lacan hinges not only upon the elision of the gaze; this 'seeing' of oneself being seen is experienced by the subject-of-consciousness—by the subject that is, who arrogates to itself a certain self-presence or substantiality—as a seeing of itself seeing itself" (*Male Subjectivity*, 127). Silverman suggests that the series of reflections and removals involved in the mirror stage might also begin to account for the broader societal phenomena of ideology: "Althusser reconceives the mirror stage as something that occurs on a mass as well as individual level. He thus suggests that societal consensus is not a matter of rational agreement, but of imaginary affirmation. And once again that affirmation is synonymous with the very constitution of the subject" (*Male Subjectivity*, 24). Imaginary affirmation visually constitutes societal consensus and is also responsible for the constitution of the subject. How, then, is subjectivity constituted in a society whose subjects operate under an oppressive visual order?

Feminist film critics initially intervened in film theory to discuss the ways in which the gaze and the look were structured and gendered male by the conventions of classical Hollywood cinema. For example, in "Visual Pleasure and Narrative Cinema," Laura Mulvey questions the assumed universality of dominant cinema's scopic gaze, contending that female bodies and the spectacle of femininity functioned within classic Hollywood cinema to create and code the gaze for the visual pleasure of male spectators, thereby reinforcing existing hegemonic forms of patriarchal oppression. Mulvey states: "The determining male gaze projects its fantasy onto the female figure, which is styled accordingly. In their traditional exhibitionist role women are simultaneously looked at and displayed . . . so that they can be said to connote *to-be-looked-at-ness*" (203).

Kaja Silverman suggests that the visual realm has the power not only to control and reflect existing power relations but also to effect subjectivity at the moment of its formation by laying claim to and manipulating this power of the gaze. Taken together, Mulvey's and Silverman's formulations indicate the power of visual representations to manipulate structures of meaning and to maintain hegemonic ideological and social control. Ultimately, their work, like that of hooks and Diawara, comes close to suggesting that processes of identification and identity formation both create and are created by the social and historical specificity of the group in which the processes occur.

Black Action! Blaxploitation Film Production and the African American Image

An examination of Black action films produced both independently by African Americans and by major Hollywood studios during the Black film explosion of the 1960s and 1970s raises important questions about the African American experience of visuality and identity formation, and the ways in which the look and the gaze of the African American are inextricably linked to a culture of oppression. The widespread popularity of films produced for mass, popular African American audiences, such as *Uptight!* (1968), *Cotton Comes to Harlem* (1970), *Shaft* (1971), *Sweet Sweetback's Baadasssss Song!* (1971), *Super Fly* (1972), *Coffy* (1973), *The Mack* (1973), *Willie Dynamite* (1973), *Foxy Brown* (1974), and *Dolemite* (1975), has typically been accounted for by film historians and cultural critics alike with a "false consciousness" model. In *Redefining Black Film*, Mark Reid states: "Black cultural nationalists and blacks who espoused middle-class values were the most adamant critics of Hollywood-produced black action films" (90). As early as 1971, critics and cultural workers such as Clayton Riley, Roy Innes, Imamu Amiri Baraka (LeRoi Jones), Donald Bogle, Daniel J. Leab, and Lerone Bennett began to criticize the Black moviegoing public for being misled into consuming what Alvin Poussaint, the Harvard psychologist and respected African American public intellectual, labeled in a *Psychology Today* article as "cheap thrills that degrade Blacks" (22). Poussaint, who would later become a consultant for *The Cosby Show*, claimed a direct correlation between the audience's supposed youth and cultural deprivation and a visual depravity that made this audience unusually malleable and ultimately unable to distinguish between the actual facts of their existence and the visual fantasies and ideologies of Hollywood: "Mature adults may see the movie in the context of story-telling; and the average middle-class youth coming from a comfortable home that satisfies most of his physical and emotional needs also may regard them as fiction. On the other hand, when poor young blacks view them, there is a potential for danger. Low-income youngsters who have no real role models to emulate, and an impoverished home life, may mistake fiction for reality" (26).

In discussions of Blaxploitation film, assumptions about the relation of an African American spectatorship to Hollywood in general and the particular viewing habits of that spectatorship often rely on the notion that Black spectatorship is either degraded, infantile, or polluted by the outside forces to which it is subjected. The advent of the Black film boom of the late 1960s and 1970s caused an outpouring of condemnation, ranging from the dismissive comments of Imamu Amiri Baraka that "black films haven't been made," to the outraged formation in Los Angeles of the Coalition against Blaxploitation, organized by civil rights groups to protect African Americans from "another form of cultural genocide."[5] Eric Pearson has rightfully noted in a 2005 issue (one devoted to Blaxploitation film) of *Screening Noir: Journal of Black Film, Television, and New Media Culture* that "earlier Blaxploitation research has focused largely on the negative impact the images exerted on black culture. While this research remains a valuable source for documenting the film movement, contemporary inquiries rooted in cultural studies approaches demand less deterministic assessments of the films, particularly around spectatorship and reception" (5).

By failing to account for the phenomenon of Blaxploitation and the visual pleasure that the African American spectator experiences in relation to these films, or by accounting for it with notions such as false consciousness, theories of spectatorship, and discussions of the African American's relationship to popular culture, overlooked the ambiguities of the consumption of visual culture by African Americans, as well as the complex negotiations in the experience of the gaze that occur for audiences traditionally excluded from dominant fields of visual representation. Blaxploitation films provide a telling counternarrative, not only to myths of white supremacy, but to national myths of visuality and visual culture created in traditional Hollywood cinema and through the conventions of the mass media. On the one hand, Blaxploitation's narrative of ghetto despair deliberately spoke both to the mass news media's inflammatory coverage of events such as the Watts rebellion and to the general coverage of a post–civil rights expression of Black rage in the Black Power era.[6] Mark Reid writes that "urban insurrections were nationally telecast. Images of black inner-city life were formed or reinforced by the television images that portrayed blacks looting stores while buildings burned. Destruction and the destructive seemed to define the black community" (74). On the other hand, however, the powerful imagery of African American masculinity in Blaxploitation films directly responded to Hollywood's problematic history in representing African American masculinity, which ranged from the placid, asexual Sidney Poitier model to the plantation Sambo or the comical Steppin Fetchit.[7]

The genre's reliance on narratives of destruction and hypermasculine empowerment both countered and was complicit in the growing discourse of urban African American criminality, whose foundational roots were in the urban unrest of the 1960s inner city. MGM's 1971 release *Shaft*, widely considered to be the work that began the Black film boom for Hollywood studios, features a narrative about an African American uptown detective who wages a war against the mob by using Harlem street smarts and both uptown and downtown connections. The film is typical of the boom in that its director, Gordon Parks, attempted to negotiate the ambiguous task of selling a policing narrative to an African American audience suspicious of law enforcement by aggressively using African American stylistic conventions and codes. He employed an unprecedented number of African Americans in the production of the film in positions ranging from gaffer to screenwriter in order to give it an "authentic" urban African American "feel."

In some instances, this practice of including African Americans in production arenas from which they had previously been excluded had a notable impact, such as the decision to ask Isaac Hayes to do the film's soundtrack—now widely recognized as a soul classic—and to have an African American advertising firm handle the postproduction marketing of the film. However, despite these groundbreaking production elements, political and ideological ambiguities persisted in the film as well as in the conditions of its production and exhibition. In the film's narrative, John Shaft is a renegade detective using methods outside the law in the service of the law. The audience at the New York City premiere of the movie included "hundreds of Blacks and hundreds of policemen, including Commissioner Patrick Murphy."[8] The event itself had been organized by an African American newspaper and radio station as a benefit for the children of policemen killed in the line of duty (13). Despite the seeming inconsistencies in its ideological methodology and approach, the film was a huge commercial success and sparked the production of Blaxploitation films in several Hollywood studios, helping to usher in major changes in African American film production and inclusion in mainstream filmmaking.

The genre of Blaxploitation, with its discourse of crooked cops and hypermasculine outlaw heroes and its particular visual investment in questions of the look and the gaze, readily spoke not only to Hollywood's exclusion of African Americans from film culture but also to the complicated body politics that had developed in relationship to the lived visual reality of racial hierarchies in the United States, especially as epitomized by the Los Angeles Police Department's overreliance on surveillance and visual cues to demarcate actions, individuals, and entire populations as "criminal." The proliferation of Blaxploitation films at this particular historical moment suggests that the negotiations around the presentation of African American masculine subjectivity on the screen would be a foundational ground of contestation, not only in Hollywood and Los Angeles, but also generally in establishing and defining hegemonic social consent on the role of African Americans in the post–civil rights era in the United States.

"The Revolution Will Not Go Better with Coke" African American Images and Media Culture

The complications and ambiguity in the relationship between African Americans and mass-media visual culture during the Blaxploitation era were most succinctly articulated in Gil Scott-Heron's classic 1970 spoken-word recording "The Revolution Will Not Be Televised," which appears on the record *Ghetto Style*. In this piece, Scott-Heron makes it very clear that though the revolution might not be televised, it and the reformation of African American subjectivity would clearly be a visual event that would expose the hypocrisy of previous televisual media presentations. Scott-Heron's disdain for the revolutionary possibilities of television in its previous incarnations is situated squarely in the middle of a barrage of television metaphors that are meant to mark the inevitability of media-saturated consumer culture while at the same time questioning that consumer culture. Within Scott-Heron's flattened vision of American televisual culture, African American leaders have both produced and been products of a mass media structure that "pimps" them like bottles of dishwashing liquid: "There will be no slow motion or still life of Roy Wilkins strolling through Watts in a red, black, and green liberation jumpsuit that he has been saving for just the proper occasion." Scott-Heron ends his critique of televisual culture by attacking the passivity inherent in the consumerism it presents: "The revolution will not go better with coke. The revolution will not fight the germs that may cause bad breath." Scott-Heron raises a cry for a mass-media-savvy revolution that will rise above a media cycle in which its objects are always already both exploited and exploiting. His narrative is ironically embedded with deep suspicion about whether this revolutionary proposition is even possible.

In creating the genre of Blaxploitation, the film industry took a spectatorial community that had been and was being constituted by the political and cultural configurations of Black Power discourse and simply commodified it into an audience for Blaxploitation. That process of commodification opened new opportunities for the representation of a Black Power discourse on film, but it set significant limitations on the shape of that representation as well. Because the urban African American filmgoing population was thought to be largely young and male, and also because movie-marketing "folk" wisdom dictated that only horror and action movies sold to "ethnic" audiences, formulaic action films dominated the genre.[9]

In an attempt to appeal to an African American urban youth market that was transforming its identity in relationship to Black Power discourse, the genre also focused intensely on an omnipotent, omnipresent African American masculinity, in effect catering to but also proscribing the group that could read and identify with these formulas as a spectatorial community. For Black cast film, more importantly, this created and promoted—because of the presumed and prescribed expectations of that community—a very specifically limited masculinist version of Black Power. Despite its specific limitations, however, the Blaxploitation "superspade" formula was not at all without certain narrative and visual payoffs for its audience. With outlaw heroes such as Priest Youngblood (*Super Fly*) and Willie Dynamite (*Willie Dynamite*) and the dangerous African American masculinity of characters such as Shaft and Dolemite, these films brought into extreme focus the disparate histories of representation clashing in the cultural space of Los Angeles. As such, the films acted to compound the city's complicated history of surveillance, racialized watching, and being watched by opening up a space for the articulation of a Black Power cultural agenda and for the rearticulation of African American folk and popular expressive forms, traditions, and belief systems.

Because African Americans had previously been unable to participate in mainstream film culture, Blaxploitation created unprecedented opportunities for African Americans wishing to gain entry, however tenuous or temporary, to Hollywood studios. It also created opportunities for African Americans who had been working independently or quasi-independently from Hollywood, and thus opened up to mass visual culture expressions of African American culture that had previously not been available on-screen, but only in oral culture or folklore. For example, between 1975 and 1979, Rudy Ray Moore, a legendary underground African American comedian who had already had success independently producing, promoting, and distributing his own comedy record albums, created and starred in a series of films based on the classic toasts ("the signifying monkey"), folklore narratives ("peteey wheatstraw, the devil's son-in-law"), jokes, and traditions of the African American community that had been formulated in the South and carried north to urban areas during the Great Migration. Moore's films successfully mixed this "down-home" humor and "gut bucket" stylistic tradition with a post–civil rights northern urban sensibility that attempted to call the community into the service of a greater good through a tradition of witnessing. With the rise of visual culture in the postprint era, however, the witness tradition took on new and even more significant dimensions. Images of the news-media coverage of civil rights demonstrations, particularly coverage of the March on Washington and Martin Luther King's "I Have a Dream" speech, became much more prevalent in the national imagination of the era than King's "Letter from a Birmingham Jail" or other print material from the period. Within the genre of Blaxploitation, an African American witness tradition that was in the process of developing in relation to dominant mass-media culture began to be refracted through a Hollywood tradition that had already inscribed the look and the gaze to function in the service of dominant culture. The results reveal the powerful importance of visual media in the maintenance or disruption of social and political hierarchies.

The second film in Rudy Ray Moore's "Dolemite" cycle, *The Human Tornado* (1975), which Moore produced and starred in, begins with a commentary not only on the powerful visual nature of race as a social marker but also on the power of the look and the gaze to do and undo social positioning. In the film's opening sequence, two exaggeratedly stereotypical "hillbillies" engage in a dialogue as they stop on a drive past a house where a party is taking place:

Momma: Lookee yonder, somethin's a going on at that big house!

Jethro: Of course somethin's going on up there. Them people's havin' a party.

Momma: Goddamn, Jethro! Them ain't people, them's niggers.

Jethro: By God, yer right! They gotta be niggers cause this ain't Halloween.

The characters of Jethro and Momma are framed throughout the dialogue by the window of the car, creating a visual emphasis on their act of watching as the camera cuts between Jethro and Momma and the members of the party, who are unaware of being watched and do not return the look.

Playing off a folk or "commonsense" understanding of race relations (if whites see Blacks having a good time, they will do everything in their power to break it up), the film declares and explores the aggression implicit in the look as a site of American racial contestation. It is only because Jethro is finally able to see the Blackness of the partygoers, about which he has to be told ("Them ain't people, them's niggers!"), that he decides anything is amiss at the party at all. Jethro's exaggerated stupidity is a common African American folk representation of whiteness as a cognitive failure made possible through privilege. This sort of whiteness results in an inability to see and to recognize, among other things, the basic humanity of others. Jethro's exaggerated stupidity, his privilege, does not allow him even to see what is "wrong" with the party in relation to his own position as white male racist, even as his look is directed at it. The act of looking is then encoded by the opening sequences of *The Human Tornado* as knowledge and power, but true to the logic of African American vernacular culture, it is those with the power who ultimately cannot see.

The film cuts immediately from the opening sequence to a sequence in the local sheriff's office, suggesting a direct relation between Jethro and Momma's gaze and the social and political power of a racist police force. In fact, visual reading and misreading continue to motivate and direct almost all the action that follows the opening sequence. In the scene in the sheriff's office, a deputy sheriff is almost shot when he walks in on the sheriff during a nap. The first thing the sheriff does upon waking is fire his gun, and it is only because he cannot see the deputy, who quickly ducks behind a filing cabinet, that he misses him. The film then cuts back to the party, where the guests see the sheriff's posse on the road below. The sheriff, after intimidating the party guests, discovers his wife in bed with Dolemite, the Human Tornado, in a shot/reverse shot formulation that contrasts the sheriff and the deputy's dumb shock with Dolemite's "cool."

The action of the film really begins here, as the camera cuts frantically between the sheriff's look, the startled, disgusted look of the deputy, the satisfied wife, and the unruffled gaze of Dolemite. In this sequence, it is clearly Dolemite who retains the power of the gaze as well as the ultimate claim to all masculine power that arises from a phallocentric masculinity, not only because of his position in bed with the wife of "The Man," but also through his pivotal positioning in the shot/reverse shot formulation, which continually privileges him as the mediator of all the others' reactions by continuously returning the shot to him. Though *The Human Tornado* lacks an explicitly political agenda, the ways in which it reimagines, reframes, and rescripts issues of masculinity, display, the gaze, and power are indicative of the ways in which Black Power cultural politics saturates and are at the core of the Blaxploitation boom.

"Trivial and Tasteless, Neither Revolutionary nor Black"
African American Masculinity and Body Politics

Melvin Van Peebles's 1971 film *Sweet Sweetback's Baadasssss Song!* contains a powerful critique of policing and police brutality that is informed by Black Power politics and centers on watching, performance, and the power of the gaze, but it also represents a uniquely African American perspective on issues of the spectacle, spectatorship, gender, and sexuality in the experience of visuality. Opening with the dedication "To All the Brothers and Sisters who've had enough of the Man," *Sweet Sweetback's Baadasssss Song!* revolves around Sweet Sweetback, an ostensibly "ordinary" oppressed brother who uses every available resource, including most prominently his sexual prowess, to liberate himself from the emasculating constraints of a Los Angeles ghetto existence.

Sweetback is working as a "stud"—a brothel sex-show performer—when he is "lent" out to police to "perform" as the main suspect in a murder case. On the way to the station, the police stop to break up an antipolice demonstration, and they brutalize a young activist. Sweetback reacts from a gut level of political consciousness, freeing the activist by beating the policeman with the handcuffs he is wearing and his bare hands. Thus begins Sweetback's journey not only to evade the police but also toward gaining an emancipatory understanding of his own and other African Americans' position in the ghetto. Ultimately, it is a liberatory African American consciousness, coupled with an innate resourcefulness in relation to the use of his body, that proves to be Sweetback's salvation. In the short course of his flight to freedom, Sweetback manages to kill an armed policeman with nothing but a pool cue, defeat a motorcycle gang with his penis, cure a gunshot wound with his own urine and sand, use his foot to kill a lizard and then consume it whole for nourishment, kill a pack of police dogs with his bare hands, and eventually escape to Mexico. The film ends with a still shot of the U.S./Mexican border and the promise that "A Baadasssss Nigger is coming back to collect some dues."

With this wish-fulfillment narrative of masculine emancipation, *Sweet Sweetback's Baadasssss Song!* virtually invented the "superspade" narrative formula that almost all later Blaxploitation films would follow. Van Peebles's film, however, with its experimental visual style, innovative soundtrack, and Black Power agenda, clearly attempted to do much more than simply re-create a typical Hollywood formulaic action-adventure film in blackface, as did many of the Blaxploitation films that would follow it. The film, a commercial success grossing $10 million in the first few months of its initial release, was so provocatively innovative in relation to the spectacle of Blackness in and through the body that it sparked predictable controversy about African American representation and what exactly was meant by African American empowerment.

In *Framing Blackness: The African American Image in Film*, Ed Guerrero writes, "*Sweetback* brought to the surface of African American discourse the subtle fissures and cracks of class tension, ideological conflict, and aesthetic arguments that had been simmering in the black social formation since the winding down of the civil rights movement" (87). For supporters and detractors alike, the film raised a number of questions about race, representations of masculinity, and the possibilities for Black emancipation (Bogle, 238). As Guerrero indicates, the exact ideological and aesthetic configuration that African American liberation would or should take was very much open to vigorous debate in the highly charged political context that arose immediately following the civil rights era. In one of the more polemical pieces ever printed in *Ebony Magazine*, the noted scholar and editor Lerone Bennett declared the film "trivial and tasteless, neither revolutionary nor black" (qtd. in Leab, 248–49). He went on to decry both the film's politics and its ideological underpinnings: "Nobody ever fucked his way to freedom. And it is mischievous and reactionary . . . for anyone to suggest to black people in 1971 that they are going to be able to screw their way across the Red Sea. . . . If fucking freed, black people would have celebrated the millennium 400 years ago."

The film's capacity to provoke such a strong reaction emanated from its ability to condense tensions regarding class, community, spectacle, and the African American body into a narrative formula that emphasized not only the possibilities of liberation but also ambivalences around its eventual attainment. Huey P. Newton was so taken by the film that he devoted an entire issue of *The Black Panther*, the Black Panther Party's official newspaper, to examining its relevance as an African American community event. In the long editorial analysis of the film that appeared in the paper, Newton praised it as an exemplar of Black Power politics, stating, "If you understand where the Panther is coming from, you will understand that Sweet Sweetback is a beautiful exemplification of Black Power" (*To Die for the People*, 139). He further wrote of the film: "It is the first truly revolutionary Black film made and it is presented to us by a Black man . . . it shows how the victims must deal with their situation, using many institutions and many approaches. It demonstrates that one of the key routes to survival and the success of our resistance is unity . . . it does all of this by using many aspects of the community, but in symbolic terms. That is, Van Peebles is showing one thing on the screen but saying something more to the audience. In other words he is signifying, and he is signifying some very heavy things" (*To Die for the People*, 112–13). Newton concludes his lengthy evaluation of the film by asserting that *Sweet Sweetback*'s power lay in its ability to act as an agent of community building: "*Sweet Sweetback* helps put forth the ideas of what we must do to build community. We need to see it often and learn from it" (147).

A large part of the film's relevance to Newton, Bennett, and others lay in its careful negotiation of the history and negative mythology surrounding encodings of African American masculinity, scripted with an emphasis on performance, the gaze, and visual dissimulation. As Frantz Fanon pointed out in *Black Skin, White Masks*, postcolonial encounters with African American masculinity are demarcated by a regime of visuality that heightens the symbolic fetishization of the body until "one is no longer aware of the Negro, but only of a penis: The Negro is eclipsed. He is turned into a penis. He *is* a penis" (177). *Sweet Sweetback's Baadasssss Song!* literalizes the conflation of Black masculinity and phallocentric power but empowers the bearer of the image with the ability to fight back.

Blaxploitation as a genre was primarily focused on beautiful Black phallocentric masculinity as epitomized by many of the genre's major stars—

Jim Kelly, Jim Brown, Fred Williamson—who were former professional athletes. The display of the African American male body within a discourse of sexual prowess created a need for specific negotiations regarding that display, and Blaxploitation film by necessity had to negotiate the anxiety arising out of the genre's explicit showcasing of sexuality and the explicit display of the African American male form for a mass consumption. Van Peebles's film is striking in that in establishing the formula for the Blaxploitation films that would follow, it created a masculinity that is empowered by a sexuality that, in terms of the film's visual display, it barely enacts. This is to say that Sweetback, though supposedly legendary for his sexual prowess, rarely performs anything other than the "missionary position" in the film, and even this is done with as little expressivity as possible. Sweetback's generative power to create community is thus predicated on a rigidly masculine display of emotive and physical inaction.

In the opening credits of the film, Sweet Sweetback is both named and constituted as a character through a sexual performance in which his virility is naturalized but not necessarily visually demonstrated. In this establishing sequence, a preadolescent Sweetback receives his nickname during his first sexual encounter, which occurs with a prostitute in the brothel where he works as a towel boy. The woman, who initially even has to instruct the young boy to remove his hat, is eventually so overcome by his sexual performance—a performance in which he barely moves, lacks any sort of facial expression, and doesn't speak—that she cries out, "Oh son, you got a Sweet Sweetback." The image of the boy then dissolves into an image of Sweetback as an adult in the same position with the same woman, who remains in the same throes of ecstasy. The sequence, which ends as Sweetback replaces his hat, displays the character's sexuality while distancing him, through inaction, from becoming the visual spectacle of that display. This type of prove-and-show negotiation is constantly repeated throughout the film and, in some ways, becomes the real object of display. Though within the narrative of the film Sweetback makes his living by performing sexual acts for the gratification of racially mixed audiences in a police-protected brothel, the film seems determined that the Sweetback character not provide the same gratification for the film's audience even as it is always, importantly, suggesting the possibility that he could.

Unlike most Blaxploitation films, *Sweet Sweetback's Baadasssss Song!* explicitly attempted to script the exact relationship between a sexual practice and an emancipatory practice. Sweetback's masculine power is definitely located in his male physique in general and in his penis specifically, but while Sweetback is able to use every other aspect of his environment in ways that are both innovative and active, his use of his penis remains remarkably ideologically, visually, and physically static and stationary. In fact, Sweetback barely has to move at all to please women, and as the opening sequence suggests through its use of the image of the boy dissolving into the man and its repetition of images like the hat and the prostitute, there is little difference between the performance of the preadolescent Sweetback and the adult. He is, in the words of the director Melvin Van Peebles, "a natural" (18).

Sweetback's sexual prowess and politics, the film would have us believe, are as innate as his revolutionary potential and are, therefore, beyond the need for any close examination or analysis by the film. The sequence's use of montage cuts that reference Sweetback's later run from the law—scenes of traffic, running feet, and train whistles—would seem to indicate that there are parallels between sexual movement and the other sorts of revolutionary movement that guarantee survival. It is the latter, however, that are clearly privileged. The static nature of Sweetback's sexual performance has the important consequence of closing off sexuality as a dynamic arena for a revolutionary praxis. To see that, one need only contrast Sweetback's powerful appropriative use of police handcuffs as a weapon against policemen in the service of a young African American activist with his static use of his penis and the possibilities that shuts down. Huey P. Newton writes of the film's power to say "something more to the audience" and to "signify some very heavy things" in "symbolic terms"; however, the film would seem to contradictorily suggest that though sexuality is of deadly importance to a liberation struggle, sexual politics is not a significant area for revolutionary analysis or praxis. Rather than evolve new strategies from a positive politics of desire for coping with the oppressive realities that ensnare African Americans' minds, bodies, and the way those bodies are displayed, the film ultimately seems to suggest that African American men need only do what comes "naturally" in order to survive.

"Shaft Can Do Everything—I Can Do Nothing"
Visual Pleasure and the Possibilities and Limitations of Blaxploitation Film

The *New York Times* film critic Clayton Riley was one of the first prominent African Americans to criticize the consequences of the new genre's encoding of African American masculine empowerment in an aptly titled condemnation of the 1971 film *Shaft,* "Shaft Can Do Everything—I Can Do Nothing." Though the director Gordon Parks Sr. described his film as one that people might attend "to see a Black guy winning," Riley suggests, as the title of the review implies, that Blaxploitation films provide a dangerously simplistic fantasy of African American masculine hyperempowerment, which has the effect of making American audiences more passive about the real injustices that African Americans face.

Most film reviewers, critics, and historians of African American cinema, including Ed Guererro, Donald Bogle, and Daniel J. Leab, have concurred with Riley's assessment of the visual pleasure that African American audiences experience in relation to Blaxploitation films, a visual pleasure that consists of a basic and simplistic identification with an inversion of the traditional racial ordering of Hollywood. In *From Sambo to Superspade,* Leab writes: "The industry recognized that what the mass of Black moviegoers wanted was not just black participation in films. . . . As *Variety* informed its readers, 'black moviegoers don't cotton to such pix, as they feature blacks in a losing light.' What moviegoers wanted to see was what John Shaft and Sweetback had offered them. Superspade was a violent man who lived a violent life in pursuit of black women, white sex, quick money, easy success, cheap 'pot,' and other pleasures" (253–54).

Donald Bogle speaks similarly of the appeal of *Sweet Sweetback's Baadasssss Song:* "The fact that a black man met violence with violence and triumphed over the corrupt white establishment appealed . . . to the mass black audience (particularly the young who flocked to it). Then, too, after decades of comic asexual black male characters . . . audiences were ready for a sexual black movie hero" (235). However, with its explicit political agenda that foregrounds the act of watching and witnessing as an act of resistance, combined with its emphasis on the ambiguity that surrounds performance, particularly sexual performance, and display, *Sweet Sweetback's Baadasssss Song!* suggests that more is actually at stake in the consumption of Black action films than simple visual "payback" on the part of a militant, or at least angry, African American audience in a Black Power era.

In *Redefining Black Film,* Mark Reid writes: "The emergence of studio-distributed black action films corresponds to the Black community's increasing rejection of nonviolent protest. Black action films are a popularized version of this discontent" (70). The hypothesis that studio-produced films were "the popularized version" of Black Power would seem to echo Parks's explanation that African American moviegoing audiences simply wanted to "see a Black guy winning for a change." Both these explanations ignore the complexities of how spectators were experiencing processes of identification in relation to these films, and they fail to account for how viewing communities were constituted by and in relation to these films. In film studies, the question of visual pleasure has revolved around possibilities for filmic identification. As Kaja Silverman writes in "Suture": "The classic cinematic organization depends upon the subject's willingness to become absent to itself by permitting a fictional character to 'stand in' for it, or by allowing a particular point of view to define what it sees. The operation of suture is successful at the moment that the viewing subject says 'Yes, that's me,' or 'That's what I see'" (222).

As Manthia Diawara points out, though generally the work of feminist theorists has done much to further film theory's understanding of dominance and spectatorship, it has failed for the most part to examine the dynamics of race or racialized spectatorship in either dominant or alternative cinema (211). The question of how visual pleasure is constituted for the racialized spectator, particularly in relation to the spectacle of race created in Hollywood studios, remains, according to Diawara, largely unanswered. In Diawara's model of "resistant spectatorship," African American audiences form and are formed by resistant spectatorship because of the contradictory nature of their identification in relation to Hollywood-produced movies, which deny them easy identification with either African American or non-African American characters on the screen. Quoting Frantz Fanon's declaration that "every spectator is a coward or a traitor," Diawara argues in favor of a "cinema of the real" that would challenge the passive identificatory position of the viewer, making all spectatorship "a resistant spectatorship" (219). Diawara locates this "cinema of the real" with African American independent directors such as "Charles Burnett, Billie Woodberry, and Warrington Hudlin . . . Larry Clark, Julie Dash, Haile Gerima and Alile Sharon Larkin" (219).

Diawara's model of "resistant spectatorship" and his suggestion of a "cinema of the real" provide a useful starting point for understanding the often ambiguous and contradictory nature of identification and spectatorship for racialized subjects. His model fails, however, to account for any sort of visual pleasure that African Americans spectators might experience in relation to the mainstream Hollywood film productions that he criticizes, such as *Forty-Eight Hours* and *Beverly Hills Cop*, both of which enjoyed enormous popularity among urban African American audiences. This results at least partially from Diawara's failure to theorize popular film culture in terms of resistance. He canonizes African American independent film directors, most of whom are members of what Ntogela Masilela has termed "the Los Angeles School of Black Filmmakers," without problematizing the "art house" nature of the products they produce and their limited reception within the African American community.

All the directors Diawara mentions, with the exception of Warrington Hudlin, studied filmmaking in UCLA's prestigious Theater Arts Department. The films they produced, though notable, have had extremely limited reception outside of a specialized, cinephile audience. Only Hudlin has worked regularly for Hollywood studios as well as producing his own independent films, and his work includes the popular films *Bebe's Kids* (1992) and *House Party* (1983). *Sweet Sweetback's Baadasssss Song!* and other popular culture films like it raise important questions about the identificatory possibilities widely available to African American spectators within popular culture, and begin to question notions of identification, spectacle, and spectatorship itself.

In *Sweet Sweetback's Baadasssss Song!* Van Peebles charts his lessons of resourcefulness and Black unity narratively through Sweetback's flight, which is always meant to refer to and invoke the historical memory of slavery. Yet the film does not rely on narrative strategies alone to teach resistance; instead, it institutes a unique spectatorship of resistance that calls into question the passivity and cowardice that surrounds the act of watching as constructed by Hollywood film. This strategy urges an active participation on the part of spectators that exists in but also extends beyond the experience of the film, since the film is visually and aurally structured around audience participation and "talk back." *Sweet Sweetback's Baadasssss Song!* relies on the spectator to supply the dialogue and "fill in the blanks" of the visual experience of the film and in this way alters the standard Hollywood process of suture.

The structure of *Sweetback* not only caters to audience reaction and encourages the audience to "talk back" but also actually necessitates it. Charged moments in the narrative, such as the police beating of Sweetback and the young Black activist, are cinematically structured around blank or white noise spaces in the sound track with little or no dialogue. These blank "reaction moments" are meant to be filled in with active audience participation. What is most immediately striking about the film, however, is that the main character almost never speaks. In fact, though he is almost always on the screen, he has fewer than five lines throughout the entire feature-length film. Huey P. Newton theorizes that the character of Sweetback lacks dialogue "because the movie is not starring Sweetback, it is starring the Black community. Most of the audiences at the movie are Black and they talk to the screen. They supply the dialogue because all of us are Sweetback. . . . So the thing to do is not just see the film, but also to recognize how you the viewer are also an actor in the film, for you are as much a victim of this oppressive system as Sweetback" (*To Die for the People,* 131). Van Peebles attributes the film's starring role in the opening credits to "The Black Community." Sweetback's journey is very much meant to mirror the spectators' own journey to consciousness as they participate vocally in the experience of the film. Concern with collectivity and community was foundational to Black Power politics and culture, so much so that Newton's editorial on the film was the product of carefully documented collective discussion and debate and numerous rewrites and rereadings by various Black Panther Party members and affiliated scholars. For the film, the collective journey of the spectators to consciousness is meant to be visual as well as vocal, since it is facilitated as much by Sweetback's lack of interpretive facial expressions and physical gestures as it is by the lack of dialogue.

Visually, Sweetback is foregrounded by the film as a spectator of the important events that occur around him. An extreme close-up shot of Sweetback's blank, witnessing face recurs throughout the film, and a still of this same shot was used in almost all the promotional material used to advertise the film. It is Sweetback's position as silent witness that is called into question as he watches police beat Moo-Moo, the Black activist. When he acts to save Moo-Moo, he changes narratively and cinematically from passive spectator to active resistant spectator, and this is a change the audience is supposed to make as well. Rather than passively consuming the film through the vehicle of the character of Sweetback, the spectator is asked to fill in the blanks of his visual imagery with his or her own interpretation. It is this process of filling in the blanks that creates a spectatorship of resistance, a spectatorship that requires active and vocal participation throughout and after the film, rather than creating and facilitating the quietly introspective spectators of Hollywood cinema. Nevertheless, while the film attempts to pioneer a unique relationship to spectatorship, it is, finally, the ambiguity of Sweetback's position as object of the gaze that raises the most interesting questions with respect to spectatorship and the film.

Sweet Sweetback's Baadasssss Song! garnered much attention when it received an X rating from an all-white jury of the Motion Picture Association of America, and much is made of the film's reliance on the hypermasculinized "superstud" portrayal of its main character. In this film, as in other Black action movies of the 1960s and 1970s, African American male sexuality, long suppressed in dominant visual representation, was finally foregrounded, and, in the words of Donald Bogle, "the bucks took center stage" (238). Blaxploitation's creation of the "superspade" or "buck" character put African American male sexuality on display in a manner previously unavailable to audiences. Suddenly, both aggression and sexuality were made available to African American male characters. This emphasis on sexuality and sexual display, however, positioned the "buck" character as a spectacle, thus fulfilling the function of *to-be-looked-at-ness*, a function usually assigned by Hollywood to women. Sweetback as a professional "stud"—a performer in sex shows for money—epitomizes the ambivalence of that display more than any other character of the Blaxploitation era. Rather than being hollowly empowered in the "buck" fashion that Bogle, Bennett, and others suggest, Sweetback's character serves as a commentary on the ambivalent possibilities of such representation even as it is complicit in the presentation of a shallow, stereotypical Black masculine sexual prowess.

Sweet Sweetback's Baadasssss Song! insists on a static, heterosexual, hypermasculine representation as a way of negotiating and ultimately insisting on masculinity, and this has significant consequences for the notion of spectacle as well. In "Masculinity as Spectacle," Steve Neale notes how the ambiguity around the male as the object of the gaze is negotiated in Hollywood cinema through the staging of sadomasochistic fantasies of aggression in order to disavow and repress the eroticism involved in the act of looking at the male form: "Hence both forms of voyeuristic looking . . . are especially evident in moments of contest and combat . . . those moments at which male struggle becomes pure spectacle. Perhaps the most extreme examples are to be found in Leone's westerns, where the exchange of aggressive looks marking most western gun duels is taken to the point of fetishistic parody through the use of extreme and repetitive close-ups. . . . The narrative starts to freeze and the spectacle takes over" (284). In *Sweet Sweetback's Baadasssss Song!* the spectacle and the specter of the African American male penis always have the upper hand as the eroticism that surrounds the act of looking is laid bare by both the narrative and the cinematic structure of the film. *Sweetback* successfully narrativizes the ideological fixation on African American male sexual prowess in that Sweetback's character is the embodiment of the African American phallic superman (or "supernigger") ideal. The film is equally invested in the cinematic representation of that ideal as it stages and restages the triumph of African American phallic mastery against all odds, reveling in its final display of full frontal male nudity.

Sweetback's particular investment in the spectacle of Black phallic power is especially evidenced in the "duel" sequence that occurs when Sweetback and the Black activist he has rescued are discovered hiding in the woods by a hostile motorcycle gang. When Sweetback is challenged to choose his weapon, he responds with one of only four lines of dialogue that he has in the film. Sweetback's answer to the white female gang leader's challenge to choose a weapon is, predictably, "fucking." She accepts this challenge. In this sequence, the eroticism of the duel and the highly sexual nature of voyeuristic looking are opened up as the male combat scene that Steve Neale outlines is made explicitly sexual. As a sexual performer, Sweetback is more active in this sequence than he has been in the film's previous sex scenes, using more than the standard missionary position, but the film's repetitive use of freeze-frames and stills reinforces and reinstates a masculinity that is ultimately static and all-powerful. This use of stills and freeze-frames operates, in its repetitive presentation of similar static images, to reify Black male sexuality as active and omnipotent, possessing even the power to stop narrative.

As the members of the white male motorcycle gang provide, through their cheers, a rhythm for Sweetback's sex, Van Peebles attempts to name the stereotypes of Black masculinity at the same time that he wants to claim some of their power. Van Peebles's Sweetback transcends the immobile, hidden masculine power at the heart of John Wayne and opens up the hidden exchange of masculine power encoded in the western duel scene but, typically, stops just short of transforming that paradigm. Sweetback is representative of Blaxploitation's attempt to both represent and transcend the "Negro is penis" formulation.

Sexual Politics, Film Production, and Its Implications for Black Power Culture

It is impossible to divorce Blaxploitation's means of production from its filmic outcomes. The effects and influence of the sort of ambivalent sexual politics displayed by *Sweet Sweetback* are evident not only in the visual experience of the film itself but also in its production history. One of Van Peebles's main objectives, as outlined in his film diaries, was to have "50% of my shooting crew to be third world people," though he conceded that this might cause the crew to be "relatively inexperienced" and possibly nonunion (11). In Van Peebles's own words, "any type of film requiring an enormous sophistication at the shooting stage should not be attempted"; this meant that he was forced to shoot the only kind of film that could be made when utilizing a nonunion crew: a pornographic film.

Because Van Peebles, working in great secrecy, claimed to be making a pornographic film, union production regulations of all kinds were greatly relaxed. This allowed him—the film's writer, director, producer, and star— to shoot the film quickly and cheaply, completing it in just nineteen days with a budget of approximately $500,000 (Bogle, 238). Employing a nonunion crew also allowed Van Peebles to involve more African Americans in the film's production, because although the Hollywood chapter of the NAACP had been agitating for years for more African American inclusion in Hollywood production, African Americans still constituted significantly less than 10 percent of film union membership, and most African Americans who were in film unions were trained as projectionists (Guerrero, 85).

Much of *Sweet Sweetback's Baadasssss Song!* is directly constituted by these facts of the film's production. In scripting African American subjectivity into the category typically allocated to it by mainstream culture—that of low-budget pornography—Van Peebles was able to produce a film with a revolutionary agenda, but those low-budget pornographic constrictions had a predictable and final impact on the film's narrative and visual possibilities. The consequence is the creation of a genre in which scenes "requiring an enormous sophistication at the shooting stage" would not, in Van Peebles's words, "be attempted" and in which the deployment of narrative strategies tended to ossify the notion that the "Negro is penis" (Fanon, 11).

Not unlike Van Peebles's attempts to co-opt the category of pornography in the service of revolutionary politics, Black Power cultural politics in general had long sought to exploit visuality and negotiate the dominant media's attendant stereotyping in order to create strategies of resistance and empowerment. Black Power advocates carefully articulated an image of masculine muscle and military might most trenchantly exemplified by the clenched and raised Black fist, which became its key symbol. Eldridge Cleaver, who would become the Black Panther Party's controversial Minister of Information, recalls his first encounter with the party as a moment of powerful visuality: "I spun around in my seat and saw the most beautiful sight I had ever seen; four Black men wearing Black berets, powder blue shirts, black leather jackets, black trousers, shiny black shoes—and each with a gun" (*Post-Prison Writings and Speeches*, 29).

The Black Panther Party carefully exploited the predictable hysteria and rampant media attention given to the public spectacle of an armed Black militia to redirect attention to the violation of African American bodies in the courtroom and on the streets of America. Images of the Black Panther Party cofounder Bobby Seale bound and gagged in the courtroom during the highly publicized conspiracy trial, and images of the incarcerated prison leader and party member George Jackson and other victims of police and state brutality were printed in the party's newspaper and widely distributed. According to Newton's autobiography, the paper was initially created to draw public attention to the issues surrounding the case of Denzil Dowell, murdered while in the custody of the Contra Costa County Sheriff's Department in 1967 (*Revolutionary Suicide*, 138). Images of African Americans and women brutalized by the institutions of the U.S. government competed with and also completed the mandate that the stylized dissent and militarized order of the black beret, black trousers, black leather jacket, and powder blue shirt presented.

The French poet and playwright Jean Genet noted the powerfully primal nature of their visual performance of dissent when he wrote in *Prisoner of Love*, published some years after he first encountered the Panthers, that "the world can be changed by other means than the sort of wars in which people die. Power comes at the end of a gun but it's also at the end of the shadow or the image of a gun" (98). Observing that "the Panthers attacked first by sight" (246), Genet consequently paints the Panthers' assault on the senses as so profoundly primal as to be sexually charged: "When the Panthers' Afro haircuts hit the Whites in the eye, the ear, the nostril and the neck, and even got under their tongues, they were panic stricken. How could they defend themselves in the subway, the office and the lift against all this vegetation, this springing, electric, elastic growth like an extension of pubic hair? The laughing Panthers wore a dense furry sex on their heads. The whites could only have replied with non-existent laws of politeness. Where could they have found insults fierce enough to smooth all those hairy, sweaty black faces, where every curly whisker on each black chin had been nurtured and cherished for dear life?" (252). For Genet, victory in the realm of visual culture is not substantially different from the sorts of victory celebrated by Che Guevara and Regis Debray, who understood propaganda as at best little more than a branding/advertising for revolution rather than a revolution in and of itself. Since "the Panthers' subversion would take place . . . in people's conscience," Genet declared ultimately, "The Panthers can be said to have overcome with poetry" (99, 100).

The circulation of Black Panther Party imagery and other images of Black Power was not strictly limited to "storefront-window organizing projects" and other manifestations of radical-fringe America, but had won, as Gil Scott-Heron indicated, a spot in America's prime time. American popular culture seemed to need the images of the Black Panthers and the material struggles they evoked to begin to negotiate America's changing relationship to its urban African American population every bit as much as the media-savvy Panthers needed American popular culture to disseminate its plan for radical social change. The clenched, raised fist, the Panther uniform, "Free Huey," the Black Panther symbol were all steps in symbolically articulating a theory of urban violence for mainstream America and began to offer a way to make sense of the civil disturbances and social upheaval occurring throughout the country.

Arising directly from the visual culture that the Black Panther Party had created, *Sweet Sweetback's Baadasssss Song!* arrived in 1971 to urban movie theaters in a hail of media controversy largely instigated by Van Peebles's protests against the racist practices of the Motion Picture Association of America and its designation of an X rating for the film. The roughly crafted, sexually explicit film was originally allowed to open in only two theaters nationwide, but it would end up one of the highest grossing films of the year and one of the highest grossing independent films ever. Understanding how the film sold to a mass audience the antipolice story of Sweetback's conversion to a Black Power consciousness is key in understanding the wider functioning of Black Power cultural politics in America.

Patricia A. Turner's theorization of the function of race-related rumors in the African American community contributes to an understanding of the potent need for the circulation of Blaxploitation's narratives in an American culture torn by racial conflict. For example, Turner explores the nearly parasitic attachment of rumors and riots to times of civil unrest (46). Using the turbulent times in East St. Louis in 1917, Chicago in 1919, and Belle Isle Detroit in 1943 as case studies, she investigates the way in which almost identical rumors circulated in both African American and white communities concerning the violation and violence occurring in the area. However, these narratives, which shared paradigmatic structures, did not produce similar outcomes for both groups. Rather, the circulation of these rumors resulted in a pattern of African American victimization with the white community spurred on to be victimizers.

Turner's research suggests that though reciprocally exclusive groups can share an identical paradigm, the function of that paradigm within those communities can be markedly divergent. The same narrative of violence that spurs the white community to violently attack nonwhites may function when circulated among African Americans simply to solidify group identification or to serve as a cautionary tale about the behavior of those outside the group. With its focus on the journey to consciousness of a prototypical, yet exemplary, Black brother who acts as both a stand-in and a guide for the ghetto oppressed, *Sweet Sweetback's Baadasssss Song!* fits neatly into the traditional patterns of African American folk culture, which extend back to the earliest traces of an African presence in American culture. The film's visual marking of the physicality of that journey, as well as its insistence on representing the brutalization of Sweetback's body at the hands of the police, offers its African American viewers, through the folkloric specificity of its visual coding, the opportunity to collectively reconstitute subjectivity. *Sweet Sweetback's Baadasssss Song!*, and Blaxploitation in general, allowed the African American spectator to formulate a spectatorial position based on and around a challenge to dominant cultural practices and viewing habits. Blaxploitation created a means for the African American spectator to enact the urgency in one of Frantz Fanon's concluding pronouncements in *Black Skin White Masks:* "In the world through which I travel, I am endlessly creating myself" (229).

The film allowed a mainstream audience the opportunity to maintain, and even potentially enhance, its view of African American masculinity as threatening, sexually potent, and extremely dangerous at the same time that it allowed an African American audience to enjoy the opportunity to identify with that threat and imagine the possibilities of its potential. Because the film highlights the importance of the historical and social positioning of spectatorship to the experience of film itself, *Sweet Sweetback's Baadasssss Song!* ultimately calls into question the limits of both the revolutionary and the repressive possibilities of visual culture, while highlighting its importance as a continued site for struggle.

Conclusion

DICK GREGORY AT THE PLAYBOY CLUB

> I understood nothing. I was black and they were black,
> but my blackness did not help me.
> —Richard Wright in *Black Power! A Record of
> Reactions in a Land of Pathos*

Despite the fact that Richard Wright's *Black Power! A Record of Reactions in a Land of Pathos* was one of the first widely disseminated texts to use the term "Black Power," it is profoundly ambivalent in relation to intraracial unity, the notion of a shared racial memory, and the African liberation movements that the Black Power movement would later celebrate. Wright, who went to Ghana on the eve of its liberation in 1953 as a guest of Kwame Nkrumah, experienced Africa as both intensely alienating and intensely familiar. As Wright's title suggests, his exploration of Africa was guided by his sense of it as a place of sadness and an ambivalent place of ancestry. Wright saw himself as part anthropologist, part person of African descent, part Western, and part political activist and commentator rather than as a lost son returning home. His presumption provoked an ontological crisis in which he not only continuously questioned the relationship between Africans and people of African descent in the diaspora, he also expressed apprehension with regard to racial unity as the necessary structuring foundation for national liberation. Wright's inability to translate his experiences into the familiar and the knowable becomes the book's constant refrain: "I understood nothing, nothing. . . . My mind reeled at the newness and strangeness of it. Had my ancestors acted like that? And why?" Wright says after wandering into a local funeral (144). When confronted by the enthusiasm of Nkrumah's supporters at a political rally, he wonders, "How much am I a part of this?" (63).

Black Power! is permeated with anxiety about a project of national liberation that Wright wanted to believe in, the historical reality of African economic underdevelopment, and his own misgivings about the value of calls for race-based unity. When he died an expatriate in France in 1960, he simply could not have anticipated that within fifteen years of the publication of *Black Power!* in 1954, a cultural, political, and social revolution that labeled itself "Black Power" would erupt in the United States. Kwame Nkrumah's revolutionary movement and liberation struggles like it across Africa would be one of the important catalysts to calls for Black liberation in the United States. In *Seize the Time* Bobby Seale justified naming his son after Nkrumah by observing: "All we have to do is organize a state like Nkrumah attempted to do" (157). In "Black Power in the International Context," Larry Neal examined the role of Nkrumah's revolution in African American liberation as one of exchange, noting that "the NAACP under DuBois's direction established a viable Pan-Africanism—a Pan-Africanism which greatly influenced nationalist leaders like Kwame Nkrumah" (157). Stokely Carmichael, who had made the initial call for Black Power in 1966, would eventually leave the United States for permanent residence in Africa, taking the name Kwame Ture in honor of his relationship to Kwame Nkrumah.

Though Wright was supportive of African liberation movements, he continued to express ambivalence regarding many of their practices. Chief among his concerns about Nkrumah's developing liberation movement was the difficulty of creating a unifying bond among the divergent groups to potentially constitute the free nation of Ghana, including both a large peasant class that was divided by ethnic affiliations and a European educated elite. He thought that the former might resort to a fanaticism and ritual that mystified rather than revealed the workings of power that it initially sought to undo. His section on Nkrumah opens with a quotation from Everett V. Stonequist's claim in *The Marginal Man* that "African revolts are frequently a mixture of religious fanaticism and anti-European sentiment" (35). Wright also reveals how Nkrumah's party skillfully manipulated a broadly based religiosity and developed a model of national culture that could create a unifying passion among the divergent groups of people who would eventually constitute the Ghanaian nation. The Black Power and Black Arts movements would be subjected to some of the same tensions that Wright saw developing in Ghana's liberation struggle, because they were charged not only with critiquing the models of political, social, and cultural inclusion created by the Civil Rights Movement but also with developing a cultural apparatus to help unify and address the needs of an African American community becoming fractured as a result of desegregation.

The early moments of desegregation not only provided economic possibilities but also proved to be fertile ground for hitherto unimaginable collaborative possibilities. Integration did more than change social conditions, it also created novel possibilities for innovation as cultures that had previously been segregated came into contact. In 1962 Dick Gregory's *From the Back of the Bus* was introduced by an essay from the modern lifestyle and sexual-revolution guru Hugh Hefner. Hefner notes that Gregory began his career as a controversial comedian and civil rights activist doing stand-up comedy in Hefner's Playboy Club, where he experienced success unprecedented for an African American comedian in a white nightclub and famously quipped: "Isn't this the most fascinating country in the world? Where else would I have to ride on the back of the bus, have a choice of going to the worst schools, eating in the worst restaurants, living in the worst neighborhoods—and average $5,000 a week just to talk about it?" Gregory's presence, in the words of the contemporary African American comedian Bernie Mac, "shook things the hell up" as he consistently played the Playboy Club in Chicago for over three years, regularly selling out the venue in the early 1960s and becoming the first African American comedian to enjoy such success (Mac, 226).

The combination of Gregory's timely social critique and Hefner's entrepreneurial spirit was fitting in an era in which liberation would become both business and art. The relationship between Hefner's marketing of sexual liberation as a form of urbane sophistication and Gregory's commodified social commentary as a type of insider cool typified the unique production limitations and opportunities created soon after segregation had ended. If the Civil Rights Movement successfully made racism into a moral failing, the Black Power movement successfully recast the relationship between urban culture, modernity, and African American identity, thereby establishing African American authenticity as defining hip, urban authenticity and cool. Gregory would title his autobiography *Up from Nigger* in a tongue-in-cheek vernacular wordplay on Booker T. Washington's ode to humble self-sufficiency, *Up from Slavery*. By defining African American identity outside its traditional boundaries and limitations, imagining it as empowered with both opportunity and possibility, the Black Power movement both highlighted the critique of postindustrial culture inherent in the celebration of urban vernacular culture by Black Arts Movement poets such as Haki Madhubuti, Larry Neal, and Amiri Baraka, and also created an astounding array of aesthetic and cultural innovations.

While increasing civil rights continued to recraft the relationship between African Americans and the dominant culture, participants in the Black Power movement dreamt of artistic and social change so profoundly cataclysmic that they imagined "the end of the world has already happened," as the musician Sun Ra and his Arkestra would claim in the 1974 film *Space Is the Place*. In one scene in the film, Sun Ra interviews candidates for positions in his space program, a scenario that would have been simply unimaginable even in science fiction just twenty-five years earlier. Though in the film it is representatives of NASA who joke about being equal opportunity employers who will put "a coon on the moon by June," it is ultimately Sun Ra who ridicules and dismisses the aspirations of the white male candidate for his "Outer Space Employment Agency." In *Space Is the Place*, Sun Ra and his Arkestra defy the limitations of space, time, and logic to demand that space is the place for African Americans currently trapped in the ghetto, because they are inevitably destined to leave Earth in order to repopulate the stars. Space was the place for unfettered optimism, opportunity, and free expression, or, as Sun Ra would claim in the film, "Outer space is a pleasant place. A place where you can be free. There's no limit to the things you can do. Your thought is free and your life is worthwhile. Space is the Place." And in the Black Power era Sun Ra was not alone in believing the sky was truly the limit for African American creative, political, and social aspirations and that the parameters for an African American culture free of oppression had yet to be defined. In 1971 Pharoah Sanders recorded the dreamy ode "Astral Traveling" and Ornette Coleman recorded the futuristic "Science Fiction" with the Black Arts poet David Henderson, while in *A Journey in Satchidananda*, Alice Coltrane would guide listeners on a trip through an imagined Afro-Asiatic past and a nirvanalike future mind-state, and Parliament would imagine a *Mothership Connection* in 1976.

Black Power/Black Arts–era practitioners were dreaming of more than the outer limits of the past, present, and future of African American creative experience; they were expanding the limits of aesthetic production as well. Everyday African American urban life and the urban vernacular became Black Arts poetry. African American avant-garde jazz reached new heights of musical innovation with Eric Dolphy, Archie Shepp, Albert Ayler, John Coltrane, and Pharoah Sanders, while Black Arts Movement practitioners struggled to redefine music criticism. Black radical political organizing redefined itself in the aftermath of the civil rights moment, moving away from church-based moral arguments toward a vicious urban visuality that emphasized masculine empowerment and militaristic strength. African American filmmakers struggled for inclusion in Hollywood at the same time that they struggled to articulate an aesthetic defined by the unique contours of African American visual culture.

The factors unique to African American life that were key to the articulation of a discrete Black aesthetic included a reawakening awareness of the effects of past oppression on African American culture and also an acknowledgement of the formative role that would be played by newer manifestations of Black oppression through urban poverty, policing, and mass incarceration. From social and political critiques of the Black Panther Party to poetry of the Black Arts Movement and the rise of the Blaxploitation film cycle, distrust of urbanity and distrust of the institutions governing urbanity, such as the police and the justice system, were repeatedly highlighted. In a contemporary U.S. culture in which one in every four African American males is either incarcerated or on parole or probation and convicted felons are politically disenfranchised at alarming rates, such a critique seems alarmingly prescient and deserving of reexamination if for no other reason than its status as a clarion call to impending social and political tragedy (see Angela Davis, *Are Prisons Obsolete?*).

Despite the Black Arts and Black Power movements' repeated calls for race-based unity, implicit and explicit politics surrounding intraracial class conflict were deeply foregrounded by each. The Black Arts Movement's literary and performance culture, African American radical political culture, and Black Power movement discourse were haunted by the specter of African American betrayal, one that was frequently couched in terms of class conflict. While Sam Greenlee's *The Spook Who Sat by the Door* imagines the possibility of stealthily infiltrating the "Negro middleclass" by subterfuge, it also imagines the ultimate betrayal of the urban revolution by that same class. Larry Neal, LeRoi Jones, and Eldridge Cleaver constantly rail against the new class of African American social service workers, intellectuals, and politicians who were created to manage desegregation by labeling them "poverticians" and "poverty pimps." Virtually every essay in the *Black Fire!* anthology imagines class-based enemies in the form of "Uncle Toms," "House Niggers," and "Black bourgies," as well as the more controversial enemy without. Blaxploitation movies such as *Sweet Sweetback's Baadasssss Song!* (1971), *Coffy* (1973), and *Space Is the Place* (1974) all feature African American politicians, entrepreneurs, and wealthy pimps and businessmen who betray the movement in order to curry favor and financial gain from the white establishment.

The movements' discussions of class conflict were as prescient as their critique of the rise of mass incarceration as a factor in African American life. The Black Arts Movement's discussions of class politics were as predictive of the rise of successful African American neoconservatives such as Condoleezza Rice as they were of the figure of the poverty-stuck "welfare mother" that was to haunt U.S. social policy throughout the 1980s and 1990s. When Dick Gregory opened at Chicago's Playboy Club and in so doing opened the doors for Black comedians, he unwittingly ushered in an era of millionaire African American entertainers rather than an era of Black social activists as he would perhaps have wished.

The 1970s continues to be a focus for nostalgic longing for the resolution of the political and cultural crisis of post–civil rights Black America. The specter of Black Power and the Black Arts Movement continue to haunt African American cultural production, from popular novels to hip-hop and film. Several instances of recent African American popular culture imagine African American salvation from poverty, crime, racism, and political stagnation by directly invoking incarnations of the figure of Huey P. Newton. For example, a 2006 episode of *The Boondocks* television show features a character named Huey, who is both modeled after and idolizes Huey P. Newton, and who adopts the corrective rhetorical stance of the Black Panther Party to act as "the voice of reason" for an otherwise culturally and politically confused Black community. Touré's 2004 satirical novel *Soul City* imagines the rescue of an African American city in trouble by a thuglike character named "Hueynewton," who must win the city's trust by taking a journey that literally reenacts slavery.

The 1970s continues to be a point of origin for everything from African American social and political commentators as diverse as the neoconservative John McWhorter, who sees the crisis of African Americans as situated in the oppositional politics of the Black Power movement, and such political progressives as Angela Davis and Al Sharpton, who find in the decade a powerful model not only for identity construction but also for political and social organizing. Ultimately, the aftereffects and limitations of the Black Power and Black Arts movements will be determined only through substantially revisiting the era to reconsider the questions and issues it raised, the representational strategies it employed, and the inquiries it poses for the current moment.

The vanguard model was the single most powerful model of identification in African American radical politics of the 1960s and 1970s. The reliance in African American radical politics on a vanguardist visual language and iconography that created an image of African Americans that was at once oppositional and open for broad identification formed the ways in which postwar American culture has come to construct African American culture and identity. Changes in postdesegregation African American culture have largely been naturalized as authentic outside the debates of the Black Power era that created them. A return to those debates helps to situate what we have come to think of as "authentic blackness" at the moment of its creation.

Notes

Introduction

1. Lester, *Look Out, Whitey!* 3.

2. Footage of the March against Fear and Carmichael's speech can be seen in "Ain't Gonna Shuffle No More (1964–1972)," the eleventh episode of *Eyes on the Prize II*.

3. Carmichael and Hamilton, *Black Power*, vii.

4. In *The Evolution of Islam: The Story of the Honorable Elijah Muhammad*, Jesus Muhammad-Ali claims that at the time of Muhammad's death, "the organization had amassed assets estimated at $80 million and to entail 750,000 acres of farm land in Alabama; a $1 million newspaper located on Chicago's South 26th and Federal Street; three ships under lease off the coast of Peru . . . the largest importer of whiting fish; a $1.2 million Lockheed Jet Star, four engine, ten passenger private plane; not to name each of the nearly 200 temples, grammar and high schools" (40).

5. Though the importance of *Cotton Comes to Harlem* as an early Blaxploitation film has often been overlooked, several critics and scholars have noted its influence in shaping the parameters of black culture in film as inherently urban and poor and, at the same time, dangerous and comedic. As early as 1971, Gary Null noted the significance of the film in his book *Black Hollywood*, pointing out that it was "the first black film with a black director" and heralding it as an indicator of "the emergence of truly black films which are not merely vehicles for black actors but are directed by blacks and destined for a black audience whose self-confidence has increased enormously" (206). However, the relevance of *Cotton Comes to Hollywood* was almost immediately overlooked with the release a year later of the more commercially successful film *Shaft* and the more cinematically innovative and controversial *Sweet Sweetback's Baadasssss Song!* While Ed Guerrero does devote most of his important discussion, in a chapter of *Framing Blackness* titled "The Rise and Fall of Blaxploitation," to the controversy surrounding these two films, he notes that *Cotton Comes to Harlem* "influenced the pacing and formal visual-musical elements that would go into the construction of the crime-action-ghetto Blaxploitation features that would follow" (81). In *Redefining Black Film*, Mark Reid notes the film's importance as "the first financially successful, hybrid minstrel comedy produced by a major studio" (26), and in *Black City Cinema*, Paula J. Massoud resituates it in the canon of Black city filmmaking by noting its influence in creating the urban milieu as central to the articulation of Black film culture. In 2001 David Walker declared in the influential fanzine *BadAzz MoFo*: "Perhaps the most hotly contested question when it comes to Blaxploitation is, 'What's the first Blax-

ploitation movie?' . . . Some say it's *Sweet Sweetback's Badasss Song,* others say it was *Shaft, Superfly* or even *Slaughter.* There are even those who say it was *In the Heat of the Night.* You could offer arguments why all those films were the first Blaxploitation flick (if you have the time to waste); but I'm going to make it very simple and lay down the Gospel According to *BadAzz MoFo:* The first Blaxploitation movie was *Cotton Comes to Harlem*" (23).

6. The competitive tension between Wright and Himes eventually ended their friendship. Himes writes: "I had never liked Dick since early 1957 when he had told me he organized the Paris Club, an organization of brothers, and barred me from joining. Later Dick learned that he had a prominent role in the book [*A Case of Rape*] and classified me as one of his many enemies" (*My Life of Absurdity,* 215–16).

7. The phrase "downtown changing my luck" refers to the supposed practice of white men coming to Harlem specifically to seek the services of Black prostitutes with the belief that sexual encounters with Black women would change their fate.

8. In a 1983 interview, Michel Fabre queried Himes about his Harlem experience, asking, "Did you live long in Harlem?" Himes responded, "No, I didn't. Only a few months at a time. Just long enough to absorb its atmosphere, although it keeps changing, mostly in terms of fashion, slang, and what is or isn't hip" (129).

9. Himes had actually written *Pinktoes,* a satire of interracial sexual mores in Harlem that was published in 1967 by Plon Press, much earlier, but he had set the work aside when he was unable to find a publisher.

10. Billed as "America's most popular Black Writer" by his publishing company, Donald Goines wrote nearly twenty novels in the five years between his release from prison and his murder in 1974. Goines's books have remained in print since the 1970s, and the publisher Holloway House claims that they continue to sell voraciously (see Stone, *Donald Writes No More*). The work of Iceberg Slim also inspired a generation of rap artists who came of age in the early 1980s, including Fab Five Freddie and Ice T, who created his name as a tribute to Beck.

11. See A. Davis, *Prison Industrial Complex.*

1. "Black Is Beautiful!"

1. In *Revolutionary Suicide,* party cofounder Huey P. Newton listed Che Guevara's *Guerilla Warfare,* along with Frantz Fanon's *The Wretched of the Earth* and the collected works of Mao Tse-Tung, as the books he and Bobby Seale "pored over" when initially conceiving the idea for the Black Panther Party (111), and cofounder Bobby Seale cited the same list of sources for the party's ideology in *Seize the Time* (82).

2. In *On The Real Side,* his landmark study of African American comedy, Mel Watkins lists Cecil Brown, Ishmael Reed, Al Young, Claude Brown, and David Henderson as the Bay Area writers and intellectuals who influenced Pryor in these years (541). Richard Pryor cites these literary figures as well but also significantly includes "characters worse than me," including "really scary people like Huey Newton," though he insists, "Newton didn't bother me" (*Pryor Convictions,* 119–20).

3. "God Is a Junkie" is on the album *Super Nigger* (Loose Cannon Records, 1982); "Super Nigger" is on *Richard Pryor* (Dove/Reprise Records, 1968); and "Wino and Junkie" and "Niggers vs. the Police" are on *That Nigger's Crazy* (Partee/Stax, 1974).

4. Amiri Baraka documents the social, cultural, and political atmosphere that contributed to the rise of Black Power in *The Autobiography of Leroi Jones*.

5. Huey P. Newton also cites *Negroes with Guns* as "a great influence on the kind of party we developed" in *Revolutionary Suicide*, his account of the creation of the Black Panther Party (112).

6. Timothy Tyson chronicles Robert Williams's history from the formation of the Monroe, North Carolina, chapter of the NAACP to his exile in Cuba in *Radio Free Dixie*.

7. The term "prison industrial complex" has its origins in the New Left critique of the military industrial complex—the creation of an industry around the proliferation of armed conflicts and interventions involving the United States (see A. Davis, "What Is the Prison Industrial Complex?").

8. Huey P. Newton outlined the relationship between the California state government, police brutality, and the Black community in "In Defense of Self-Defense: Executive Mandate Number One" (40). The relationship between policing and government oppression is also articulated by Seale and Newton in the "Ten Point Program," three points of which directly address the criminal justice system and focus particularly on issues of policing and courtroom justice.

9. California has the highest incarceration rate in the United States, and the United States has had the highest rates of incarceration in the world since the late 1980s (see Schlosser, "Prison Industrial Complex").

10. The Kuumba Collective, a Chicago-based art and cultural collective, issued an official response to an edition of the Black Panther newspaper that was largely devoted to celebrating the film *Sweet Sweetback's Baadasssss Song!* as a "black community event" (Newton, *To Die for the People*, 146). The collective remarks, "We don't know what film Huey Newton watched (or any other perverted, confused, or badly misguided folks who agree with him). . . . In terms of black aesthetics, 'Sweetback' fails an essential principle—that black art must be functional." The Kuumba Collective specifically criticized the film's graphic violent and sexual content and its glorification of street life. The collective characterized several of the scenes as "more fit for stag films—to be shown to white people—than as part of any film for black people" (Kumba Collective, unpublished position paper, Dr. Huey P. Newton Foundation Collection, Stanford University Special Collections, Palo Alto, CA).

11. Seale's *Seize the Time* provides a detailed account of the early history of the Black Panther Party.

12. The official history of the paper is given in "The Black Panther: Mirror of the People" (see Foner, *Black Panthers Speak*, 8–14). David Hilliard also speaks at length about the creation and daily importance of the paper in his autobiography, *This Side of Glory*, and Mumia Abu-Jamal mentions the paper's importance in helping to educate and coalesce Panther ideology for Panther recruits in *We Want Freedom* (111–14).

13. Huey P. Newton details the community patrols in his autobiography, *Revolutionary Suicide* (120–27). Bobby Seale discusses the formation and implementation of the patrols at length in *Seize the Time* (85–99), and David Hilliard writes about the patrols in relation to the formation of the party and their effect on the community in *This Side of Glory* (117–19).

14. The details of Newton's arrest and his trial are provided by Edward M. Keating, a member of Newton's legal defense team, in *Free Huey!*

15. Newton devotes an entire chapter of *Revolutionary Suicide* to "the brother on the block" as an integral force in the Black Panther Party (73–78). Chris Booker considers the "lumpenization" of the party its "critical error," claiming, "The criminal element within the lumpen developed a modus operandi that created a sociocultural milieu inimical to a stable political organization" ("Lumpenization," 38).

16. Elaine Brown gives a detailed account of the incident in her autobiography, *Taste of Power*. Huey P. Newton contends that the shooting was carried out by two FBI informants, who were subsequently convicted and sentenced to prison but, according to Newton, were allowed to escape and were never apprehended (*Revolutionary Suicide*, 78–81). Ward Churchill and Jim Vander Wall discuss the murder of Huggins and Carter in relation to the effective propaganda campaign created by the FBI's Counter Intelligence Program (COIN-TELPRO) to foment dissent between radical Black activist groups in Los Angeles (*Agents of Repression*, 42–43).

17. COINTELPRO was the code name for actions taken by the Federal Bureau of Investigations Counter Intelligence Program to disrupt a wide array of political groups between 1940 and 1971 through the now infamous use of often illegal tactics ranging from organized harassment and wiretaps to outright assassination (Churchill and Vander Wall, *Agents of Repression*, 37–39).

18. Me'Shell NdegéOcello, "I'm Diggin' You (Like an Old Soul Record)," *Plantation Lullabies* (Warner Brothers, 1993).

19. *This Side of Glory* provides an important firsthand account of the paper's significance to the party.

20. The Random House contract with the Black Panther Party and Mary Clemmy's 24 January 1972 letter to Huey Newton can be found in the Dr. Huey P. Newton Foundation Collection, Stanford University Special Collections, Palo Alto, CA.

21. John Holden, Agreement between San Francisco Mime Troupe and the Black Panther Party, 2 October 1970, Dr. Huey P. Newton Foundation Collection, Stanford University Special Collections, Palo Alto, CA.

22. From 1964 to 1970, SNCC members published a newsletter called the *Movement*, SNCC's closest equivalent to the *Black Panther*. Even a brief comparison of the two demonstrates the relative sophistication of the Black Panther Party's use of this type of mass media in comparison with that of established civil rights organizations. The *Black Panther* is professionally typeset, with professionally rendered illustrations and photographs; most of the work was done in-house by party members themselves, and the paper was able to maintain a fairly consistently large national distribution. The *Movement*, in comparison, never had more than a limited circulation and more closely resembled a high school newspaper than a national newsweekly. C. T. Vivian writes that "publicity was of the highest strategic importance" in winning the hearts and minds of the general public to the cause of civil rights, but the focus of movement strategists tended to be on using mainstream media to reveal the horrors of segregation. The Black Panther Party borrowed that technique from the Civil Rights Movement but also went further in attempting to use other avenues available in popular culture. For example, Brian Ward highlights "the difficulties faced by enthusiastic but inexperienced SNCC members when they attempted to take

their beg-steal-and-borrow fundraising philosophy into the cutthroat world of commercial entertainment and record production" (qtd. in Clayborne, 270). The Black Panther Party was also inexperienced, but it managed to create a far more professional product in almost every instance than comparable civil rights organizations.

23. Panther ideology was also successfully disseminated through the posters that advertised various party events, many examples of which are available in the Dr. Huey P. Newton Foundation Collection at Stanford University, including the Assassinated Malcolm X Poster of 21 February 1971 and the Revolutionary Intercommunal Day of Solidarity [with] Bobby Seale, Erika Huggins, Angela Davis, Ruchell Magee and Post-Birthday Celebration for Huey P. Newton, 5 March 1971.

24. Both the greeting cards and the Eldridge Cleaver watch are in the Dr. Huey P. Newton Foundation Collection, Stanford University Special Collections, Palo Alto, CA.

25. The watch was to be produced by the Bell Time Company, a wing of the Dirty Time Company, the novelty watch company that also produced the high-selling "Spiro Agnew Watch" (see Donald A. Marton's letter to the Black Panther Ministry of Information, 12 July 1971, Dr. Huey P. Newton Foundation Collection, Stanford University Special Collections, Palo Alto, CA). For a discussion of how the Huey Newton Foundation trademarked the slogan "Burn, Baby Burn" in order to use it to market hot sauce, see Rick DelVecchio, "Black Panthers Hot Again," *San Francisco Chronicle*, 20 July 2005, A2. Also, David Hilliard stressed the importance of being "creative with our radical marketing" and "using our history as a marketing resource" in "Using the Black Panther Name to Market New Products" on National Public Radio's *All Things Considered* on 16 August 2005.

26. A copy of the Bell Time Company advertisement is housed in the Dr. Huey P. Newton Foundation Collection, Stanford University Special Collections, Palo Alto, CA.

2. Radical Chic

1. Michael E. Staub's "Black Panthers, New Journalism, and the Rewriting of the Sixties" explores the way in which *New York Times* coverage that characterizes support for Mumia Abu-Jamal as "radical chic" reflects the ways in which New Journalism participated in the rewriting of the 1960s that continues to shape the way in which the mainstream media views radical politics and its supporters.

2. Robert Sandarg chronicles Genet's time with the Panthers in "Jean Genet and the Black Panther Party"; Edmund White writes extensively about Genet's time with the Panthers in *Genet*; and Genet himself extensively explores his encounter with the Panthers in his interview with Hubert Fichte reprinted in *The Declared Enemy* and in *Prisoner of Love*.

3. Fiona Handyside examines the contradictions of Jean Seberg's image as an icon of the French New Wave in "Stardom and Nationality: The Strange Case of Jean Seberg."

4. Mel Gussow explores the events surrounding Seberg's suicide in his article "The Seberg Tragedy," which appeared in the *New York Times* on 30 November 1980.

5. Judy West, memo to Comrade Herman, 30 August [no year given], Dr. Huey P. Newton Foundation Collection, Stanford University Special Collections, Palo Alto, CA.

6. Amiri Baraka gives a detailed account of the political and cultural elements that went into the founding of the Black Arts Theater in a self-published essay entitled "The Black Arts Movement." He mentions Wingate on page 7.

7. "Leonard Bernstein Asserts F.B.I. Used Dirty Tricks against Him," *New York Times*, 22 October 1980, A20.

8. Kenneth O'Reilly details the F.B.I.'s use of charges of anti-Semitism to fracture what it saw as a growing coalition between African Americans and Jews on the left in *"Racial Matters": The FBI's Secret File on Black America, 1960–1972.*

9. The Bernstein quote is from "Leonard Bernstein Asserts F.B.I. Used Dirty Tricks against Him."

10. Romain Gary would himself commit suicide in 1980; see "Romain Gary Is Dead; Novelist Shot in Head, Apparently a Suicide," *New York Times* 3 December 1980, A1.

11. *The Glass House Tapes* tells of how a group of activist journalists formed the Citizens Research and Investigation Committee in order to document claims by Louis Tackwood that he had been paid by the Los Angeles Police Department to provide information about Black radical groups in Southern California. Tackwood was married to the sister of James Carr, George Jackson's closest prison confidante, and was able to establish ties to the Black Panther Party in Los Angeles. According to him, the LAPD systemically planned to infiltrate and destroy the Black Panther Party in Los Angeles. He and Melvin "Cotton" Smith later offered testimony that was used to convict members of the party who were involved in the confrontation between the Panthers and the LAPD. In *Agents of Repression*, Ward Churchill and Jim Vander Wall use declassified COINTELPRO documents to substantiate their claims that the police raids of Panther offices and homes were coordinated by the FBI (84–87). Bobby Seale discusses the destruction of the Los Angeles Black Panther Party as part of a systematic plan to destroy the Panthers in *Seize the Time* (370–77).

12. The New York 21, as the defendants in the conspiracy trial of the leadership of the New York Black Panther Party came to be known, tell their story collectively in *Look for Me in the Whirlwind.*

13. The murders of Mark Clark and Fred Hampton are discussed in detail by Ward Churchill and Jim Vander Wall in *Agents of Repression* (64–77) and by Huey P. Newton in *War against the Panthers* (71–77).

14. Seale explores the use of police harassment and raids to disrupt the party's daily operation in a chapter of *Seize the Time* entitled "Why They Raid Our Offices" (369–73). Gail Sheehy examines the New Haven trial in detail in *Panthermania.*

15. Churchill and Vander Wall provide the most complete account of the FBI's involvement in the destruction of the Black Panther Party in *Agents of Repression*. O'Reilly places the assault on the Black Panther Party in the context of other acts of anti-Black violence perpetuated by the FBI during the civil rights and early postsegregation era in *"Racial Matters."* Jonathan Jackson's attempt to free George Jackson and the controversies surrounding George Jackson's murder are explored by Jo Durden-Smith in *Who Killed George Jackson?*

16. Newton chronicles the efforts of "law enforcement agencies to 'neutralize,' contain, and/or destroy organizations and individuals thought to be 'enemies' of the American government (or status quo)" in *War against the Panthers* (8).

17. Sheehy documents the events that led to the murder of Alex Rackley by members of the New Haven chapter of the Black Panther Party who suspected him of being a police informer. The murder and subsequent trial contributed to the growing public furor over the party's supposed support of violence as a political tactic.

18. Earl Anthony suggests in *Spitting in the Wind* that Black House was largely funded by white communist radicals led by Beverly Axelrod, the lawyer who had helped secure Cleaver's release; according to Anthony, "she was the front for a group of white influential Communists who were planning to promote Eldridge Cleaver as the next Malcolm X" (15).

19. Elaine Brown discusses the success and contradictions in the campaign for city council in her autobiography, *A Taste of Power* (321–27).

20. While recent academic studies have done much to address questions of visibility, performativity, and the media's reception of the party, little attention has been devoted to examining the party's attempts to affect popular consumer culture.

21. Tupac Shakur commemorated Huey P. Newton in an unpublished poem titled "Fallen Star/4 Huey P Newton" that now appears on Shakur's own memorial page on Davey D's Hip Hop Webpage http://www.daveyd.com/pacpoemfall.html. Shakur creates a more sympathetic picture of Newton's spiral into drugs and crime and his death than does Pearson, offering a more complicated view of the relationship between Newton, his fame, and his youthful admirers. In the poem, Shakur writes, "How could they understand what was so intricate / 2 be loved by so many, so intimate." While Pearson suggests that ignorance of the "real" Newton accounts for the huge following he enjoys among African American youth, Shakur's tribute suggests that Newton's imperfections heighten, rather than diminish, his appeal to young people, who feel directly and indirectly victimized by similar cycles of addiction, alienation, and incarceration.

22. In *Are Prisons Obsolete?* Angela Y. Davis explores the historical factors that have created incarceration as the major factor governing the lives of African Americans in the United States.

3. "We Waitin' on You"

1. In Harper's words, the Black Arts project calls for the liberation of "'all Black people' but not, evidently for 'you'" (*Are We Not Men?* 53).

2. Ellison, *Shadow and Act*, 253; Baker, *Afro-American Poetics*, 161.

3. L. Neal, *Visions of a Liberated Future*, 63, 76.

4. This has been somewhat rectified by the recent publication of several literary and cultural histories of the movement, including work by Cheryl Clarke, Harry J. Elam, James Smethurst, and Komozi Woodard.

5. David J. Garrow's *The FBI and Martin Luther King, Jr.* provides documentation of government excesses under COINTELPRO and the FBI's systematic campaign of harassment against King. Philip Melanson's *Who Killed Martin Luther King?* examines some of the most glaring inconsistencies in the investigation into the murder of King by the House Select Committee on Assassinations. Both books extensively document the U.S. government's attempts to derail the Civil Rights Movement, and both implicate government agencies in King's assassination.

6. Larry Neal, LeRoi Jones, Houston Baker, Ossie Davis, and Clayton Riley, among others, all contributed to the *Liberator* either as writers or by serving on its editorial board.

7. In *Beyond Black and White*, Marable goes on to cite the following factors as evidence of this crisis: "The infant mortality rate for black infants is twice that for whites. Blacks, who represent only 13 per cent of the total United States population, now account for ap-

proximately 80 per cent of all premature deaths of individuals aged fifteen to forty-four—those who die from preventable disease and/or violence. There are currently more than 650,000 African-American men and women who are incarcerated, and at least half of these prisoners are under the age of twenty-nine. In many cities the dropout rate for non-white high-school students exceeds 40 per cent." (129).

8. Komozi Woodard gives the most complete account of the conflicts and infighting that surrounded the cultural projects of the Black Arts/Black Power era, including the Black Arts Repertory Theater School, in *A Nation within a Nation*, 63–68.

9. A partial list of significant anthologies produced during the period of the Black Arts Movement includes R. Baird Schuman's *Nine Black Poets*, J. Saunders Redding and Arthur P. Davis's, *Cavalcade: Negro American Writing from 1760 to the Present*, Dudley Randall's *Black Poetry: A Supplement to Anthologies which Exclude Black Poets*, Ed Bullins's *New Plays from the Black Theatre*, Gwendolyn Brooks's *A Broadside Treasury*, Toni Cade Bambara's *Tales and Stories for Black Folks*, Ahmed Alhamisi and Harun Kofi Wangara's, *Black Arts: An Anthology of Black Creations*, Etheridge Knight's *Black Voices from Prison*, and Orde Coombs's *We Speak as Liberators: Young Black Poets*.

10. Lorenzo Thomas explores the formation and impact of literary collectives such as Umbra in "The Shadow World." James Smethurst explores the impact of the Black Left-ist tradition on emerging Black nationalism in literary journals such as *Liberator*, *Journal of Black Poetry*, and *Black Dialogue* in "Poetry and Sympathy." Smethurst gives the most complete history to date of the Black Arts Movement's literary collectives and Black Arts publications in *The Black Arts Movement*.

11. In "The Black Arts Movement and Its Critics," David Lionel Smith cites Henry Louis Gates's dismissal of the Black Arts Movement and his desire "to take the 'mau-mauing' out of the black literary criticism that defined the 'Black Aesthetic Movement' of the 60s and transform it into a valid field of intellectual inquiry" as formative for the way in which the Black Arts Movement continues to be received.

12. Nielsen, *Black Chant*, 101, 98; Thomas, "The Shadow World," 54.

13. Joe Goncalves served as the editor of *Journal of Black Poetry* and the poetry editor of *Black Dialogue*. "Now the Time Is Ripe to Be" and "Sister Brother" appear in *Black Fire!* (265–66).

14. For example, in "Controversies of the Black Arts Movement," a section in his longer discussion of the Black Arts Movement that appears in the 1997 *Norton Anthology of African American Literature*, Houston A. Baker Jr. uses such troublesome subcategories as "anti-Semitism" and "misogyny, homophobia" in discussing the movement (1804–6).

15. It is not surprising, given the post–civil rights era context in which *Black Fire!* appeared, that the figure of the Black preacher is the most frequently castigated repre-sentational figure in the anthology. Ben Caldwell's "Prayer Meeting, or the First Militant Preacher" goes so far as to suggest a conversion scenario for a civil rights–era Black mem-ber of the clergy based on his encounter with a Black criminal.

4. "People Get Ready!"

1. L. Neal, "Some Reflections on a Black Aesthetic," 257.

2. In *The Autobiography of Leroi Jones*, Baraka explains how the Black Arts Theater be-came the literal as well as figurative vehicle for avant-garde jazz when it created mobile

stages on the back of trucks for musicians to perform on throughout Harlem (211). These stages were, Baraka claims, an important precursor to the Harlem Community Council's highly successful "jazzmobiles," which operated into the late 1970s and 1980s. (See also Wilmer, *As Serious as Your Life*, 219.)

3. The Ayler tracks can be found on *Live in Greenwich Village*. The Baraka statement is from *Autobiography of Leroi Jones*, 195; Joans is quoted in Wilmer, *As Serious as Your Life*, 95.

4. Albert Ayler's interview with Kiyoshi Koyama for *Swing Journal*, recorded on 25 July 1970, is available on *Holy Ghost*, disc 9 (Revenant Records, 2004).

5. McCartney lists Ayler as a major influence in Barry Miles, *Paul McCartney*. The quote is taken from C. Fox, "An Avant-Garde McCartney," 2.

6. Ayler interview, *Holy Ghost*, disc 9.

7. In *The Crisis of the Negro Intellectual*, Harold Cruse reprints a description of a Garvey meeting at Carnegie Hall in the 1920s in order to illustrate that group's reliance on music by European composers to the complete exclusion of "a spiritual, not to mention jazz or a classical melody by an Africanized composer" (539). Paul Gilroy offers an important critique of the ways in which Garvey's movement was influenced by the European nationalist movements after which he styled the UNIA in *Against Race*. In *Keep Cool*, Ted Vincent notes that the Black working-class constituency of the UNIA ensured that it had popular jazz at its center and discusses the ways in which the "endorsements by Garvey and his lieutenants of Black achievements in classical music" have been misinterpreted by scholars. According to Vincent, though "these endorsements have been interpreted as anti-jazz sentiment," it might be more productive to think of them as evidence of the organization's ability to negotiate and appreciate the complex reality of the popular music culture of the 1920s (128).

8. In *Funk*, Rickey Vincent writes of this incident and many others that characterized Brown's famous perfectionist, "workaholic" attitude, which won him the title of "the hardest working man in show business" (72).

9. Guralnick writes: "There was a great deal of feeling among church people that Sam's death had come as a judgment" (*Sweet Soul Music*, 48).

5. "You Better Watch This Good Shit!"

The quotation in the chapter title is a voice-over line that accompanies the stunt action of Rudy Ray Moore's legendary Dolemite character in *Dolemite II: The Human Tornado* (1976).

1. Morton, "Beach Party Films."

2. It is important to situate *Black Looks* and hooks's work in general in relation to the traditions it was both drawing on and attempting to bridge, including the interest in spectatorship and the gaze found in feminist theory initiated by Laura Mulvey's influential 1975 essay "Visual Pleasure and Narrative Cinema," and the interest in the body, the experiential, and historical recovery found in Black feminist studies in the work of Audre Lorde, Barbara Smith, Barbara Christian, and Gloria T. Hull, among others.

3. In *Black Women as Cultural Readers*, Jacqueline Bobo offers a more nuanced account of the ways in which African American female spectators might receive and rework *The Color Purple*.

4. Wells's writings on lynching are collected in *On Lynchings*.

5. Leab, *From Sambo to Superspade*, 258; Guerrero, ed., *Framing Blackness*, 101.

6. Between 1967 and 1968 there were 384 violent rebellions in 298 U.S. cities. The 1968 assassination of Martin Luther King Jr. resulted in full-scale civil unrest in 160 cities (Guerrero, *Framing Blackness*, 71, 29).

7. A full history of Hollywood's stereotyping of African Americans can be found in Donald Bogle's *Toms, Coons, Mulattoes, Mammies, and Bucks*.

8. Murray, "Do We Really Have Time for *Shaft?*" 13.

9. Ed Guerrero notes that the film industry targeted Black audiences with "a specific product line of cheaply made, black cast films [that were] marketed to a basically inner-city, black youth audience in anticipation of substantial box office profits" (*Framing Blackness*, 69). Dan Streible makes similar observations in his historiography of an urban theater in "The Harlem Theater," 229.

Bibliography

Books and Articles

Abu-Jamal, Mumia. *Live from Death Row.* New York: Harper Perennial, 1996.

———. *We Want Freedom: A Life in the Black Panther Party.* Cambridge, MA: South End Press, 2004.

Alexander, Elizabeth. "Can You Be Black and Look at This? Reading the Rodney King Video(s)." In *Black Male: Representations of Masculinity in Contemporary American Art,* edited by Thelma Golden, 77–94. New York: Harry N. Abrams, 1994.

Algarin, Miguel. "The Sidewalk of High Art: Introduction." In Algarin and Holman, *Aloud,* 3–28.

Algarin, Miguel, and Bob Holman, eds. *Aloud: Voices from the Nuyorican Poets Cafe.* New York: Henry Holt, 1994.

Alhamisi, Ahmed, and Harun Kofi Wangara, eds. *Black Arts: An Anthology of Black Creation.* Detroit, MI: Black Arts Publications, 1969.

Allen, Robert. *Black Awakening in Capitalist America.* Garden City, NY: Doubleday, 1969.

Anthony, Earl. *Picking Up the Gun: A Report on the Black Panthers.* New York: Pyramid Books, 1971.

———. *Spitting in the Wind: The True Story behind the Violent Legacy of the Black Panther Party.* Malibu, CA: Roundtable Publishing, 1990.

Athill, Diana. *Make Believe: A True Story.* South Royalton, VT: Steerforth Press, 1993.

Attali, Jacques. *Noise: The Political Economy of Music.* Minneapolis: University of Minnesota Press, 1985.

Baker, Houston A., Jr. *Afro-American Poetics: Revisions of Harlem and the Black Aesthetic.* Madison: University of Wisconsin Press, 1988.

———. "The Black Arts Movement." In McKay and Gates, *Norton Anthology of African American Literature,* 1791–1805.

Bambara, Toni Cade, ed. *Tales and Stories for Black Folks.* Garden City, NY: Doubleday, 1971.

Baraka, Amiri. *The Autobiography of LeRoi Jones.* New York: Freundlich Books, 1984.

———. "The Black Arts Movement." Self-published essay. 1997.

Bell Time Company Advertisement. Dr. Huey P. Newton Foundation Collection. Stanford University Special Collections, Palo Alto, CA.

Bennett, Lerone. "The Emancipation Orgasm: Sweetback in Wonderland." *Ebony,* September 1971, 106–19.

Benston, Kimberly W. "Introduction to the Special Edition." *Callaloo* 8 (1985): 5.

————. *Performing Blackness: Enactments of African American Modernism.* New York: Routledge, 2000.

Berguist, Laura. "Interview." In *Che: Selected Works of Che Guevara,* edited by R. E. Bonachea and N. P. Valdes, 384–87. Cambridge, MA: MIT Press, 1969.

Bobo, Jacqueline. *Black Women as Cultural Readers.* New York: Columbia University Press, 1995.

Bogle, Donald. *Toms, Coons, Mulattoes, Mammies, and Bucks: An Interpretive History of Blacks in American Films.* New York: Continuum, 1989.

Booker, Chris. "Lumpenization: A Critical Error of the Black Panther Party." In C. Jones, *Black Panther Party Reconsidered,* 337–62.

Boyd, Herb. *The Black Panthers for Beginners.* New York: Writers and Readers Press, 1995.

Brooks, Gwendolyn, ed. *A Broadside Treasury.* Detroit, MI: Broadside Press, 1971.

Brown, Elaine. *A Taste of Power: A Black Woman's Story.* New York: Pantheon Books, 1992.

Brown, H. Rap. "Free Huey Rally Speech, February 1968." The Pacifica Radio/UC Berkeley Social Activism Sound Recording Project/The Black Panther Party. http: www.lib .berkeley.edu/MRC/rapbrown.html.

Bullins, Ed, ed. *New Plays from the Black Theater.* New York: Bantam Books, 1969.

Caldwell, Ben. *The King of Soul (or The Devil and Otis Redding).* In Bullins, *New Plays from the Black Theater,* 77–83.

————. "Prayer Meeting, or the First Militant Preacher." In L. Neal and L. Jones, *Black Fire!* 589–94.

Caldwell, Earl. "Brandeis Negroes Get Amnesty after They Relinquish Building." *New York Times,* 19 January 1969, 24.

————. "2nd Man Surrenders on Coast in Slaying of 2 Black Panthers." *New York Times,* 22 January 1969, 24.

"Campus Disruption in City and Elsewhere." *New York Times,* 30 April 1969, 29.

Carmichael, Stokely, and Charles V. Hamilton. *Black Power: The Politics of Liberation in America.* New York: Vintage Books, 1967.

————. "Free Huey Rally Speech, February 1968." The Pacifica Radio/UC Berkeley Social Activism Sound Recording Project/The Black Panther Party. http: www.lib.berkeley .edu/MRC/carmichael.html.

Carr, James. *Bad: The Autobiography of James Carr.* Oakland, CA: AK Press, 2002.

Carson, Clayborne. *In Struggle: SNCC and the Black Awakening of the 1960s.* Cambridge, MA: Harvard University Press, 1981.

Castro, Fidel. *The Second Declaration of Havana.* New York: Pathfinder Press, 1994.

Chang, Jeff. "Stakes Is High: Conscious Rap and the Hip Hop Generation." *Nation,* 13 January 2003, 17–21.

Churchill, Ward, and Jim Vander Wall. *Agents of Repression: The FBI's Secret War against the Black Panther Party and the American Indian Movement.* Boston, MA: South End Press, 1990.

Clarke, Cheryl. *After Mecca: Women Poets and the Black Arts Movement.* New Brunswick, NJ: Rutgers University Press, 2005.

Cleaver, Eldridge. *Post-Prison Writings and Speeches.* New York: Vintage, 1969.

————. *Soul on Ice.* New York: Dell, 1968.

Clemmy, Mary. Letter to Huey Newton. 24 January 1972. Dr. Huey P. Newton Foundation Collection. Stanford University Special Collections, Palo Alto, CA.

Cobb, Charlie. "Ain't That a Groove." In L. Neal and L. Jones, *Black Fire!* 524.

Cohen, Jerry, and William S. Murphy. *Burn, Baby Burn! The Los Angeles Race Riot, August 1965.* New York: Avon, 1967.

"College Reopens to Empty Rooms." *New York Times,* 21 November 1968, 35.

Collins, Lisa Gail, and Margo Crawford, eds. *New Thoughts on the Black Arts Movement.* Rutgers University Press, 2006.

Coombs, Orde. *We Speak as Liberators: Young Black Poets.* New York: Dodd, Mead, 1970.

Crouch, Stanley. "The Incomplete Turn of Larry Neal." In *Visions of a Liberated Future: Black Arts Movement Writing,* edited by Michael Schwartz, 3–6. New York: Thunder's Mouth, 1989.

Crouchett, Lawrence, et al. *Visions toward Tomorrow: The History of the East Bay Afro-American Community, 1852–1977.* Oakland, CA: Northern California Center for Afro-American History and Life, 1989.

Cruse, Harold. *The Crisis of the Negro Intellectual.* New York: William Morrow, 1967.

Cullaz, Maurice. "Chester Himes's Crusade: An Interview." In *Conversations with Chester Himes,* edited by Michel Fabre and Robert E. Skinner, 143–44. Jackson: University of Mississippi Press, 1995.

Davis, Angela Y. "Afro Images: Politics, Fashion, Nostalgia." In *Soul: Black Power, Politics, and Pleasure,* edited by Monique Gillory and Richard C. Green, 23–31. New York: New York University Press, 1998.

———. *Are Prisons Obsolete?* New York: Hyperion, 1999.

———. *The Prison Industrial Complex.* New York: Hyperion, 1999.

———. "What Is the Prison Industrial Complex? What Are the Goals of Critical Resistance?" Speech given at the Critical Resistance to the Prison Industrial Complex Conference, 25 September 1998, University of California, Berkeley.

Davis, Mike. *City of Quartz: Excavating the Future in Los Angeles.* New York: Vintage, 1990.

Davis, Miles, and Quincy Troupe. *Miles: The Autobiography of Miles Davis.* New York: Simon & Schuster, 1989.

Debray, Regis. *Revolution within the Revolution? Armed Struggle and Political Struggle in Latin America.* New York: Grove Press, 1967.

Decker, Jeffrey Louis. "The State of Rap: Time and Place in Hip Hop Nationalism." In *Microphone Fiends: Youth Music and Youth Culture,* edited by Tricia Rose, 99–121. New York: Routledge, 1994.

DelVecchio, Rick. "Black Panthers Hot Again." *San Francisco Chronicle,* 20 July 2005, A2.

Dent, Gina, ed. *Black Popular Culture.* Seattle, WA: Bay Press, 1992.

DePalma, Anthony. "Massachusetts Campus Is Torn by Racial Strife." *New York Times,* 18 October 1992, 20.

Diawara, Manthia. "Black Spectatorship: Problems of Identification and Resistance." In *Black American Cinema,* edited by Manthia Diawara, 211–20. New York: Routledge, 1993.

Dougan, Clark, and Stephen Weiss. *The Vietnam Experience: Nineteen Sixty-Eight.* Boston, MA: Boston Publishing Company, 1983.

Du Bois, W. E. B. *The Souls of Black Folk*. Chicago, IL: A. C. McClurg and Company, 1903.

Durden-Smith, Jo. *Who Killed George Jackson? Fantasies, Paranoia and the Revolution*. New York: Alfred A. Knopf, 1976.

Early, Gerald. *One Nation under a Groove: Motown and American Culture*. Hopewell, NJ: Ecco Press, 1995.

Elam, Harry J. *Taking It to the Streets: The Social Protest Theater of Luis Valdez and Amiri Baraka*. Ann Arbor: University of Michigan Press, 2001.

Ellison, Ralph. *Shadow and Act*. New York: Quality Paperbacks, 1964.

Ely, Melvin Patrick. *The Adventures of Amos 'n' Andy: A Social History of an American Phenomenon*. New York: Free Press, 1991.

Emanuel, James A. "Blackness Can: A Quest for Aesthetics." In Gayle, *The Black Aesthetic*, 182–211.

Fabre, Michel. *Conversations with Chester Himes*, edited by Michel Fabre and Robert E. Skinner. Jackson: University of Mississippi Press, 1995.

Fanon, Frantz. *Black Skin, White Masks*. New York: Grove Press, 1967.

———. *The Wretched of the Earth*. New York: Grove Press, 1968.

Foner, Philip S., ed. *The Black Panthers Speak*. New York: Da Capo Press, 1995.

Fox, Chris. "An Avant-Garde McCartney." *Rubberneck*, November 2000, 1–6.

Fox, Sylvan. "C.C.N.Y. Shut Down, Then Racial Clash Injures 7 Whites: Club Swinging Negroes Cap Violent Day with Battle on South Campus." *New York Times* 6 May 1969, 1.

———. "225 Radical Students Picket 8 Buildings at Columbia in One-Day Strike." *New York Times*, 26 March 1969, 28.

Franklin, Clarence. "Two Dreams (for m.l.k.'s one)." In L. Neal and L. Jones, *Black Fire!* 364.

Fraser, Gerald C. "F.B.I. Files Reveal Moves against Black Panthers." *New York Times*, 19 October 1980, 1.

Fuller, Hoyt. "Towards a Black Aesthetic." In Addison, *The Black Aesthetic*, 3–11.

Garrow, David J. *The FBI and Martin Luther King, Jr.* New York: Penguin, 1981.

Gayle, Addison, ed. *The Black Aesthetic*. New York: Doubleday, 1971.

Genet, Jean. Interview with Hubert Fichte. In *The Declared Enemy: Texts and Interviews*, edited by Albert Dichy, 118–51. Stanford: Stanford University Press, 2004.

———. *Prisoner of Love*. 1986. New York: New York Review of Books Classics, 2003.

George, Nelson. *The Death of Rhythm & Blues*. New York: Pantheon, 1988.

———. *Where Did Our Love Go? The Rise and Fall of the Motown Sound*. New York: St. Martin's Press, 1985.

Gilroy, Paul. *Against Race: Imagining Political Culture beyond the Color Line*. Boston: Harvard University Press, 2001.

———. "Wearing Your Art on Your Sleeve: Notes toward a Diaspora History of Black Ephemera." In *Small Acts: Thoughts on the Politics of Black Cultures*, 237–51. London: Serpents Tail, 1993.

Giovanni, Nikki. "For Saundra." In *Black Writers of America: A Comprehensive Anthology*, edited by Richard Barksdale and Kenneth Kinnamon, 823. New York: Prentice-Hall, 1972.

Gitlin, Todd. "On the Line at San Francisco State." In *Black Power and Student Rebellion: Conflict on the American Campus*, edited by James McEvoy and Abraham Miller, 298–306. Belmont, CA: Wadsworth Publishing Company, 1969.

Goncalves, Joe. "Now the Time Is Ripe to Be" and "Sister Brother." In L. Neal and L. Jones, *Black Fire!* 265–66.

Greenlee, Sam. *The Spook Who Sat by the Door.* Detroit, MI: Wayne State University Press, 1989.

Gregory, Dick. *From the Back of the Bus.* New York: E. P. Dutton, 1962.

———. *Up from Nigger.* New York: Fawcett, 1977.

Guerrero, Ed. *Framing Blackness: The African American Image in Film.* Philadelphia, PA: Temple University Press, 1993.

Guevara, Ernesto "Che." *Che: Selected Works of Che Guevara.* Edited by R. E. Bonachea and N. P. Valdes. Cambridge, MA: MIT Press, 1969.

———. *Guerilla Warfare.* New York: Vintage, 1968.

Guralnick, Peter. *Sweet Soul Music: Rhythm and Blues and the Southern Dream of Freedom.* New York: Harper & Row, 1986.

Gussow, Mel. "The Seberg Tragedy." *New York Times,* 30 November 1980, Section 6, Column 4, Magazine Desk.

Handyside, Fiona. "Stardom and Nationality: The Strange Case of Jean Seberg." *Studies in French Cinema* 2.3 (2003): 165–76.

Harper, Phillip Brian. *Are We Not Men? Masculine Anxiety and the Problem of African-American Identity.* New York: Oxford University Press, 1996.

Harris, William J. Introduction. *The LeRoi Jones/Amiri Baraka Reader,* edited by W. J. Harris, xvii–xxxi. New York: Thunder's Mouth Press, 1991.

Hartman, Saidiya V. *Scenes of Subjection: Terror, Slavery, and Self-Making in Nineteenth-Century America.* New York: Oxford University Press, 1997.

Haskins, Jim. *Power to the People: The Rise and Fall of the Black Panther Party.* New York: Simon and Schuster, 1997.

The Hate that Hate Produced. CBS special with Mike Wallace and Malcolm X. Produced by Mike Wallace and Louis Lomax. First broadcast 13–17 July 1959, WNTA-TV, New York.

Hayes, Floyd W., and Francis A. Kiene. "'All Power to the People': The Political Thought of Huey P. Newton and the Black Panther Party." In C. Jones, *Black Panther Party Reconsidered,* 157–76.

Heath, Joseph, and Andrew Potter. *The Rebel Sell: How the Counterculture Became Consumer Culture.* West Sussex: Capstone Publishing, 2005.

Hilliard, David, and Lewis Cole. *This Side of Glory: The Autobiography of David Hilliard and the Story of the Black Panther Party.* Boston, MA: Little, Brown, 1993.

———. "Using the Black Panther Name to Market New Products." *All Things Considered.* Narrated by Mandalit Del Barco. National Public Radio News, 16 August 2005. Transcript.

Himes, Chester. *Blind Man with a Pistol.* 1969. New York: Vintage, 1989.

———. *A Case of Rape.* 1980. Washington, DC: Howard University Press, 1984.

———. *Cotton Comes to Harlem.* 1965. New York: Vintage, 1988.

———. *If He Hollers Let Him Go.* 1945. New York: Thunder's Mouth, 1995.

———. *Lonely Crusade.* 1947. New York: Thunder's Mouth, 1997.

———. *My Life of Absurdity: The Later Years.* 1976. New York: Thunder's Mouth, 1995.

———. *Pinktoes.* 1961. Paris: Plon Press, 1967.

————. *Plan B.* Jackson: The University Press of Mississippi, 1993.

————. *The Quality of Hurt: The Early Years.* 1973. New York: Thunder's Mouth, 1995.

————. *The Real Cool Killers.* 1959. New York: Vintage, 1988.

Holden, John. Agreement between San Francisco Mime Troupe and the Black Panther Party. 2 October 1970. Dr. Huey P. Newton Foundation Collection. Stanford University Special Collections, Palo Alto, CA.

hooks, bell. "The Oppositional Gaze." In *Black Looks: Race and Representation,* 115–31. Boston, MA: South End Press, 1992.

Hughes, Langston. *The Big Sea: An Autobiography.* New York: Hill and Wang, 1993.

Hughes, Langston, with Milton Meltzer. *Black Magic: A Pictorial History of the Negro in American Entertainment.* New York: Prentice Hall, 1967.

Jackmon, Marvin E. (Marvin X). "Flowers for the Trashman." In L. Neal and L. Jones, *Black Fire!* 541–58.

Jackson, George. *Blood in My Eye.* New York: Random House, 1972.

————. Last Will and Testament. Dr. Huey P. Newton Foundation Collection. Stanford University Special Collections, Palo Alto, CA.

————. *Soledad Brother.* New York: Bantam, 1970.

James, Darius. *That's Blaxploitation: Roots of the Baadasssss 'Tude.* New York: St. Martin's Griffin, 1995.

Johnson, Alicia Loy. "on my blk/ness." In *Nine Black Poets,* edited by R. Baird Schuman, 47. Durham, NC: Moore Publishing.

Jones, Charles E., ed. *The Black Panther Party Reconsidered.* Baltimore, MD: Black Classic Press, 1998.

Jones, Charles E., and Judson L. Jeffries. "'Don't Believe the Hype': Debunking the Panther Mythology." In C. Jones, *Black Panther Party Reconsidered,* 25–56.

Jones, LeRoi. "Black Art." In L. Neal and L. Jones, *Black Fire!* 302–3.

————. *Black Music.* New York: Quill, 1967.

————. *Blues People: The Negro Experience in White America and the Music that Developed from It.* New York: Morrow Quill, 1963.

————. *Home: Social Essays.* New York: William Morrow, 1966.

————. "le roi jones talking." In *Home,* 179–89.

————. *The LeRoi Jones/Amiri Baraka Reader,* edited by W. J. Harris. New York: Thunder's Mouth Press, 1991.

————. "The Myth of Negro Literature." In *Home,* 124–36.

————. "STATE/MEANT." In *Home,* 251–52.

Joseph, Peniel E. *The Black Power Movement: Rethinking the Civil Rights–Black Power Era.* New York: Routledge, 2004.

Jost, Ekkerhard. *Free Jazz.* New York: Da Capo Press, 1994.

Karenga, Maulana. "Black Art. Mute Matter Given Force and Function." In *Black Poets and Prophets,* edited by W. King and E. Anthony, 174–79. New York: Mentor Press, 1974.

————. "Black Cultural Nationalism." In Gayle, *The Black Aesthetic,* 31–37.

<3m.> "Kawaida and Its Critics: A Socio-Historical Analysis." *Journal of Black Studies* 8.2 (December 1977): 125–48.

Keating, Edward M. *Free Huey!* New York: Dell, 1970.

Kgositsile, K. William. "Towards a Walk in the Sun." In L. Neal and L. Jones, *Black Fire!* 228–29.

Kifner, John. "Cornell Negroes Seize a Building." *New York Times*, 19 April 1969, 1.

King, Martin Luther, Jr. "Letter from a Birmingham Jail." In *Crossing the Danger Water: Three Hundred Years of African-American Writing*, edited by Deirdre Mullane, 633–46. New York: Doubleday, 1993.

———. *Where Do We Go from Here: Chaos or Community?* Boston, MA: Beacon Press, 1968.

Kinnamon, Kenneth, ed. *New Essays on* Native Son. Cambridge, UK: Cambridge University Press, 1990.

Knight, Etheridge, ed. *Black Voices from Prison*. New York: Pathfinder Press, 1970.

Labrie, Peter. "The New Breed." In L. Neal and L. Jones, *Black Fire!* 64–77.

Leab, Daniel J. *From Sambo to Superspade: The Black Experience in Motion Pictures*. Boston, MA: Houghton Mifflin, 1975.

Lee, Don L. "Toward a Definition: Black Poetry of the Sixties (After LeRoi Jones)." In Gayle, *The Black Aesthetic*, 222–23.

———. "a poem to compliment other poems." In McKay and Gates, *Norton Anthology of African American Literature*, 1982.

Lehman, Nicholas. *The Promised Land: The Great Black Migration and How It Changed America*. New York: Vintage, 1992.

"Leonard Bernstein Asserts F.B.I. Used Dirty Tricks against Him." *New York Times*, 22 October 1980, A20.

Lester, Julius. *Look Out, Whitey! Black Power's Gon' Get Your Mama!* New York: Grove Press, 1968.

Levy, Peter B., ed. *Documentary History of the Modern Civil Rights Movement*. New York: Greenwood Press, 1992.

Llorens, David. "The Fellah, the Chosen One, the Guardian." In L. Neal and L. Jones, *Black Fire!* 169–77.

"Louisiana Students Hold Building, Police Action Hinted." *New York Times*, 7 November 1972, 75.

Mac, Bernie. *Maybe You Never Cry Again*. New York: Regan Books, 2004.

Mailer, Norman. "The White Negro: Superficial Reflections on the Hipster." *Dissent* 4.3 (Summer 1957): 276–93.

Marable, Manning. *Beyond Black and White: Transforming African American Politics*. London: Verso, 1995.

Marighella, Carlos. *The Terrorist Classic: The Manual of the Urban Guerilla*. Chapel Hill, NC: Documentary Publications, 1985.

Martinez, Gerald, Diana Martinez, and Andres Chavez. *What It Is . . . What It Was: The Black Film Explosion of the Seventies in Words and Pictures*. New York: Hyperion, 1998.

Marton, Donald A. Letter to the Black Panther Ministry of Information. 12 July 1971. Dr. Huey P. Newton Foundation Collection. Stanford University Special Collections, Palo Alto, CA.

Massoud, Paula J. *Black City Cinema: African American Urban Experiences of Film*. Philadelphia, PA: Temple University Press, 2003.

McEvoy, James, and Abraham Miller. "San Francisco State: 'On Strike . . . Shut It Down.'"

In *Black Power and Student Rebellion: Conflict on the American Campus,* 12–30. Belmont, CA: Wadsworth, 1969.

McKay, Nellie, and Henry Louis Gates, eds. *Norton Anthology of African American Literature.* New York: W. W. Norton, 2004.

McWhorter, John. *Winning the Race: Beyond the Crisis in Black America.* New York: Penguin, 2005.

Melanson, Philip. *Who Killed Martin Luther King?* Berkeley, CA: Odonian, 1993.

Mercer, Kobena. "'1968': Periodizing Politics and Identity." In *Welcome to the Jungle: New Positions in Black Cultural Studies,* 287–308. New York: Routledge, 1994.

Milner, Ronald. "Black Theater—Go Home!" In Gayle, *The Black Aesthetic,* 288–94.

Montgomery, Paul L. "100 Negro Students Loot New Campus Store as 'Payment' for the Burning." *New York Times,* 7 April 1970, 31.

Morton, Jim. "Beach Party Films." In *Research: Incredibly Strange Films,* edited by Andrea Juno and V. Vale, 166–68. San Francisco: V/Search Publications, 1986.

Moten, Fred. *In The Break: The Aesthetics of the Black Radical Tradition.* Minneapolis: University of Minnesota Press, 2003.

Muhammad-Ali, Jesus. *The Evolution of Islam: The Story of the Honorable Elijah Muhammad.* Birmingham, AL: JMA Publishing, 2002.

Mulvey, Laura. "Visual Pleasure and Narrative Cinema." In *Feminism and Film Theory,* edited by Constance Penley, 57–68. New York: Routledge, 1988.

Muntaqim, Jalil. *We Are Our Own Liberators: Selected Prison Writings.* Toronto: Abraham Guillen Press, 2003.

Murray, Albert. *Stomping the Blues.* New York: Da Capo Press, 1976.

Murray, James P. "Black Movies and Music in Harmony." *Black Creation* 5.1 (Fall 1973): 9–12.

———. "Do We Really Have Time for *Shaft?*" *Black Creation* 3.2 (Winter 1972): 12–14.

———, ed. "The Expanding World of Black Film: A Black Creation Special Issue." *Black Creation* 4.2 (Winter 1973): 25–43.

———. "Running with Sweetback: The Life and Trials of Melvin Van Peebles." *Black Creation* 3.1 (Fall 1971): 10–12.

———. "West Coast Gets the Shaft." *Black Creation* 3.4 (Summer 1972): 12–14.

Murray, Timothy. *Like a Film: Ideological Fantasy on Screen, Camera and Canvas.* New York: Routledge, 1993.

Naipaul, V. S. *Guerillas.* New York: Penguin, 1975.

Neal, Larry (Lawrence P.). "The Black Arts Movement." In Gayle, *The Black Aesthetic,* 257–74.

———. "Black Power in the International Context." In *The Black Power Revolt,* edited by Floyd Barbour, 156–72. New York: Macmillan, 1968.

———. "Black Revolution in Music: A Talk with Drummer Milford Graves." *Liberator* 5.9 (September 1965): 14.

———. "A Conversation with Archie Shepp." *Liberator* 5.11 (November 1965): 24–25.

———. "The Cultural Front." *Liberator* 5.6 (June 1965): 27.

———. "The Genius and the Prize." *Liberator* 5.10 (October 1965): 11.

———. "Ghost Poem #1." In *Hoodoo Hollerin' Bebop Ghosts,* 7.

———. *Hoodoo Hollerin' Bebop Ghosts*. Washington, DC: Howard University Press, 1968.

———. "On Malcolm X." In *Visions of a Liberated Future*, 125–32.

———. "A Reply to Bayard Rustin." *Liberator* 5.7 (July 1965): 6–8.

———. Review of *New Grass*, by Albert Ayler. *The Cricket* 4 (1968): 37–38.

———. "Shine Swam On." In L. Neal and L. Jones, *Black Fire!* 639–56.

———. "Some Reflections on a Black Aesthetic." In Gayle, *The Black Aesthetic*, 12–15.

———. "Towards a Relevant Black Theatre." *Black Theater* 4 (1969): 14–15.

———. *Visions of a Liberated Future: Black Arts Movement Writing*. Edited by Michael Schwartz. New York: Thunder's Mouth, 1989.

Neal, Larry, and Leroi Jones, eds. *Black Fire! An Anthology of Afro-American Writing*. New York: William Morrow, 1968.

Neal, Mark Anthony. *Soul Babies: Black Popular Culture and the Post-Soul Aesthetic*. New York: Routledge, 2002.

Neale, Steve. "Masculinity as Spectacle." In *The Sexual Subject: A Screen Reader in Sexuality*, 277–90. London: Routledge, 1992.

Newton, Huey P. "The Correct Handling of the Revolution." In Foner, *Black Panthers Speak*, 41–44.

———. "He Won't Bleed Me: A Revolutionary Analysis of Sweet Sweetback's Baadasssss Song." In Newton, *To Die for the People*, 112–47.

———. "Huey P. Newton Talks to the Movement about the Black Panther Party, Cultural Nationalism, SNCC, Liberals, and White Revolutionaries." In Foner, *Black Panthers Speak*, 50–66.

———. "In Defense of Self-Defense: Executive Mandate Number 1." In Foner, *Black Panthers Speak*, 000–000.

———. *Revolutionary Suicide*. New York: Writers and Readers, 1995.

———. *To Die for the People: The Writings of Huey P. Newton*, edited by Toni Morrison. New York: Writers and Readers Press, 1995.

———. *War against the Panthers*. 1980. New York: Harlem Rivers Press, 1996.

New York 21. *Look for Me in the Whirlwind: The Collective Autobiography of the New York 21*. New York: Vintage Books, 1971.

Nielsen, Aldon. *Black Chant: Languages of African-American Postmodernism*. New York: Cambridge University Press, 1997.

Null, Gary. *Black Hollywood: From 1970 to Today*. New York: Citadel Press, 1993.

Ogbar, Jeffrey O. G. *Black Power: Radical Politics and African American Identity*. Baltimore, MD: Johns Hopkins University Press, 2004.

O'Reilly, Kenneth. "*Racial Matters*": *The FBI's Secret File on Black America, 1960–1972*. New York: Free Press, 1989.

Pearson, Eric. "Introduction: Blaxploitation Revisited." *Screening Noir: Journal of Black Film, Television and New Media Culture* 1.1 (Fall/Winter 2005): 5–8.

Pearson, Hugh. *The Shadow of the Panther: Huey Newton and the Price of Black Power in America*. New York: Addison-Wesley, 1994.

Phallon, Richard. "Fire Destroys the Black Studies Center at Cornell." *New York Times*, 2 April 1970, 21.

"Police Break Up Campus Protests." *New York Times*, 12 February 1969, 25.

Poussaint, Alvin F. "Stimulus/Response: Blaxploitation Movies—Cheap Thrills that Degrade Blacks." *Psychology Today*, February 1974, 22–98.

"Protesters Disrupt Duke and CCNY: 1,000 Quelled at Durham." *New York Times*, 14 February 1969, 1.

Pruter, Robert. *Chicago Soul*. Urbana: University of Illinois Press, 1991.

Pryor, Richard, with Todd Gold. *Pryor Convictions and Other Life Sentences*. New York: Pantheon Books, 1995.

Randall, Dudley. *Black Poetry: A Supplement to Anthologies Which Exclude Black Poets*. Detroit, MI: Broadside Press, 1969.

Redding, J. Saunders, and Arthur P. Davis. *Cavalcade: Negro American Writing from 1760 to the Present*. Boston: Houghton Mifflin, 1971.

"Reed College Barricade." *New York Times*, 12 December 1969, 21.

Reid, Mark A. *Redefining Black Film*. Berkeley: University of California Press, 1993.

Reilly, John M., ed. *Richard Wright: The Critical Reception*. New York: Lennox Hill, 1978.

Revolutionary Intercommunal Day of Solidarity, Bobby Seale, Erika Huggins, Angela Davis, Ruchell Magee, and Post-Birthday Celebration for Huey P. Newton. Poster. 5 March 1971. Dr. Huey P. Newton Foundation Collection. Stanford University Special Collections, Palo Alto, CA.

Richards, David. *Played Out: The Jean Seberg Story*. New York: Random House, 1981.

Riggins, Roger. "Respect." *The Cricket* 4 (1968): 12–13.

Riley, Clayton. "On Black Theater." In Gayle, *The Black Aesthetic*, 295–315.

———. "Shaft Can Do Everything—I Can Do Nothing." In Guerrero, *Framing Blackness*, 69–112.

Robinson, Cedric J. "Blaxploitation and the Misrepresentation of Liberation." *Race and Class* 40 (1998): 1–12.

Robinson, Douglas. "Duke Settlement Reached; Black Studies Program Set." *New York Times*, 17 February 1969, 1.

Rodgers, J. A. "Jazz at Home." In Gayle, *The Black Aesthetic*, 104–11.

"Romain Gary Is Dead; Novelist Shot in Head, Apparently a Suicide." *New York Times*, 3 December 1980, A1.

Rout, Leslie B., Jr. "Reflections on the Evolution of Post War Jazz." In Gayle, *The Black Aesthetic*, 143–53.

Rowley, Hazel. "The Shadow of the White Woman: Richard Wright and the Book-of-the-Month Club." *Partisan Review* 66.4 (Fall 1999): 624.

Rubin, Jerry. *Do It! Scenarios of the Revolution*. New York: Touchstone, 1970.

Sandarg, Robert. "Jean Genet and the Black Panther Party." *Journal of Black Studies* 16.3 (March 1986): 269–82.

Savio, Mario. "An End of History." In *Documentary History of the Modern Civil Rights Movement*, edited by Peter B. Levy, 149–98. New York: Greenwood Press, 1992.

Schaefer, Eric. *"Bold! Daring! Shocking! True!": A History of Exploitation Films, 1919–1959*. Durham, NC: Duke University Press, 1999.

Schlosser, Eric. "The Prison Industrial Complex." *Atlantic Monthly*, December 1998, 51–72.

Schumach, Murray. "35 Negro Girls Seize Part of a Building at Vassar and Sit In." *New York Times*, 31 October 1969, 28.

Schuman, R. Baird. *Nine Black Poets.* Durham, NC: Moore, 1968.

Scott, Robert L., and Wayne Brockside, eds. *The Rhetoric of Black Power.* New York: Harper & Row, 1969.

Seale, Bobby. *Seize the Time: The Story of the Black Panther Party and Huey P. Newton.* New York: Random House, 1970.

——, with Huey P. Newton. "The Ten-Point Program." In Foner, *Black Panthers Speak,* 2–3.

Sell, Mike. *Avant-Garde Performance and the Limits of Criticism: Approaching the Living Theater, Happenings, Fluxus, and the Black Arts Movement.* Ann Arbor, MI: University of Michigan Press, 2005.

Shakur, Assata. *Assata: An Autobiography.* Chicago, IL: Lawrence Hill, 1987.

Shakur, Tupac. "Fallen Star/4 Huey P Newton." Online posting. 26 April 1999. Davey D's Hip Hop Webpage. http://www.daveyd.com/pacpoemfall.html.

Shaw, Arnold. *The World of Soul: Black America's Contribution to the Pop Music Scene.* New York: Cowles, 1970.

Sheehy, Gail. *Panthermania: The Clash of Black against Black in One American City.* New York: Harper & Row, 1971.

Shoats, Russell. "Black Fighting Formations: Their Strengths, Weaknesses and Potentialities." *New Political Science* 21.2 (1998): 53–71.

Silverman, Kaja. *Male Subjectivity at the Margins.* New York: Routledge, 1992.

——. "Suture." In *Narrative, Apparatus, Ideology,* edited by Philip Rosen, 219–35. New York: Columbia University Press, 1986.

Simon, Richard. "The Stigmatization of Blaxploitation." In *Soul: Black Power, Politics, and Pleasure,* edited by Monique Guillory and Richard C. Green, 236–249. New York: New York University Press, 1998.

Singh, Nikhil Pal. *Black Is a Country: Race and the Unfinished Business of Democracy.* Cambridge: Harvard University Press, 2004.

Smethurst, James. *The Black Arts Movement: Literary Nationalism in the 1960s and 1970s.* Chapel Hill, NC: University of North Carolina Press, 2005.

——. "'Pat Your Foot and Turn the Corner': Amiri Baraka, the Black Arts Movement, and the Poetics of a Popular Avant-Garde." *African American Review* 37.2–3 (2003): 261–70.

——. "Poetry and Sympathy: New York, the Left, and the Rise of Black Arts." In *Left of the Color Line: Race, Radicalism, and Twentieth-Century Literature of the United States,* edited by Bill V. Mullen and James Smethurst, 259–78. Chapel Hill, NC: University of North Carolina, 2003.

Smith, David Lionel. "The Black Arts Movement and Its Critics." *American Literary History* 3.1 (Spring 1991): 93–110.

Smith, Roger Guenveur. *A Huey P. Newton Story.* One-man show. Produced by California Theater Works. Los Angeles: 2001.

Spain, Johnny, with Lori Andrews. *Black Power, White Blood: The Life and Times of Johnny Spain.* Philadelphia, PA: Temple University Press, 2000.

Spellman, A. B. *The Beautiful Days.* New York: Poets Press, 1965.

——. *Four Lives in the BeBop Business.* New York: MacGibbon & Kee, 1967.

———. "Not Just Whistling Dixie." In L. Neal and L. Jones, *Black Fire!* 159–68.

Staub, Michael E. "Black Panthers, New Journalism, and the Rewriting of the Sixties." *Representations* 57 (Winter 1997): 53–72.

Stewart, James T. "The Development of the Black Revolutionary Artist." In L. Neal and L. Jones, *Black Fire!* 3–10.

Stone, Eddie. *Donald Writes No More*. Los Angeles: Holloway House, 1986.

Streible, Dan. "The Harlem Theater: Black Film Exhibition in Austin, Texas: 1920–1973." In *Black American Cinema*, edited by Manthia Diawara, 221–36. New York: Routledge, 1993.

"Student Blinded in Coast Bombing." *New York Times*, 7 March 1969, 1.

"Students at Los Angeles Rampage in Protest." *New York Times*, 11 March 1969, 30.

"Student Unrest in Brief." *New York Times*, 24 April 1969, 1.

Tackwood, Louis, and the Citizens Research and Investigation Committee. *The Glass House Tapes*. New York: Avon, 1973.

Thomas, Lorenzo. "The Shadow World: New York's Umbra Workshop and the Origins of the Black Arts Movement." *Callaloo* 4.1 (October 1978): 53–73.

Thompson, Julius E. *Dudley Randall, Broadside Press, and the Black Arts Movement in Detroit, 1960–1995*. Jefferson, NC: McFarland & Company, 1999.

Touré. *Soul City*. New York: Little, Brown, 2004.

Turner, Patricia A. *I Heard It through the Grapevine: Rumor in African American Culture*. Berkeley: University of California Press, 1993.

Tyson, Timothy. *Radio Free Dixie: Robert Williams and the Roots of Black Power*. Chapel Hill, NC: University of North Carolina Press, 1999.

Van Deburg, William L. *New Day in Babylon: The Black Power Movement and American Culture, 1965–1975*. Chicago, IL: University of Chicago Press, 1992.

Van Peebles, Melvin. *The Making of Sweet Sweetback's Baadasssss Song*. Edinburgh: Payback Press, 1996.

Vincent, Rickey. *Funk: The Music, the People, and the Rhythm of One*. New York: St. Martin's Press, 1996.

Vincent, Ted. *Keep Cool: The Black Activists Who Built the Jazz Age*. East Haven, CT: Pluto Press, 1995.

"Violence at San Francisco." *New York Times*, 22 November 1968, 40.

Waldron, Martin. "Louisianian Hints An Error in Killings." *New York Times*, 18 November 1972, 77.

———. "2 die in Clash with Police on Baton Rouge Campus." *New York Times*, 17 November 1972, 1.

Walker, David. Review of *Cotton Comes to Harlem*, directed by Ossie Davis. *Badazz MoFo: Pop Culture at Its Baddest* 6 (Winter 2001): 23.

Ward, Brian. *Just My Soul Responding: Rhythm and Blues, Black Consciousness, and Race Relations*. Berkeley: University of California Press, 1998.

Washington, Booker T. *Up from Slavery: An Autobiography*. 1901. New York: Dover, 1995.

Watkins, Mel. *On The Real Side: Laughing, Lying, and Signifying—The Underground Tradition of African-American Humor That Transformed American Culture, from Slavery to Richard Pryor*. New York: Simon and Schuster, 1994.

Welburn, Ron. "The Black Aesthetic Imperative." In Gayle, *The Black Aesthetic*, 126–42.

Wells, Ida B. *On Lynchings: Southern Horrors, a Red Record, Mob Rule in New Orleans*. New York: Arno Press, 1969.

West, Cornel. "Nihilism in Black America." In Dent, *Black Popular Culture*, 37–47.

West, Judy. Memo to Comrade Herman. 30 August [n.d.]. Dr. Huey P. Newton Foundation Collection. Stanford University Special Collections, Palo Alto, CA.

White, Edmund. *Genet: A Biography*. New York: Vintage, 1993.

Williams, Barbara Morrows. "Filth vs. Lucre: The Black Community's Tough Choice." *Psychology Today*, February 1974, 22–98.

Wilmer, Valerie. *As Serious as Your Life: John Coltrane and Beyond*. London: Serpent's Tail, 1992.

Williams, Raymond. *Keywords: A Vocabulary of Culture and Society*. Oxford: Oxford University Press, 1985.

Williams, Robert. *Negroes with Guns*. 1962. Detroit, MI: Wayne State University Press, 1998.

Wilson, C. E. "The Screens." In L. Neal and L. Jones, *Black Fire!* 133–43.

Wolfe, Tom. *Radical Chic and Mau-Mauing the Flak Catchers*. New York: Farrar, Strauss & Giroux, 1970.

Woodard, Komozi. *A Nation within a Nation: Amiri Baraka (LeRoi Jones) and Black Power Politics*. Chapel Hill, NC: University of North Carolina Press, 1999.

Wright, Richard. *Black Power! A Record of Reactions in a Land of Pathos*. 1954. New York: Harper Perennial, 1995.

———. "Blueprint for Negro Writing." In Gayle, *The Black Aesthetic*, 315–26.

Discography

Afro Asian Music Ensemble. *Black Panther Suite: All Power to the People*. Written and directed by Fred Ho. Innova Records, 2003.

Ayler, Albert. *Holy Ghost*. 9 CDs. Revenant Records, 2004.

———. *Live in Greenwich Village: The Complete Impulse Recordings*. GRP Records, 1998.

———. *New Grass*. Impulse Records, 1968.

Brown, James. *Prisoner of Love*. With Billy Eckstine and Etta James. Medacy Records, 1999.

Coleman, Ornette. "Science Fiction." *The Complete Science Fiction Sessions*. Sony Records, 2000.

Coltrane, Alice. *Journey in Satchidananda*. Impulse Records, 1970.

Common. *Be*. Geffen Records, 2005.

Funkadelic. *Free Your Mind and Your Ass Will Follow*. Westbound Records, 1989.

Huey! Folkways Records, 1972.

Mayfield, Curtis. *Super Fly*. Curtom Records, 1972.

NdegéOcello, Me'Shell. "I'm Diggin' You (Like an Old Soul Record)." *Plantation Lullabies*. Warner Brothers, 1993.

Parliament. *Mothership Connection*. Mercury Records, 1976.

Pryor, Richard. *Bicentennial Nigger*. Warner Brothers, 1976.

———. "God Is a Junkie." *Super Nigger*. Loose Cannon Records, 1982.

———. "Niggers vs. the Police." *That Nigger's Crazy*. Partee/Stax, 1974.

————. "Super Nigger." *Richard Pryor*. Dove/Reprise Records, 1968.

Public Enemy. "Burn, Hollywood, Burn." *Fear of a Black Planet*. Def Jam, 1994.

Pump Ya Fist: Hip Hop Inspired by the Black Panther Party. Avatar Records, 1995.

Sanders, Pharaoh. "Astral Traveling." *Thembi*. Impulse Records, 1970.

Scott-Heron, Gil. "The Revolution Will Not Be Televised." *Ghetto Style*. BMG International, 1970, 1990. Transcription appears in McKay and Gates, *Norton Anthology of African American Literature*, 61.

Simone, Nina. *The Best of Nina Simone*. Polygram Records, 1990.

————. *I Put a Spell on You*. New York: Da Capo Press, 1993.

Filmography

Bebe's Kids. Directed by Bruce W. Smith. Paramount, 1992.

Black Panther. Third World Newsreel, 1968.

Coffy. Directed by Jack Hill. MGM, 1973.

Cotton Comes to Harlem. Directed by Ossie Davis. MGM, 1970.

Dolemite. Directed by D'Urville Martin. Xenon, 1975.

Dolemite II: The Human Tornado. Directed by Cliff Roquemore. Xenon, 1976.

Eyes on the Prize II: America at the Racial Crossroads. Directed by Harry Hampton. Blackside, 1990.

Foxy Brown. Directed by Jack Hill. MGM, 1974.

Hallelujah. Directed by Charles Vidor. MGM, 1929.

House Party. Directed by Reginald Hudlin. New Line, 1983.

A Huey P. Newton Story. Directed by Spike Lee. Performed by Roger Guenveur Smith. Urban Works, 2004.

Lilies of the Field. Directed by Ralph Nelson. MGM, 1963.

The Mack. Directed by Michael Campus. New Line, 1973.

May Day Panther. Black Panther Party, Third World Newsreel, 1969.

Petey Wheatestraw: The Devil's Son-in-Law. Directed by Cliff Roquemore. Xenon, 1973.

Shaft. Directed by Gordon Parks. Warner Brothers, 1971.

Song of the South. Directed by Harve Foster. Disney, 1946.

Space Is the Place. Directed John Coney. Plexifilm, 1974.

Stagolee: A Conversation with Bobby Seale in Prison. American Documentary Films, 1970.

Super Fly. Directed by Gordon Parks Jr. Warner Brothers, 1972.

Sweet Sweetback's Baadasssss Song! Directed by Melvin Van Peebles. Oh Yeah Productions, 1971.

Sympathy for the Devil. Directed by Jean Luc Godard. Abcko, 1968.

Uptight! Directed by Jules Dassien. Paramount, 1968.

Willie Dynamite. Directed by Gilbert Moses. Universal, 1973.

Index

Abu-Jamal, Mumia, 20, 197n12, 199n1
Afro (hairstyle), 51, 52, 72, 183
Alameda County Courthouse, 45, 48
Alexander, Elizabeth, 64–65
anthologies, 23–24, 109–10, 202n9
Attali, Jacques, 146–47
authenticity, 12, 14, 23, 89, 95, 118, 129, 136, 166, 193
Ayler, Albert, 25, 90, 111, 124, 132, 133–35, 140, 141, 191, 203
Ayler, Donald, 141
"back to Africa," 10
Baldwin, James, 120

Baraka, Amiri, 39, 97, 105, 107, 123, 131, 132, 133, 134, 140, 190, 197n4, 199n6, 202n2. *See also* Jones, LeRoi
Bennett, Lerone, 164, 172–73, 180
Benston, Kimberly, 92, 139
Bernstein, Leonard, 58–59, 61–62, 65, 67, 69, 70–71
Black aesthetic, 7, 15, 16, 22, 24, 25, 89, 93, 97, 103, 106, 110, 111, 113, 122, 129, 130, 137, 139, 191
Black Aesthetic, The, 90, 92, 97, 102, 104, 105, 110, 122, 138, 139, 141, 155
Black Arts Repertory Theater School of Harlem, 23, 70, 88, 89, 105, 106, 108, 109, 111, 140, 141, 199n6, 202n8, 202n2
Black Arts Movement, 15, 16, 18, 22–26, 89–90, 101, 104, 112, 113, 117–23,

142, 188, 190, 191, 192, 202nn10–11, 202n14; and African American music, 105–7, 131–33, 137–40, 143, 202n2; and Black Arts Repertory Theater, 88–89, 111, 202n8; and *Black Fire!* anthology, 101, 107, 109–10, 115–17, 137, 202n9; influence on contemporary African American culture, 92–96, 125; as reaction to Civil Rights Movement, 91–92, 97–98, 103
black consciousness, 24, 90, 138
Black Fire! An Anthology of Afro-American Writing, 24, 90, 93, 97, 99, 101, 107, 109, 110, 111, 114, 115–16, 119, 124, 130, 137, 140, 192, 202n13
black masculinity, 11, 21
black nationalists, 39, 65, 78, 98, 101, 202n10
Black Panther Party, 2, 11, 21, 22–23, 29–38, 41, 77–79, 108, 142, 173, 179, 191, 192, 197n5, 197nn10–13, 198n19–21; cross-racial identifications with, 60, 68, 71–72, 199n2; harassed by law enforcement, 74–77, 200nn11–17; negative depictions of, 58–60, 61–62, 69, 72, 82–87; use of mass media and visual image, 17–19, 42–57, 73–74, 77, 79–81, 183–84, 198n22, 199n23, 199n25; valorization of the "brother on the block," 12, 19–20, 42, 198n15
Black Power, 2, 4, 11, 26, 27, 69, 81, 97, 187, 188, 189, 192, 193, 197n4; and

CPSIA information can be obtained at www.ICGtesting.com
Printed in the USA
LVOW090513181111

255555LV00005B/41/P